Perspectives on Leadership

A compilation of thought-worthy essays from the faculty and staff of the Army's premier educational institution for Civilian Leadership and Management, the Army Management Staff College.

★

2008

This essay compilation is intended for the further education, motivation and inspiration of leaders and those who will lead. Perspectives on Leadership presents professional information, but the views expressed herein are those of the authors, not the Army Management Staff College (AMSC), Department of the Army, Department of Defense, or the U.S. Government. The content does not reflect the official U.S. Army position and does not change or supersede any information in other official U.S. Army publications. Authors are responsible for the accuracy and source documentation of material they provide. AMSC is the leader development element of Army Civilian University.

Executive Editor:	Colonel Garland H. Williams, Ph. D.
Managing Editor:	Jennifer A. Brennan
Editor:	Deanie Deitterick
Design & Desktop Publishing:	Patrick B. Morrow
Support Staff:	David S. Burdick
	Jennifer M. Spangler
	Heather Deitterick

Published by Books Express Publishing
Copyright © Books Express, 2010
ISBN 978-1-907521-72-0
To purchase copies at discounted prices please contact
info@books-express.com

★

Army Management Staff College Perspectives on Leadership *is dedicated to the Civilians and Soldiers of the United States Army who defend America's ideals and freedoms, both at home and in distant lands.*

★

AMSC Mission - Vision - Goals - Values

MISSION:

- Educates and prepares civilian and Military leaders to assume leadership and management responsibilities throughout the Army
- Acts as Army Training and Doctrine Command's lead agent for the Civilian Education System curriculum
- Conducts research on Civilian Leadership and Installation Management

VISION:

- A Recognized Source for Leader Development
- Guiding Principles: Inspiring lifelong learning and service for the Army Civilian Corps
- The Center of Excellence in leadership and management for Army, Joint, and Interagency professionals
- Educating leaders in support of the Warfighter
- Relevant for the Army and the Nation
- A collaborative, meaningful research and learning environment

GOALS:

- Graduates who can lead and manage organizations
- An environment conducive to learning in both resident and Distributed Learning
- Recruit, support, and retain a highly qualified workforce

VALUES: In all its activities, the Army Management Staff College will promote:

- Excellence: Relevant commitment to leadership management, knowledge development, and innovation
- Communication: Respect academic exchange of diverse ideas and thoughts that encourage mutual creativity and trust
- Community: Recognize the importance of people and show concern for their health and well-being
- Professionalism: Reflect the highest standards of Military and Civilian service

Table of Contents

FOREWORD   **1**
Pete Geren, Secretary of the Army

PREPARING TO LEAD   **2**
1. **Followership: The Underappreciated Component of Leadership**   **3**
   Colonel Garland H. Williams, Ph.D., Commandant
   The Army expends most of its resources educating a fraction of its members,
   communicating their value to the institution, and establishing career paths
   founded on assessing selected leadership characteristics—while ignoring the
   vast majority who "merely" follow. This strategy is inadequate for honing
   the required skills within the rapidly transforming strategic environment that
   will prevail for the foreseeable future.

2. **Interpersonal Skills: A Key to Effective Leadership**   **19**
   Charles Stokes, Professor of Civilian Leader Development
   In order to affect success while in a leadership position, there are certain
   skills that effective leaders must have. These skills can be collectively
   referred to as interpersonal skills or "people skills."

3. **Intergenerational Diversity: A Leadership Tool**   **33**
   Arthur P. McMahan, Ph.D., Director of Educational Services
   Awareness of generational diversity and the implications of having three
   or four generations of followers working on the same team can prove
   beneficial to leaders interested in maximizing efficiency and effectiveness.

LEVERAGING LEADER ASSETS   **44**
1. **Leadership via the Eyes of the Follower: Somebody's Watching You** **45**
   Darrin Graham, Ed.D., Professor of Civilian Leader Development
   Leaders solve complex ill-structured problems daily, but many fail to
   understand their role through the eyes of their followers, which if handled
   incorrectly could become a problem.

2. **Core Values: The Essence of Leadership in the 21ˢᵗ Century**   **56**
   James Jarrett, Professor of Civilian Leader Development
   Establishing core values is a critical function if leaders are to lead their
   organization to greatness. The goals, decisions, and actions of leaders
   must be inextricably aligned with their true core values to obtain personal
   and organizational success.

3. **Mastering Teambuilding Principles**   **66**
    Kathy Strand, Professor of Civilian Leader Development
    *Investigating theories surrounding effective teambuilding using sports
    teams as a reference point for exploration.*

4. **Leadership and Emotional Intelligence**   **78**
    Constance Yelverton, Professor of Civilian Leader Development
    *Focussing on the cornerstone belief that Emotional Intelligence Quotient is
    key for effective leadership skills that are needed to meet the challenges
    the Army faces today and in the future.*

5. **Women and Minority Leaders in the Federal Government**   **86**
    Angela Parham, Ph.D., Professor of Civilian Leader Development
    *Focussing on the under-representation of women and minorities in middle
    and advanced leadership positions in the Federal Government*

6. **Distributed Learning: A Leadership Multiplier**   **97**
    Sidney Ricks, Professor of Civilian Leader Development
    *Diminishing resources and additional requirements for the Global War on
    Terrorism will force the Army to look at different methods of training and
    developing leaders that are cost conscious and get maximum bang for the
    buck.*

7. **Leveraging Self-Synchronization - A Leaders Art in Network
    Centric Warfare**   **106**
    Jim Geter, Technology and Operations Specialist
    *Leaders should explore the vast capability realized from self-synchronization
    in a network-centric Military organization and leverage the capability in
    Network Centric Warfare.*

STRENGTHENING **LEADERSHIP SKILLS**   **115**
1. **The Leader's Role in Increasing Ethical Reasoning Ability of Followers**   **116**
    Pamela Raymer, Ed.D., Dean of Academics
    *To translate a set of values, abstractly defined, to the ability to act ethically
    means moving those values across a chasm filled with ambiguous, complex,
    multiple variables. The challenge for leaders is to find ways to enhance the
    ethical reasoning ability of followers to more successfully cross that chasm
    and, in so doing, personify moral character.*

2. **The Role of Transformational Leadership: Lessons Learned from Visionary Leaders**   **127**
   Deloris Willis and Judy Thompson-Moore, Professors of Civilian Leader Development
   The positive aspects of having the attributes of a transformational leader.

3. **Redefining Army Leadership: Has the Be, Know, Do Model Been All that it Can Be?**   **145**
   Fiona J. Burdick, Ph.D., Professor of Civilian Leader Development, and David S. Burdick, Professor of Installation Management
   Army leadership is much more than occupying a position of influence, power, and responsibility over others—rather, it is the quality of the relationships developed and sustained among unit members that contribute most significantly to an Army unit is success.

4. **Civilians as Micro-Strategists**   **157**
   Roy Eichhorn, Director of Research and Development
   While much has been written about building strategists for the Military side of the Army, this essay addresses various questions as they relate to the Army Civilian Corps and the Army's Generating Force.

5. **The Motivation Factor: The Invisible Barriers to Organizational Effectiveness**   **169**
   Alton Dunham and Karen Spurgeon, Ed.D., Professors of Civilian Leader Development
   Common sense look at how the real meaning of motivation becomes obvious when people look below the surface at underlying de-motivators and then recognize the significance these elements play in organizational failure.

6. **Leading Change Through Investment**   **178**
   John Plifka, Civilian Education System Basic Course Director, and Wayne Ditto, Professor of Civilian Leader Development
   If the Army fails to change its thinking about Leader Development investment, we will become ineffective and fail to build the bench.

AUTHOR BIOGRAPHIES   **196**

AMSC HISTORY   **202**

ARMY MANAGEMENT STAFF COLLEGE

1987

BUILDING THE TOTAL TEAM

FOREWORD

In this era of constant engagement, the role of our Civilian workforce is increasingly vital to the accomplishment of the Army's mission. Army Civilians serve at the forefront of operations, provide direct and indirect support to our Soldiers, and make enormous contributions to the Global War on Terror. As the proponent for Army Civilian leadership, I am proud to announce the publication of Perspectives on Leadership, the first book-length publication by the Army Management Staff College (AMSC), the Department of the Army's premier educational institution for Civilian Leadership and Management.

The Army is a lifelong learning organization, with a strong focus on leader development. The work accomplished in recent years by the Army Training and Leader Development Panels and the Review of Education, Training, and Assignments for Leaders resulted in the development and implementation of the Civilian Education System at AMSC, which is in direct support for Army Initiative No. 5. All of these efforts have further accelerated the Army Civilian leader development program.

Perspectives on Leadership, authored by serving faculty and staff at AMSC, is a welcome addition to the program and serves as a guide for Army Civilian Corps leaders throughout their careers. It is written to guide the reader sequentially across an Army civilian career and serves as a leadership reference that we can all add to our toolboxes of knowledge.

Perspectives on Leadership is a broad examination of leadership that is useful for those just starting their careers, as well as those who have been in leadership positions for decades. I would like to thank my predecessor, Secretary of the Army Francis Harvey, for his vision to educate and prepare our Army civilians to lead during time of war as well as during peacetime. This book serves as a tangible reminder of his effort.

Army Strong!

Pete Geren
Secretary of the Army

PREPARING

TO LEAD

1. **Followership: The Underappreciated Component of Leadership**
   Colonel Garland H. Williams, Ph.D., Commandant

2. **Interpersonal Skills: A Key to Effective Leadership**
   Charles Stokes, Professor of Civilian Leader Development

3. **Intergenerational Diversity: A Leadership Tool**
   Arthur P. McMahan, Ph.D., Director of Educational Services

Colonel Garland H. Williams, Ph.D.

Followership:
The Underappreciated
Component of Leadership

Introduction

During the Army Management Staff College 3rd Annual Leadership Symposium in 2008, one of the keynote speakers claimed that we are all *leaders*. But is he right? Are you always a *leader* . . . or does the term *follower* better represent what you do in your current position? There is no simple answer to this question, and the hard reality is that we fulfill both roles simultaneously from the day we enter the workforce, throughout our careers, and well into our "golden years." Following is a natural part of life, and *follower* is an essential role we play in fulfilling our responsibilities and missions. Since most of the Army's institutions are hierarchical in design, the majority of any Military institution's members are, by definition, *followers*. But therein lies the problem. Few professional development programs spend time developing effective follower cultures and skills. Instead, officer commissioning sources, college business programs, professional Military education curricula, and the Army Management Staff College's own Civilian Education System focus on developing leaders.

Some may argue that the various functional technical schools fill the gap in follower development for career-minded individuals. This approach, however, diminishes the value that followers contribute to organizational success. If technical training and continuing education/leadership development is the accepted learning method for developing effective followers, the same line of reasoning would argue to implement a similar strategy to shape effective leaders. It would certainly be less resource-intensive, especially in the constrained environment of government service, and it would limit the amount of the time an individual is away from the job attending school. But these measures fall far short of the requirement to attract and retain people of the caliber the Army needs in the future. The Army expends most of its resources educating a fraction of its members, communicating their value to the institution, and establishing career paths founded on assessing selected leadership characteristics—while ignoring the vast majority who "merely" follow. This strategy is inadequate for honing the required skills within the rapidly transforming strategic environment that will prevail for the foreseeable future.

To successfully create and maintain a high performing organization, there must be a comfortable mix of leaders and followers. Leaders, in broad terms, are those who develop the long-term vision and organizational direction, while followers execute those concepts to successful conclusion. Leadership is the incremental influence exerted on people that encourages them to go that extra mile—that is to perform over and above the minimally acceptable level of performance. This influence, however, must be accepted because leaders can only exert as much persuasion over others as they are willing to accept. The other half of the equation, then, is followers. The organization requires far more good followers to meet its objectives than it does leaders. The followers are the implementers; they accept and support the visions of the leaders. We depend upon followers to build the organizations of tomorrow; it is the followers who will move the organization forward into the future.

Scholarship Support for Followership Development

An organization demands many people to accomplish its goals, yet all these people cannot serve as organizational heroes who operate in the limelight. Many followers are those who comfortably work in the background to help meet the organizational goals. They are, in essence, the unsung heroes by today's standards. Followership is so young as an area of study that it is currently in a stage where most thoughtful academics and professionals are trying only now to justify its importance. The role of followership has changed drastically to maintain its currency and relevancy. Changes in the global economy, for example, are promoting new models of followership to sprout. Ira Chaleff explains that in the past, strong leadership was imperative to get things accomplished, such as digging the Panama Canal or laying the Transcontinental Railroad. In the Information Age, there are so many interconnected units working for the success of a specific organization (all reporting to a long chain of leaders and usually in an independent virtual environment) that many people are needed to simultaneously coordinate their business by acting upon clear information.[1] A new model needs to be re-thought as management processes change to become more elaborate, and follower skill sets need to be revised to guide the development of followers to promote leadership success.

Others successfully argue that leaders must spend considerable time developing their followers to be successful. John Maxwell, in *The 21 Irrefutable Laws of Leadership*, asserts that "more than four out of five of all the leaders that you have ever seen will have emerged as leaders because of the impact made on them by established leaders who mentored them."[2] Using football as his teaching platform, he shows that the leader development of half of the head coaches in the National Football League (NFL) can be traced to two remarkable former professional football leaders—Bill Walsh and Tom Landry. As of 1998, 10 NFL head coaches spent a year or longer working for three-time Super Bowl champion Bill Walsh or for one of the top assistants he trained. And five NFL coaches have a direct or indirect mentoring connection with two-time Super Bowl winner Tom Landry or one of the men he trained.[3] Looking at the other side of the equation, what follower traits did Bill Walsh or Tom Landry demand from their assistants?

Scholars argue that there needs to be a shift to a team and follower focus because a leader without followers is not a leader. Robert Kelley states that "in the office and on the factory floor . . . we see increased emphasis on teams, collaboration, follower ownership, and grass-roots movements."[4] In this shift, the lines are blurred between leaders and followers—if one perspective of leadership or followership is promoted over another, it weakens the ability to manage followers efficiently, leading to a sense of groupthink and conformism. Due to the increased demands of the global economy, this type of conformism views followers as "blindly obeying sheep" and is dysfunctional.[5]

Not only is the focus shifting to followership to address global changes in industry, but followers are the impetus behind organizational productivity. Kelley's research shows that followers contribute 80 percent of the work in an organization, where leaders provide 20 percent. Even if we are in the leadership position, we actually spend more time reporting to our superior than leading our followers.[6] In high performing organizations, the leader and the follower (individually and collectively) are serving common organizational goals. How well this relationship works, specifically the quality of followership skills, directly impacts the organization's success.

Follower Traits

The limited literature on followership offers a large number of characteristics that exemplary followers should share. In categorizing the numerous claims that writers and researchers have made, there are six different dimensions that can offer insight to the components of followership and can be developed using the three domains of learning— organizational learning, institutional learning, and self-development. The first two are skill-based and can be formally learned in a classroom or an institutional educational setting: *interpersonal communication skills* and *conflict orientation.* The next two dimensions are personal traits that can be developed through operational experience: *initiative* and *integrity.* The final two dimensions (also personal traits) are defined as characteristics that make up the disposition of the personality of the follower and can be enhanced through self-development: *professionalism* and *intelligence.*

Skill-Based Characteristics in the Institutional Domain

Of the three domains of learning, followers first begin their development in the schoolhouse. Follower development is a deliberate, continuous, sequential, and progressive process grounded in Army Values and grows Soldiers and Civilians into competent and confident followers capable of working well on teams and within organizations to execute decisive action. Initial follower development is achieved through the synthesis of the knowledge, skills, and experiences gained through institutional training. To that end, the Army leverages professional development education (professional Military education and the Civilian Education System) and uses resident and distributed Learning education to enhance the followers' ability to influence their organization. No longer are followers expected to follow their leaders blindly; rather the expectation is that followers serve as active influencers in their organizations, oriented around the organization's goals and objectives, and they will actively seek out institutional opportunities to develop their skills in an institutional setting. This knowledge gained at the institution is then augmented at the local level by mentoring, coaching, and counseling, as well as selecting the right talent for specific job assignments.

Interpersonal Communication

Interpersonal communication skill is the first dimension that is paramount to developing exemplary followers. The ability to interact with one another, regardless of age, gender, culture, and status is crucial to being a versatile follower and making a difference in the organization's success. Exemplary followers are aware of their role with other people, how they are perceived through their communication efforts, and the expectations attached to those developed relationships. It is logical to claim that interpersonal communication is integral to followership development because of the sheer number of interactions that occur on a daily basis in the workplace. Interpersonal communication is such an important aspect to being a functional member of society that all areas of communication would be helpful to enrich the development of exemplary followers; however, areas of emphasis would include intercultural communication, gender communication, understanding stereotyping, and nonverbal communication. Followers who expand their background in these different areas would have the versatility and the breadth to be able to work with a diverse population.

The Army profession is rich with opportunities for worldwide travel to interact with people from many different backgrounds; however, communication differences create barriers to aligning leaders and followers. In Albania, for example, shaking the head from side-to-side indicates agreement whereas the Western cultures interpret this as *no.* This misalignment has the potential to cause considerable confusion if speakers do not understand these differences at the outset of the conversation. Followers from a low-context culture may be more direct, and may be seen as more assertive and confident. However, followers from a high-context culture (where they rely less on verbal communication and more on the context of nonverbal actions and environment) may not connect as easily with someone who was raised in a different environment. Conscious, directed study of these cultural nuances will help followers minimize cultural barriers and enhance the success of the communication exchange.[7]

As important as intercultural communication is, interpersonal communication (primarily in regards to gender) can considerably aid followers in their interactions. Gender communication is dynamic and sometimes emotive; it happens all the time, every day, and in all contexts; and it is a constant source of change when considering the social norms surrounding the issues of gender. Linda Ford explains that men and women tend to have different approaches to questions.

For example, if a woman has a fact or opinion, she may choose to raise her issue in the form of a question. On the other hand, even when a man doesn't have facts, he may express his view as a definitive statement. For men and women, questions may be heard as a sign of weakness or lack of knowledge; statements can sound like arrogance.[8]

To excel as followers, people must be able to aptly adapt their interpersonal communication in interactions with the opposite gender. It is specifically important for followers to be aware of how their own behavior changes when crossing gender lines; the development of this trait calls for intense study. Followers greatly enhance their professionalism when communication inherently respects gender differences without compromising mission accomplishment.

The two generations most prevalent in the workplace are Generation Xers (1960-1980) and Baby Boomers (1946-1964). Additionally, on the younger side, there are a few members of Millennials (1980-2000) and on the other side there are members of the Traditionalists (1920–1946). Dr. Arthur P. McMahan says,

When you begin to design activities that address generational diversity issues, pay close attention to communication preferences. The newest followers in the workforce grew up with computers, Internet, and electronic communication devices. Baby Boomers and Traditionalists had radio, TV, and newspapers as their primary sources of information during their developing years. The experiences that each generation has during formative years could result in differences in the way each group prefers to receive and absorb information.[9]

Effectively communicating ideas across the generational divides allows the potential of each member to be maximized and becomes a key to success within the organization.

Equally important is the awareness of perpetuating stereotypes in interpersonal relationships. If followers are skilled at identifying stereotypes, they can be equipped to defeat the impact in the workplace. A working environment void of negative stereotyping and the misunderstanding that can result creates a comfortable working environment that promotes the organization's mission effectiveness. Stereotyping, by definition, breeds false, possibly negative perceptions of co-followers and peers, which hinders organizational success. There can be a broad and pervasive tendency for people to perceive and interpret others in terms of their feelings at the time; awareness and study can significantly empower them to overcome negative stereotyping in organizations, specifically followers in their interactions with their leaders.

Finally, 65 percent of interpersonal communication is nonverbal.[10] The use of eye contact, facial expressions, gestures, and posture can emphasize, deemphasize, contradict, or undermine what the spoken language is trying to say. When followers align their nonverbal communication with their verbal communication, they express their ideas much more clearly and appear much more confident. Professional followers ensure that all communication (verbal and nonverbal) is in agreement to avoid miscommunication. The bottom line is that followers skilled in interpersonal skills will have the versatility to be able to work with different types of people, specifically regarding culture, gender, stereotypes, and age.

Interpersonal Skills
- *Cultural Awareness*
- *Gender Communication*
- *Generational Communication*
- *Stereotyping Awareness*
- *Nonverbal Communication*

Follower Trait Summary: Interpersonal Skills

Conflict Orientation

The second dimension that is key to effective followership is conflict orientation. Effective followers have a thorough understanding of the organizational goals and can make intelligent decisions in regard to leadership guidance. Willingness to confront decisions or policies and knowing how to do so in a supportive and effective way are critical skills for high-performance followers. In the workplace, conflict is inevitable because people do not perceive things in exactly the same way, nor should they. Organizational success is predicated on how well the workforce deals with business conflicts.

Followers are constantly exposed to conflict. In fact, Robert Lussier and Christopher Achua suggest that one-fifth of the workday is devoted to handling conflict and is, thus, an important followership skill. The ability to resolve conflicts has a direct impact on an organization's success and (with the trend towards teamwork) conflict skills are increasingly important to team building and team decision making. Conflict is often thought of as fighting and is viewed as disruptive; however, conflict is an inherent part of organizational activity. When conflict is not resolved effectively, negative consequences occur and prevent the achievement of organizational objectives. Functional conflict, on the other end of the spectrum, exists when disagreement and opposition supports the achievement of organizational goals and objectives and increases the quality of group decisions leading to innovative changes. The important question to ask is not whether conflict is disruptive or functional, but how to manage conflict effectively to benefit the organization.[11]

Stephen Lundin highlights confrontation skills well in a discussion on the importance of integrity. "This type of communication requires a number of skills, including a willingness to seek the truth, the ability to cope with conflict, and the confidence to take personal risks to benefit the common good."[12]

Tom Brown agrees, claiming that followers have the important role to "speak up . . . forcefully, not timidly" if the leader is defying the vision of the organization.[13] Specific skills that would be ideal for followership training are problem-solving, coping with change, and conflict management.

Communication Studies may be the right avenue to specifically address the skill of positive conflict orientation required in followers. Training programs for various organizations can include the development of conflict orientation skills as a part of follower or member orientation. Since the groundwork has already been laid for understanding varying means of conflict, communication scholars can now provide these tools for followers to empower their organizations.

Conflict Orientation

- *Willingness to Seek the Truth*
- *Speak up Forcefully . . . Not Timidly*
- *Problem Solving*
- *Coping with Change*
- *Conflict Management*

Follower Trait Summary: Conflict Orientation

Personal Characteristics in the Operational Domain

In many instances, the best development opportunities for followers occur in the workplace. As a lifelong learning institution, the Army continually determines the potential differences between operations today and those the Army will encounter in the future and develops the capabilities to meet those changes. Followers who examine their organizational experiences critically will ultimately learn from them to find better methods to accomplish the organization's mission. Open mindedness and imagination create an effective organizational learning environment; however, followers should not be afraid to make mistakes. If a follower is reaching into unexamined areas in an effort to improve the organization, mistakes will be made and learning will take place from those mistakes. Followers must stay positive, learn from those mistakes, and remain confident in their own ability to make learning a lifelong commitment. French Military theorist Ardant Du Picq stressed the importance of learning. "The instruments of battle are valuable only if one knows how to use them . . . ."[14]

Initiative

A great challenge for leaders is to encourage their followers to exercise proper initiative. Followers who have never walked in a leadership position are often reluctant to recognize that a situation requires them to take responsibility and step forward. This could be as minor as speaking up when the individual has technical knowledge or situational information that the boss lacks. Organizational climate can largely determine the extent to which initiative and input are encouraged. Leaders set the conditions for initiative by guiding followers to think through problems for themselves, thus building confidence in their followers' competence and ability to solve problems.

Followers, however, must understand that leaders cannot possibly be experts in every part of their broad spans of control and that leaders must rely on the expertise of their followers to achieve the goals of the organization. Followers must take action, using their resident expertise to promote the organizational goals and mission. The second Army Value is Duty—fulfill all required obligations; however, duty extends beyond just those things required by law, regulation, and orders.[15] Professionals work not just to meet the minimum standard, but consistently strive to excel in their professional responsibilities. Professional followers anticipate what needs to be done before being told what to do. They exercise initiative when they fulfill the purpose (not merely the letter) of the tasks they have been assigned and the orders they have received; the task is not complete until the intent is achieved.

Innovation is a subset of initiative and describes the Army followers' ability to develop something new when an opportunity arises. Innovative organizations spark creativity in the production of ideas that are original and worthwhile. At times, new problems present themselves or old problems require new solutions. Effective Army followers seize those opportunities to think creatively and demonstrate initiative and innovation. A key concept of critical thinking is to develop new approaches and ideas to challenge organizations. Effective followers come up with new ways for peers and leaders to accomplish tasks and missions using adaptive approaches and drawing from previous similar circumstances or methods. Followers who exemplify initiative battle organizational complacency by challenging their peers with forward-looking approaches and ideas. Combining innovation with initiative, followers rely on intuition, experience, knowledge, and input from their peers and "reinforce team building by making everybody responsible for, and consequently stakeholders in, the innovation process."[16]

Initiative and Innovation	• *The tendency to introduce new ideas when the opportunity exists or in the face of challenging circumstances* • *Strive to excel in professional responsibility* • *Creativity in the production of ideas and objects that are both novel or original and worthwhile or appropriate* • *Reinforce team building*

Follower Trait Summary: Initiative and Innovation

Integrity

Followers must, at all times, demonstrate integrity in everything they do. This can best be summed up by the phrase "do what's right, legally, morally, even when nobody is looking." Integrity refers to behavior that is honest and ethical, in effect making people trustworthy. Honesty inspires truthfulness rather than deception, and many researchers found that integrity is the most prized asset that followers can possess. According to Lussier and Achua, "Trustworthiness is an important part of organizational success; trusting relationships are at the heart of profit making and sustainability in the global knowledge-based economy. Honesty and trust are so important at CompUSA that any follower who is caught telling a lie is fired immediately; according to the CEO, 'We all trust each other.'"[17]

Followers must be able to trust their leaders, and leaders must be able to trust their followers. To be viewed as trustworthy and a person of integrity, followers must be honest to a fault, support their leaders with actions replete with the truth, and keep their confidences. If peers discover that their co-follower has lied or has manipulated the truth for personal gain, that follower will be seen to be undependable and, most importantly, not to be trusted. Integrity is the number one trait that managers want in their followers. At General Electric, integrity is its core value. At GE's website (http://www. ge.com), former CEO Jack Welch told followers to do everything with integrity.[18]

This is not to say that unanticipated events never happen. If followers inadvertently present bad information, they should correct the error upon discovery. Followers of integrity do the right thing not because it is convenient or because they have no other choice. They choose the path of truth because their character permits nothing less, assuming the followers inherently understand right versus wrong. Just as important, followers should do what is right, even at personal cost. They demonstrate the Army Values personally and inculcate them into their everyday lives. Personal values may extend beyond Army Values, to include "such things as political, cultural, or religious beliefs; however, as Army followers and persons of integrity, these values should reinforce, not contradict, Army values."[19]

Integrity	• *Do what is right legally, morally, and when nobody is looking* • *Honesty and Truthfulness* • *Trusting Relationships* • *Integrity is a Core Value*

Follower Trait Summary: Integrity

Personal Characteristics in the Self-Development Domain

Of all the learning domains, self-development is continuous and must be pursued during institutional and operational assignments. Successful self-development begins with motivated individuals and is augmented by a concerted team effort. Quality feedback from multiple sources—peers, followers, and superiors—is imperative and leads to the establishment of self-development goals. The followers' Individual Development Plans become the key documents to improve individual performance by enhancing acquired skills, knowledge, behaviors, and experience, further demonstrating the potential for progressively more complex and higher-level assignments. In general, self-development for followers is structured and focused; however, the focus significantly broadens as individuals identify their own strengths and weaknesses, determine individual needs, and become more independent.[20]

Professionalism

The most encompassing aspect of followership (and possibly the hardest to explain in concrete terms) is professionalism. Followers who act in accordance with accepted appropriate standards enable others to work collaboratively and efficiently. If followers are to perform on exemplary levels, they must be aware of certain unprofessional actions or omissions that will certainly damage their credibility. Professional behavior as a follower must include dependability, technical competence, and complete honesty. William Crockett adds "self-discipline" and "self-management" and states that followers who are professional are responsible for themselves and for their own behavior. Good followers are fully accountable for the actions they take and are aware of how their actions affect the success of the organization.[21]

Ethical and honest communication, workplace appearance, effective listening, and planned, pertinent writing are inherent in professionalism. Effective followers constantly examine their habitual standards of dress, nonverbal expressions, and speech patterns. To determine if they are presenting a competent image to their peers, followers must seek feedback on their capabilities and take responsibility for their own development; this requires self-awareness, humility, and objectivity about their own performance. Though these skills can be obtained through experience, pursuing formal education in these areas allows less experienced followers to assimilate in productive organizations much faster. Using a 360 degree assessment, for example, will help followers gain honest appraisal of their strengths and weaknesses.

Self-presentation is vital. The appropriate use of language, for instance, greatly enhances one's professionalism. Language should reflect the formality of the situation, and more formal language should be spoken to those with higher power. Jargon and slang, if used at all, should be contingent on the specific audience so that communication is understood. Profanity should be avoided, as its use demonstrates a significant linguistic deficit on the part of the speaker. Finally, appropriate dress and grooming show respect and consideration for the organization and for the people with whom you interact. In the end, demonstrating these attributes of professionalism not only lends immense credibility to followers when working with their leader, but also ensures a strong and favorable working relationship. Followers who are professional display confidence, assurance, interest, and respect, thus furthering the goals and missions of the organization.

Professionalism

- *Dependability*
- *Competence*
- *Honesty*
- *Self-Discipline*
- *Self-Management*
- *Self-Presentation*
- *Use of Language*
- *Appropriate Dress*

Follower trait summary: Professionalism

Intelligence and Mental Agility

Intelligence is an expression of the mental tendencies and resources that mold conceptual abilities, which then can be applied to one's duties and responsibilities. It enables sound judgment before implementing concepts and plans, helps one think creatively, and promotes analytical reason replete with cultural sensitivity to consider unintended as well as intended consequences. Like a basketball player trying to anticipate an opponent's moves, followers must think through what they expect to occur because of a decision. Some actions may set off a chain of events; therefore, followers must attempt to anticipate the second- and third-order effects of their actions.[22]

Mental agility, as a subset of intelligence, is an ability to anticipate or adapt to changing conditions. Because the Army is forced to operate in times of ambiguity, agility encourages the contemplation of all ramifications when current decisions or actions fail to achieve expectations. "It breaks habitual thought patterns, promoting improvisation when faced with conceptual impasses and provides quick application of multiple perspectives to consider new approaches or solutions."[23] The ability to reason critically while remaining open to multiple possibilities allows discovery of the truth in instances where direct observation is insufficient, impossible, or impractical. It allows the full contemplation of problems to develop solutions—central to a follower's exercise of judgment and contribution to decision making.

As the Army leadership manual states, "Critical thinking is the key to understanding changing situations, finding causes, arriving at justifiable conclusions, making good judgments, and learning from experience."[24] Followers must be well-versed in critical thinking skills to better promote their organizations' vision and intent.

Intelligence and Mental Agility	<ul><li>*Flexibility of mind*</li><li>*The tendency to anticipate or adapt to uncertain or changing situations; to think through second- and third-order effects when current decisions or actions are not producing the desired effects*</li><li>*The ability to break out of habitual thought patterns*</li><li>*The ability to quickly apply multiple perspectives and approaches to assessment, conceptualization, and evaluation*</li></ul>

Follower trait summary: Intelligence and Mental Agility

Conclusion

The Army is a bureaucracy with a rigid hierarchical structure. This structure tends to highlight its leaders and develop institutional mechanisms to further enhance their leadership capabilities. But what about those whom the leader leads? What should the Army do? In a world where everyone answers to someone else along highly bureaucratic lines, where leaders on top may be distant from their followers, followers can face the danger of setting precedents of passivity that could deny them power in the future. Organizationally, the Army should counter this passivity, empower followers to be thinking agents of the bureaucratic structure, and allow them ownership of the organization's growth and success. The Army should grant followers the power to challenge and change the future direction of their organizations. There are voices that have spoken out in defense of followers, some louder than others, all with the purpose to promote the development of followership. Kelley states:

> We are a nation of followers. The United States is a 200-year old experiment in the belief that common people like you and me - the follower, if you will - believe enough in ourselves to govern ourselves. The spirit of American democracy elevates and elaborates the role of the follower.[25]

Empowering resources are available to answer their calls. Skill-based traits of *interpersonal communication skills* and *conflict orientation* are key institutionally-driven dimensions that enhance followership development. Additionally, *initiative* and *integrity* acquired on the job, when coupled with the personal-based traits of *professionalism* and *intelligence*, provide a developmental roadmap for followers to use as they empower themselves to strengthen their leaders and their organizations.

Notes

1. Ira Chaleff, *The Courageous Follower* (San Francisco, CA: Berrt-Kuehler Publishers, Inc., 1995), 4.
2. John C. Maxwell, *The 21 Irrefutable Laws of Leadership* (Nashville, TN: Thomas Nelson Publishers, 1998), 134.
3. Ibid.
4. Robert E. Kelley, *The Power of Followership* (New York, NY: Bantam Doubleday Dell Publishing Group, Inc., 1992), 8.
5. Ibid., 12-13.
6. Ibid., 20-21.
7. Judee K. Burgoon, David B. Buller, and W. Gill Woodall, *Nonverbal Communication: The Unspoken Dialogue* (New York, NY: Harper & Row Publishers, 1989), 26-29.
8. Linda Ford, *The Fourth Factor: Managing Corporate Culture* (Indianapolis, IN: Dog Ear Publishing, 2008), 38.
9. Arthur P. McMahan, "Intergenerational Diversity," *Army Management Staff College Perspectives on Leadership,* (Fort Belvoir, VA: Army Management Staff College, 2008).
10. Burgoon, Buller, and Woodall, *Nonverbal Communication*, 4.
11. Robert N. Lussier and Christopher F. Achua, *Leadership: Theory, Application, Skill Development*, 2nd ed. (Eagan, MN: South-Western, Thompson, 2004), 245-246.
12. Stephen C. Lundin, Lynne C. Lancaster, and John W. Gardner, "The Importance of Followership," *The Futurist* 24, no. 3 (May-June 1990): 18 (5). Academic OneFile. Gale. Remote access for CFSC; available on the Internet at http://find.galegroup.com/itx/start.do?prodld=AONE (Accessed 1 April 2008)
13. Tom Brown, "Great Leaders Need Great Followers," *Industry Week* 244, no. 16, (4 September 1995); Available on the Internet at http://proquest.umi.com/pqdlink?did=8 80047&sid=1&Fmt=3&clientid=30287&RQT=309&VName=PQD
14. *Army Leadership: Competent, Confident, and Agile* [Field Manual 6-22] (Washington, D.C.: Department of the Army, 12 October 2006), 8-11.
15. Ibid., 4-5.
16. Ibid., 6-2 to 6-3.
17. Lussier and Achua, 35.
18. Ibid.
19. *Army Leadership*, 4-8.
20. Ibid., 8-7.

21. William J. Crockett, "Dynamic Subordinancy," *Training and Development Journal* (May 1981): 162.
22. *Army Leadership*, 6-1.
23. Ibid.
24. Ibid.
25. Kelley, 24.

Charles Stokes

Interpersonal Skills: A Key to Effective Leadership

Introduction

Schermerhorn states that leadership is a special case of interpersonal influences that gets an individual or group to do what the leader wants done.[1] Leadership is defined in Army Field Manual 6-22, *Army Leadership,* as "influencing people, by providing purpose, direction, and motivation, while operating to accomplish (an objective, mission, or to improve the organization)."[2] In order to be effective in leadership positions, there are certain skills that leaders must demonstrate and possess. These skills can be collectively referred to as interpersonal skills or "people skills." They can be learned and captured succinctly. This chapter addresses communicating, supervising, and counseling as vital interpersonal skills for successful leaders.

Communicating

Speaking is the most common form of communication used to relay messages, thoughts, and ideas from one person to another. Effective oral communication skills are one of the hallmark traits of a leader. Leaders are consistently able to influence the actions of followers to accomplish organizational objectives, goals, and vision. They must master the skill of speaking effectively by knowing their audience and being able to communicate with them. President John F. Kennedy and Rev. Dr. Martin L. King, Jr. were great leaders, and their success was in part due to their ability to communicate effectively. This skill enabled them to depict their vision clearly and succinctly to their staff as well as to the public. The quality and characteristics of their oral communications serve as a model for all communications skills. The learned use of logic, organization, directness, and precision can ensure effective flow of ideas in oral communication.

Speakers cannot learn how to speak effectively simply by reading books. Skill in presenting a speech or briefing requires knowledge of the principles of speech and experience gained only through considerable practice, rehearsal, and performance. Even the most accomplished speakers learn something every time they brief or make a speech. With each speaking engagement, they are afforded an opportunity to further perfect their personal speaking techniques and develop the confidence to speak to a variety of audiences. There are universal attributes that make both the speaker and the speech effective, regardless of the type of speech presented. These attributes include integrity, character, knowledge, and skill.

Integrity and Character

Integrity is a reflection of personal qualities such as high moral and ethical standards and character. Ralph Waldo Emerson once said that "Character is higher than intellect . . . a great soul will be strong to live, as well as to think" and of integrity. "What you are . . . thunders so that I cannot hear what you say to the contrary."[3] The great philosopher Aristotle said, "The speaker's character is the most potent of all the means of persuasion."[4] These timeless quotes show that integrity and character play into the ability to communicate. One cannot communicate without eventually revealing the true self. If the self revealed is perceived as false, inaccurate, or pompous, the audience will refuse to accept what is being said. There will be a lingering suspicion that will prevent the listeners from responding wholeheartedly and accepting the speaker's point of view.

Knowledge

It is imperative that speakers have comprehensive knowledge of the subject material presented. Speakers in public forums are often in positions to influence others; this carries with it an obligation to speak knowledgably about the topic being presented. They must also know and have consideration for their audience, remembering that the attendees may have come to obtain new ideas, encouragement, or information. Speakers must have up-to-date mastery of their subject material. Alfred North Whitehead put it another way when he said, "A merely well-informed man is the most useless bore on God's earth."[5] An effective speaker must not only have something to say, but must also have the knowledge and skill to say it well.

Skill

Presenting

Delivery of the message in a clear, concise, succinct, and logical manner requires skill. While integrity and character can be considered as internal or not readily known; knowledge and skill are readily observed and may be developed through specific study and practice. The first skill needed is that of organizing material for the audience. Most effective speeches have patterns of organization that the audience can recognize, understand, and follow as an introduction, body, and conclusion. In addition to organizing the speech to flow smoothly and in a logical order, speakers must have the skill to deliver the presentation. They must be able to project main ideas and thoughts to the audience; however, delivery alone cannot replace substance. The manner in which the speech is delivered lends credibility as speakers project ideas that give dignity, force, and effectiveness to their presentations.

All ideas and feelings communicated through speech occur in the form of audible or visible symbols. Speakers should talk loudly enough to be heard, be fluent, be forceful; and use body language, gestures, and animation to help get their ideas across to the audience. Visual aids, such as charts and graphics should be clear and uncluttered. Charts should be used to make the speaker's point and to clarify specific information.

The ability to handle questions and questioners is another skill that leaders need. This skill is especially acute during Military briefings because they normally include a question-and-answer period. Experienced speakers anticipate the possible questions that may arise in the minds of their listeners and incorporate the answers into the briefing itself. Because listeners can interrupt a briefing with questions at any time, speakers need additional facts available to respond to them.

The steps to create a presentation or briefing are basically the same— know the role as briefer; know the audience; and know the subject matter. Speakers should expertly "sell" their ideas to the audiences. The introduction has three purposes, to gain attention, establish goodwill, and disclose and clarify the subject. A technique used by many established speakers is to first gain the audiences' attention and establish goodwill. The noted American psychologist and philosopher William James said, "What holds attention determines action."[6] If you can get the attention of the audience and can keep that attention sharply focused on the speech, the audience will tend to respond as desired. The first requisite of effective speech is to engage the attention of the listeners. Unless someone attunes to what speakers are saying, they are not communicating. It is the speaker's job to ensure that the audience receives the intended message. An effective way to grab the audience's attention is to begin with an interesting narrative to illustrate a point or the message to be conveyed.

A striking incident that dramatizes the central idea of a speech can be one of the most effective openings for a speech. For example, this classic attention-getter was used by Arthur Taylor, President of Columbia Broadcasting at the Los Angeles World Affairs Council in 1973. To capture the audience's attention, he began his speech by stating the little known fact that the last major battle of the War of 1812 (the Battle of New Orleans) was fought on January 8, 1815, after the Treaty of Ghent (which ended the war) was signed on December 24, 1814.[7]

The heart of the speech is the body. Building the body of the speech involves arranging or rearranging the main points of the tentative outline, so that the speaker's thoughts and ideas flow smoothly, and each point is developed as effectively as possible. Regardless of how long the speech may be, it should not have more than three or four main points and almost never more than five. Ideas should be carefully analyzed and reduced to a few basic parts. If the speech has too many main points, the analysis is likely faulty and follower ideas have been substituted for main ideas.

Nothing weakens a speech more than the speaker breaking off suddenly, just stopping, or saying, "Well, that's it." A conclusion should contain at least three elements. First, it should summarize the main ideas to remind the audience of the objectives of the speech. Second, it may contain a brief recapitulation of main points, a quotation that epitomizes the argument, an illustration or narrative that dramatizes the central ideas, or any device that focuses attention on the main ideas and ties them together. Finally, the conclusion should leave the audience favorably disposed toward the speaker. It is a way of saying goodbye. Speakers should strive in composition and delivery in order to achieve closure—a tone of finality that clearly indicates that the talk is finished. The public speaking checklist (Figure 1) is a useful guide that may help when preparing to present a speech or briefing.[6]

Supervising

Supervision is a key people skill (much akin to leadership) that can be further developed by using interpersonal skills. Carter McNamara, in his article, " Basics-Definitions (and Misconceptions) about Management" states that leaders typically are responsible for directly reporting progress and productivity in the organization. Supervision often includes:

- Using basic management skills (i.e., decision-making, problem-solving, planning, delegation, and meeting management)
- Organizing teams
- Noticing the need for and designing new job roles in the group
- Hiring new followers
- Training new followers
- Managing follower performance (setting goals, observing and giving feedback, addressing performance issues, and initiating disciplinary actions, etc.)
- Ensuring conformance to personnel policies and other internal regulations.[8]

Supervision encompasses a multitude of responsibilities that involves more tasks than the leader can handle alone. In order to be successful, the leader must use time wisely and employ a full array of interpersonal skills. For example, the leader empowers and delegates, which is a process of assigning responsibility and giving authority to followers to perform and accomplish specific tasks that they may not normally perform. These practices lead to improved time management and allow the leader to focus on other important issues.

In the book, *Leadership: Theory, Application, Skill Development*, Robert Lussier and Christopher Achua say that delegating refers to giving followers new tasks to perform. The new task may become part of a redesigned job, or it may simply be a one-time event.[9] The true art of delegation lies in the leader's ability to know when and how to delegate. Leaders should delegate work when there is not enough time to attend to priority tasks and when followers seek more challenges and opportunities. Coaching is a useful tool if the delegated task is one with which the follower is unfamiliar. Coaching a follower on how to perform a new task not only increases a leader's span of delegation, but allows the leader increased flexibility; it frees up time to perform tasks of higher importance.

Lussier and Achua also suggest the use of a four-step delegation model to help the leader determine which tasks to delegate to followers. The leader must:

- Explain the need for delegating and the reason for selecting the follower.
- Set objectives that define responsibility, the level of authority, and deadlines.
- Write objectives, assign a coach, and empower the follower with levels of authority necessary to perform the assigned tasks.
- Establish control check points and hold the follower accountable.[10]

Counseling, Coaching, and Mentoring

Effective leaders continually seek opportunities to improve their leadership skills. The ability to counsel, coach, and mentor are key interpersonal skills that help make leaders effective. Using these skills enables them to interact with followers to improve job performance and increase two-way communication, which allows for direct transmission of information equally between the leader and the follower. These interactions result in opportunities to discuss specific follower concerns and job performance and to make recommendations with the ultimate goal of increasing organizational effectiveness and working relationships between followers, leaders, customers, and peers.

Generally, anytime leaders communicate with followers, it is an opportunity to use interpersonal skills for individual development or discussion of training. These sessions will hold to be particularly true if the followers are performing below standard. Coaching, counseling, and mentoring sessions provide opportunity to recognize high performers and recommend training that will enhance future organizational goals and personal goals of the follower.

Counseling

Interpersonal opportunities for recognition of performance can be presented during counseling sessions, which are basically a follower-centered communication activity. During counseling sessions, plans outlining actions necessary to achieve individual training, education, or organizational goals are acknowledged. Army Field Manual 6-22, *Army Leadership: Confident, Competent, and Agile*, describes counseling as the process used by leaders to review (with followers) the follower's demonstrated performance and potential. During counseling, followers are not passive listeners but rather active participants in the process.[11]

When leaders prepare to counsel their people, they mentally organize themselves in order to isolate relevant issues. They use standard formats or create their own, which normally includes four elements:

- The need for counseling is identified; this need may stem from an organizational requirement such as counseling prior to an evaluation. The need may also stem from observing the followers' performance compared to expected standards or from a developmental need.
- Leaders select a suitable location and time that is convenient for both the leader and the follower. Followers are notified well in advance and leaders have a structured counseling plan.
- The session is conducted by the leader and follower discussing the issues together. Leaders adhere to the developed plan of action and record and close the sessions.
- Leaders follow up to ensure that required actions are taken.

During counseling, leaders help followers identify their strengths and weaknesses and create plans of action. To make the plans work, leaders actively support their followers throughout the implementation and assessment processes. Followers are encouraged to invest themselves in the process by being forthright in their willingness to improve and be candid in their assessment and goal-setting. The Army recognizes three types of counseling for Soldiers and Civilians—event counseling, performance counseling, and professional growth counseling.[12]

Event Counseling

Leaders conduct event counseling to cover a specific event or situation. It may precede events such as going to a promotion board or attending a school. It may also follow events such as exceptional duty performance, a performance problem, or a personal problem. Event counseling is also recommended for reception into a unit or organization, for crises, and for transition from an organization or unit, or separation from the Army.

Performance Counseling

Leaders use performance counseling as a means to review a follower's duty performance during a specified period. The leader and the follower jointly establish performance objectives and clear standards for the next counseling period. The counseling focuses on the follower's strengths, areas to improve, and potential. Effective counseling includes providing specific examples of strengths and areas needing improvement and providing guidance on how followers can improve their performance. Performance counseling is required under the officer, noncommissioned officer (NCO), and *Army Civilian evaluation reporting systems.*

Professional Growth Counseling

Professional growth counseling includes planning for the accomplishment of individual and professional goals. It has a developmental orientation and helps followers identify and achieve organizational and individual goals. Professional growth counseling includes a review of performance (to identify and discuss the follower's strengths and weaknesses) and creation of an Individual Development Plan. The plan builds on existing strengths to overcome weaknesses.

A part of professional growth counseling is a discussion characterized as a "pathway to success." It establishes short- and long-term goals for the follower. These goals may include opportunities for Civilian or Military education, future duty assignments, special programs, or reenlistment options. Leaders help develop specific courses of action tailored to each individual.

Approaches to Counseling

Inexperienced leaders are sometimes uncomfortable when confronting a follower who is not performing to standard. Counseling is not about leader comfort; it is about correcting the performance or developing the character of a follower. To counsel effectively, leaders must demonstrate certain qualities, such as respect for followers, self-awareness, cultural awareness, empathy, and credibility. Effective leaders are self-aware; they are conscious of personal behaviors, traits, and feelings that contribute to their personalities. The first step to becoming an effective leader is to know self. This saying is especially true when counseling. Self-aware leaders are knowledgeable of cultural differences; they identify with followers by showing empathy and respect, regardless of the circumstances. Leaders must be fair, honest, and respectful to gain the trust of the followers they counsel. Observance of these basic leader attributes adds credibility to the counseling session.

One challenging aspect of counseling is selecting the proper approach for specific situations. For leaders to counsel effectively, they use a technique that fits the situation. Some cases may only require providing information or listening. A follower's improvement may call for just a brief word of praise. Other situations may require structured counseling, followed by specific plans of action. Leaders should approach each follower as an individual. Counseling includes nondirective, directive, and combined approaches. The major difference between the approaches is the degree to which the follower participates and interacts during the counseling session.

The nondirective approach is preferred for most counseling sessions. Leaders use their experiences, insight, and judgment to help followers develop solutions. Leaders partially structure this type of counseling by telling the follower about the counseling process and explaining the expectations.

The directive approach works best to correct simple problems, make on-the-spot corrections, and correct aspects of duty performance. When using the directive style, the leader does most of the talking and tells the follower what to do and when to do it. In contrast to the nondirective approach, the leader directs a course of action for the follower.

In the combined approach, the leader uses techniques from both directive and nondirective approaches and adjusts them to articulate what is best for the follower. The combined approach emphasizes the follower's planning and decision-making responsibilities.[13]

Coaching

Another opportunity for leaders to use their interpersonal skills effectively is during coaching sessions, they might be assessing the follower's performance based on observations and feedback. Leaders may find that some followers may want to take on more responsibilities or new assignments. Coaching is a cost-effective way to train followers in new skills or tasks.

Skilled leaders will guide their followers on the details and requirements of the job while the followers actually perform the tasks. The benefits of coaching are that it allows followers to upgrade their skills and their performance levels; it is a form of follower-development without formal off-the-job training time. Another benefit is that coaching frees up time by allowing work to be distributed to a larger work pool. Coaching can be used to help followers and improve performance by working with leaders (or skilled peers) under a developed coaching plan of action to sustain strengths and overcome weaknesses.

Lussier and Achua refer to coaching as a process of giving motivational feedback to maintain and improve performance. Coaching is designed to maximize follower strengths and minimize weaknesses. Coaching helps leaders concentrate on goals, develop resiliency, and build interpersonal savvy.[14] As with counseling, many leaders use guidelines to map out a coaching strategy. Lussier and Achua created the following coaching guidelines for that purpose:

- Develop a supportive working relationship
- Give praise and recognition
- Avoid blame and embarrassment
- Focus on the behavior, not the person
- Have followers assess their own performance
- Give specific and descriptive feedback
- Give coaching feedback
- Provide modeling and training
- Make feedback timely, but flexible
- Do not criticize
- Be specific, descriptive, and non-judgmental

The tasks may seem simple to the leader; but for a new trainee, it may be difficult[15]

Mentoring

One of the most powerful interpersonal skills is mentoring. As a mentor, the leader serves as a trusted counselor or teacher, especially in occupational settings. Two-way communication exists between the follower being guided and the mentor, who is usually the senior person. The mentor "shows the ropes" of the organization to the protégé, pointing out organizational norms and other pertinent information for success. Army Regulation 600-100, *Army Leadership*, defines mentoring as the voluntary developmental relationship that exists between a person of greater experience and a person of lesser experience that is characterized by mutual trust and respect.[16] Army Field Manual 6-22, *Army Leadership*, further explains that mentorship takes place when the mentor provides a less experienced leader with advice and counsel over time to help with professional and personal growth. The developing leader often initiates the relationship and seeks counsel from the mentor. The mentor takes the initiative to check on the well-being and development of that person.

Mentorship affects both personal development (maturity, interpersonal, and communication skills) and professional development (technical and tactical knowledge and career path knowledge).[17] It is interesting to note here that both Army Regulation 600-100 and Field Manual 6-22 stress that mentoring is a mutual trust relationship between the mentor and the protégé. In many organizations formal mentoring programs are established where upcoming followers are arbitrarily assigned to a mentor. Caution should be exercised before embarking on this type of formal mentoring program. Consideration should be given to the following possible shortfalls: Personality incompatibility (conflict) between the mentor and protégé. Gender preference, some protégés prefer same- or opposite-gender mentors; failure to meet this personal requirement will result in a mismatch. Mismatched hours of availability and proximity of work locations can deter a successful mentoring relationship. Intergenerational Diversity (age differences) can be harmful if senior members (mentors) of the workforce are unaware of the younger generation's expectations.

The strength of individual mentoring relationships or mentoring programs is based on mutual trust and respect. The mentored should carefully consider assessments, feedback, and guidance; these considerations become valuable for the growth that occurs. Contrary to common belief, mentoring relationships are not confined to the senior-junior relationship. They are found between peers and notably in the Army between senior NCOs and junior officers.[18] These relationships are also found between leaders and followers; protégés must be active participants in the developmental process; they should not wait for a mentor to choose them, but rather be proactive in their own development and request the mentor of their choice.

Conclusion

Leadership is a multifaceted art that must be studied, nurtured, and developed to be at its best. Simply following each of the steps outlined in this chapter will not make one an effective leader. However, being aware of the skills presented here (especially for the inexperienced leader) will enhance performance if leaders practice and fine-tune them to fit their needs and their personality. Entire regulations, pamphlets, manuals, and books are written on any one topic addressed in this chapter.

Effective leadership and interpersonal skills are not developed overnight, but are accomplished and learned over time. The leaders' use of the tools available to them and their ability to connect with others (through the use of interpersonal skills) is essential to leadership success. Mastery of oral presentation, counseling, coaching, and mentoring skills, supervising, and empowering are hallmark qualities that benchmark outstanding leaders from the mediocre. These are skills that can be taught and learned and will assuredly increase any leader's overall effectiveness.

Public Speaking Checklist[19]

ORGANIZATION: (Discernible, balanced plan of presentation)

Introduction. Identify yourself and use professional courtesy when addressing the person(s) being briefed. Establish the significance of the subject, the direction, and the purpose of the speech; identify your thesis.

Body. Present the main ideas in a logical order, transitioning smoothly to provide continuity and coherence from point to point. Clearly state the facts that bear on the problem and any assumptions. Present advantages and disadvantages of each option presented. The presentation should reflect a careful analysis of the subject and audience.

Conclusion/Summary. Tie the summary together with the main points of the speech in a meaningful way. Make an appropriate concluding statement and ask for questions.

ANALYSIS: (Clear development of the issues; justification for judgments and assertions)

Thesis/Focus. Make the thesis clear and unambiguous and (more importantly) identify it up front. Is the topic manageable and is it developed in sufficient detail without pointless departures from the subject?

Logic. Make arguments unfailingly consistent and not contradict stated positions. Conclusions are reasonable and follow from the available evidence; avoid emotional language.

Depth. Address the complexities of the issue, and avoid superficiality.

Breadth. Consider other points of view when addressing the issue, and present information in an unbiased manner?

Support. Present facts clearly, ensuring that they are accurate, credible, and objectively support the argument presented.

DELIVERY: (How the speaker communicates)

Appearance and Movement. Maintain a professional demeanor, and be well-groomed. Use gestures that are well-timed and natural, with purposeful movement to enhance the presentation. Eliminate distracting mannerisms such as repeated gestures, uh's , um's, and ok's.

Sincerity and Enthusiasm. Be openly enthusiastic and positive; show genuine concern for the subject and audience. Sell your ideas; do not just talk about them.

Eye Contact. Establish eye contact with the audience, right, left, and center. Maintain eye contact throughout the presentation.

Voice Quality. Use a rate of speech that is neither too fast nor too slow; use a tone and pitch that is natural and varied and not monotonous, too loud, or too soft.

Visual Aids. Integrate simple, concise, easily visible, and neat visual aids throughout the presentation to strengthen communication. Check for spelling errors.

Questions. Remain poised, and handle questions in a credible manner.
Adherence to Time. Stay within the stated time limits!

Figure 1 Public Speaking Checklist

Notes
1. John R. Schermerhorn, Jr., James G. Hunt, and Richard N. Osborn, *Organizational Behavior*, 7th ed. (New York: John Wiley & Sons, Inc., 2000), 287.
2. *Army Leadership: Competent, Confident, and Agile* [Field Manual 6-22] (Washington, D.C., Headquarters, Department of the Army, October 2006), 1-2.
3. Ralph Waldo Emerson, *The Complete Works of Ralph Waldo Emerson* (Centenary Edition, edited and with notes by Edward Waldo Emerson), available on the Internet at http://quod.lib.umich.edu/e/emerson/ (accessed 21 May 2008).

4. William A. Haskins, "Ethos and Manager's Credibility: Lessons From the Classroom," *Global Virtue Ethics Review*, January 2003; Available on the Internet at http://goliath.ecnext.com/coms2/gi_0199-2800993/Ethos-and-manager-s-credibility.html#abstract (accessed March 2008).

5. H. Johnson, ed., *The Wit and Wisdom of Alfred North Whitehead* (Whitefish, MT: Kessinger Publishing Company, 2007), 82.

6. William James, *Psychology: Briefer Course* (New York, N.Y.: Penguin Putman, Inc., 1992), 10.

7. Battle of New Orleans; Available on the Internet at http://en.wikipedia.org/wiki/Battle_of_New_Orleans (accessed 10 May 2008).

8. Carter McNamara, "Basics - Definitions (and Misconceptions) About Management," from the *Free Management Library*; available on the Internet at http://www.managementhelp.org/mgmnt/defntion.htm (accessed 20 May 2008).

9. Robert N. Lussier and Christopher F. Achua, *Leadership: Theory, Application, Skill Development*, 2nd ed. (Eagan, MN: South-Western, Thompson, 2004), 245-246.

10. Ibid., 247-249.

11. *Army Leadership*, 8-12.

12. Ibid.

13. Ibid., 8-12 to 8-13.

14. Lussier and Achua, 185.

15. Ibid., 186-189.

16. *Army Leadership* [Army Regulation 600-100] (Washington, D.C.: Headquarters, Department of the Army, 8 March 2007), 6.

17. *Army Leadership*, 8-14.

18. Ibid.

19. "Oral Presentation Assessment," *Army Management Staff College Student Guide, Version 1, Advanced Course Resident Curriculum* (30 May 2008), 62 (adapted by author).

Arthur P. McMahan, Ph.D.

Intergenerational Diversity: A Leadership Tool

Introduction

From leadership 101 to studies in advanced leadership, we learn that a leader must be competent. One particular aspect of competence is awareness of the environment around us and those variables that may impact it. Leaders must know what is right and what is right for the situation if they are to convince followers to do the right thing. Peter Drucker said, "Leadership is lifting a person's vision to high sights; the raising of a person's performance to a higher standard; the building of a personality beyond its normal limitations."[1] In order to be successful, leaders must understand their people and the way they interact in the workplace. Awareness of generational diversity and the implications of having three or four generations of followers working on the same team can prove beneficial to leaders interested in maximizing efficiency and effectiveness.

Notter says, "Diversity in the workplace is generally focused on working effectively with people who are different from you in the categories outlined in the law, i.e. race, gender, religion, etc."[2] Another aspect of diversity that is getting a lot more attention today is generational diversity. Many organizations have followers in their seventies or late sixties and some as young as 25. The knowledge and understanding about the values and interests of each generation can arm you with tools that can enhance organizational performance. The following quote from the Generational Imperative Inc. sums up the point:

By understanding each generation's unique core values and attitudes, employers can enhance their ability to: 1) recruit the best followers, 2) retain them, 3) maximize their loyalty and fulfillment, and 4) improve intergenerational cooperation and understanding.[3]

What is Generational Diversity?

Generation refers to a cohort of people born into *and* shaped by a particular span of time events, trends and developments.[4] Notter defines generation as "a group of people defined by age boundaries—those who were born during certain eras. They share similar experiences growing up, and their values and attitudes (particularly about work-related topics) tend to be similar based on their shared experiences during their formative years."[5] The boundary years for each generation vary by a few years, but there is general agreement on the years listed below. Researchers were more adamant about the Baby Boomer parameters than any other because they saw a clear physical indication after World War II of the increase in the number of births in the United States starting in 1946.

Individuals born on the fringes (early or late) of a generation may be quite different from those in the middle and could hold the values and interests of either the preceding or next generation. For as much as there is flexibility in the date parameters of generations, there is also a bit of flexibility in what each generation is called. The most commonly referenced names found throughout the research have been chosen for this chapter. The four generations likely to be represented in your workforce (see table 1) are 1) Traditionalists (1920-1945), 2) Baby Boomers (1946-1964, 3) Generation Xers (1960-1980) and 4) Millennials (1980-2000).

Generational diversity is having two, three, or four of these generations represented in your organization or on your team. According to Dr. Constance Patterson, "Every generation is influenced by its period's economic, political, and social events—from the Great Depression to the Civil Rights and women's movements to the advent of television and advanced computer technologies."[6] The leader's responsibility is to understand the values and interests of each group. Patterson further explains,

While obviously not every Traditionalist, Baby Boomer, Gen Xer, or Millennial may fit within their generational stereotype, taking note of generational diversity is still important, especially since intergenerational conflict in the workplace may keep plans, products, and ideas from moving forward.[7]

Understanding the characteristics of each group will allow leaders to appreciate groups and facilitate a cooperative and collaborative environment where different generations work in harmony.

Generational Characteristics

The Generations

TRADITIONALIST	BABY BOOMERS	GENERATION Xers	MILLENNIALS
Born 1920-1945	*Born* 1946-1964	*Born* 1960-1980	*Born* 1980-2000
Current Age 63-88	*Current Age* 44-62	*Current Age* 28-48	*Current Age* <28
Percent of Workforce 5	*Percent of Workforce* 43	*Percent of Workforce* 42	*Percent of Workforce* 10

Table 1

Table one above shows each generation and the span of years in which its members were born. Below is a description of some of the key characteristics of each generation and some of the implications for leaders to consider.

Traditionalists

Traditionalists are sometimes called the Silent Generation, and its members were born roughly from 1920-1945, although some experts have them born as early as 1900. They hold the key to many of the formulas your organization has used in the past. These are your elder statesmen, your longest tenured, and (in some cases) your senior ranking members.

Key events that shaped or influenced the lives of this generation are The Great Depression and World War II. Some key words to describe the traditionalists are dedication, sacrifice, conformity, and duty. This generation was loyal to their employers and often found themselves with one company or organization throughout their entire careers.

One observation about this group (from the follower point of view) is that they could be overbearing and somewhat rigid in their thinking, making them unwilling to accept other points of view. You may find them to be more conservative than their younger counterparts and a bit less prone to embrace technology and all of its many applications. Leaders should be aware that the traditionalist in your organization may retire at any moment and take away a host of institutional knowledge that is invaluable to your organization.

Baby Boomers

Baby Boomers (also referred to as Boomers) were born from 1946-1964, although some experts have the range at 1940-1962. The Vietnam War, the Civil Rights Movement, and television greatly influenced Boomers' lives. The boom in Baby Boomers refers to a noticeable rise in the number of children born in the U.S. after World War II.

> While austerity and restraint were the norms during the stress of the war years, after the war couples reunited and returned to traditional roles. Returning (mostly male) soldiers re-entered the workforce, and many women left wartime work to concentrate on childbearing and child rearing.

Researchers report that over 76 million babies were born during the Baby Boom era. Marriage became (again) a cultural and career norm for most women—and one result was babies.[8]

The Baby Boomer generation holds many of the leadership jobs today in business, government, and industry. Some of the prosperity that boomers experienced is a result of the hard work and frugality of their Traditionalist parents. Key words that describe this generation are personal gratification, optimism, team orientation, and involvement. This group is more technology savvy than the previous generation, but all have not fully embraced technology. A significant number of boomers are also eligible for retirement. Leaders should begin to develop succession plans to soften the impact that will be felt when boomers exit the workforce.

Generation Xers

Generation Xers are the children of Baby Boomers. Boomers who gained substantial socio-economic advantages over their Traditionalist parents passed those advantages on to their children. Born roughly from 1960-1980, this generation is smaller in number than previous generations. They are also referred to as Post Boomers.

One story has it that no one could come up with a name for this generation, so they called it "X." Some significant events that influenced Xers' lives were computers, Watergate, MTV, and an increase in single parent homes. Some key words that describe this generation are diversity, balance, fun, and self-reliance. Gen Xers grew up using computers and are technology-savvy. Compared to the two previous generations, they have a heightened expectation of the use and advantages of automation.

Millennials

Also known as Generation Y, the Internet Generation, and Generation Next, this is the newest group to join the workforce. Born from 1980-2000, this generation fully embraces the Internet and the art of multi-tasking. You should not be surprised to see a Millennial on the computer, text-messaging, listening to an iPod, and doing homework all at the same time.

Morley Safer said, "The workplace has become a psychological battlefield, and the Millennials have the upper hand because they are tech savvy, with every gadget imaginable almost becoming an extension of their bodies. They multitask, talk, walk, listen, type, and text. And their priorities are simple: they come first."[9] Millennials bring energy and enthusiasm into the workplace and present a distinct challenge for leaders on how to monitor and mentor without stifling creativity and technology skills. Some key words that describe Millennials are optimism, confidence, achievement, and diversity.

As a result of high school and college curricula that emphasize volunteerism and student employment, this group enters the workforce having been shaped or influenced by those experiences. Damian Oliver cites student employment experiences as a primary reason for this group's attitudes about work.[10]

Why is Intergenerational Diversity Important?

Leaders must understand human behavior in order to be effective. Understanding how values and interests differ across generations is a valuable tool for leadership. Notter offers that:

> Awareness of the generalized differences among the generations can help all followers work more productively with each other. Knowing in advance how each generation can be triggered (either positively or negatively) can help organizations develop balanced policies and can help individual managers and followers structure their work interactions in ways that benefit all types of people."[11]

Many questions may confront leaders faced with a multigenerational workforce. Ron Zemke, Claire Raines, and Bob Filipczak identify (below) some of those questions in their book, *Generations at Work*:

- How can I get older followers to sit down and discuss projects with the younger ones?
- How can I convince younger followers to listen to their older counterparts?
- How can I unite these different groups to focus on our common goal, despite their individual preferences?
- How do I mentor and nurture the younger followers so that they do not go off unsupervised and cause problems for the organization?
- How do I account for the differences in dress, communication preferences, and workplace etiquette preferred by the different generations?[12]

Baby Boomers who currently occupy many of the leadership positions in government, industry, and business are often skeptical that Millennials are too fast on the trigger and reject conforming to organizational norms. Millennials, on the other hand, often feel that Boomers are too rigid and often play the politics game in the workplace. While these statements are not true for all members of these groups, it is worthwhile to understand that these opinions exist. If leaders understand that these views could create potential conflicts, they may be able to resolve issues and turn the differences into positives. However, you cannot adjudicate generational differences if you are not aware that they exist.

Implications for Leaders

First, recognize that there are differences between the values and interests of individuals from different generations. Then ask yourself (or your Human Resources Chief) how many or what percent of your workforce is represented in each generation (see Table 1)? The numbers alone may indicate that you should be proactive in this area.

The inventory will show that you have multiple generations in your workforce or that you are a homogenous organization that is predominately one generation. Whatever the representation, the awareness of those numbers can lead you to action that can increase productivity and morale within your organization.

For example, if most of your followers are Traditionalists and Baby Boomers, you should have or be in the process of developing a succession plan that will allow you to capture the experience and institutional knowledge of your senior workforce. Part of that plan should include a strategy that builds a bench to replace the retiring followers. If all or most of your followers are Generation Xers and Millennials, you will have a fairly young workforce and should pay particular attention to their values and interests.

Understanding what the group likes or prefers can help drive the on-boarding and orientation programs. It could also lead to a better understanding of how to capture their enthusiasm and take advantage of their lifelong association with computers and technology.

If you have three or four generations in your workforce, then you should have an education program that will identify and address generational differences and bring the groups together in an effort to build diverse teams. "If we do not talk about why we're different and our different perspectives, we do not come to the best decisions," Patterson says, "The more people are willing to invest in honest communication about these issues, the better the outcome."[13]

In organizations that show the most success in addressing intergenerational diversity, over-communication is the rule. Further, these organizations have multiple methods of communication such as generationally diverse teams, small group discussions, email messages, and open conversation on vital issues. There is as much listening going on as there is talking, and listening to others' points of view and compromising in the end are key behaviors that identify organizations that address generational diversity.[14]

When leaders begin to design activities that address generational diversity issues, they should pay close attention to communication preferences. The newest followers in the workforce grew up with computers, the Internet, and electronic communication devices. Baby Boomers and Traditionalists had radio, TV, and newspapers as their primary sources of information during their developing years. The experiences that each generation has during formative years could result in differences in the way each group prefers to receive and absorb information. Again, understand that one cannot broad-brush all members of each generation and assume that they have the same preferences; but literature shows there is consistency within generations when it comes to values, interests, and other preferences (like communication). The high-performing organizations mentioned above have multiple modes of communication to account for variances in preferences. The Resilience Report, from Booz Allen Hamilton, highlights the dynamics of communication preferences between organizations and their millennial followers. The report states:

> The U.S. Department of Defense (DoD) took an unprecedented step on May 15, 2007, blocking troop access to MySpace, YouTube, and other popular Web sites. The official reason was to conserve bandwidth and safeguard security. But the DoD's ban also highlighted a gap in understanding between senior Military leaders and what demographers call Generation Y (alternatively known as the Millennial Generation or the Baby-Boom Echo). Few members of this generation (born after 1978) can recall a time when the Internet was not at their disposal.[15]

On the surface you may say, so what? But, in essence, they blocked some of the preferred methods of communication of its targeted recruiting pool. The group that may be the hardest sell and the one they need to sustain the force is most affected by the technology prohibition. This situation is complicated by security and access concerns, but it highlights a dilemma for the Army not unlike that of many organizations trying to recruit young, intelligent Millennials. How does an organization provide an environment that can accommodate the rapid-fire, high-tech communication that this generation is accustomed to and at the same time balance security issues, tradition, and the values and interests of older followers?

> This case illustrates that organizations with multi-generational workforces must be aware that there are communication preferences tied to generational groups and that those preferences must be accounted for in policy and regulations. The organization does not have to give in to all of the interests or whims of generational groups, but it must be aware of differences and be willing to discuss them among its members. The Army is addressing this issue head-on and may resolve it, perhaps by using an intergenerational team.

The Human Resources arena is an area where you may find a plethora of issues related to generational differences. Specific areas such as workplace behavior, hours of work, pay, rewards and dress codes all have the potential to break along generational lines. Traditionalists were loyal to their company, and many worked at the same place all of their adult lives. Each generation since has favored more mobility and focus on self. When you look at the resumés of Generation Xers and Millennials, you need to apply a different metric than the one used for Boomers or Traditionalists because the younger groups are apt to change jobs more frequently in pursuit of happiness, self satisfaction, and salary. Leaders should look closely at rewards and compensation to ensure the organization is competitive in both its approach to retaining talented young followers and compensating valued seasoned followers.

Younger generation followers question why they must adhere to dress codes that seem obsolete. More specifically with males, they wonder why they cannot just wear jeans and a T-shirt to work instead of a shirt and tie. One effective way to engage this topic is through a cross-generational team, where the leader consciously builds a team with representatives from all of the generations present in the workforce. The discussion about dress, if handled properly, could be the beginning of an open dialog that allows each generation to voice preferences and could perhaps lead to a compromise.

Solutions for Leaders

Twenty-first century leaders will have to deal with generational diversity, whether they want to or not. In the United States (as individuals continue to work longer and organizations continue to bring in younger followers) there is the potential that leaders will have three or four generations in their workforce. Educating themselves and their organization on the possible impact of generational diversity is one of many tools that they can use to become more effective. Here are some actions that leaders can take that will improve their chances of successfully addressing generational differences in the workplace and building intergenerational teams that are productive and efficient.

- Leaders should educate and prepare themselves and their organization on the values, implications, and interests of each generation. They may hire a consultant/trainer or appoint an intergenerational team to study the topic and present it to the organization.
- Assess the organization's generational posture. How many followers belong to each generation?
- Develop a mentoring program that pairs generationally diverse followers so that they can learn about and from each other.
- Make a conscious effort to build teams composed of members from each generation in the workforce, where applicable.

- Develop a succession plan that stipulates the intent to garner the experience and knowledge of seasoned followers, and set forth a method to replace the aging workforce as they retire.
- Build a salary, rewards, and recognition program that accounts for generational preferences and concerns and addressees the needs of the organization relative to the generational groups.
- Consider telework, flexible work schedules, and other options to address generational preferences and concerns.
- Place extra emphasis on communication, and try (where applicable) to use multiple communication options to maximize coverage and comprehension
- Create a specific plan to develop Millennials.
- Be an adaptive leader that recognizes their own generational preferences and is open to suggestions and comments from all followers from all generations.

There are some who think (as reported by Fran Giancola) that this entire "generational" discussion may be overblown. Even some advocates agree that there are limitations to the generational approach, particularly in regards to minorities and recent immigrants.[16] However, there is great utility in addressing generational diversity issues for leaders. An aware leader who understands that individuals from different generations might have differing values and interests and (therefore) may perceive group and workplace dynamics differently can proactively address these issues. Intergenerational diversity is in and of itself neither positive nor negative but can be used to the organization's advantage if leadership is proactive. The dynamics created by generational differences can manifest as issues that confront leaders directly or that loom beneath the surface.

Conclusion

Generational diversity is an "X" factor that compounds all existing variables in the workplace such as gender, race, education, leader/follower, personality type, etc. Generational differences can be channeled into strengths by skillful leaders or if not checked may lead to disorder (such as the 'us against them' attitude) and a drain on effectiveness and efficiency. Audiences seem to be able to wrap their arms around this topic and find application in their work and private lives. As aging Baby Boomers retire and more Gen Xers and Millennials fill their jobs, the workplace will continue to become more generationally diverse. To prepare for this transformation, leaders should equip themselves with knowledge and understanding of how generational differences (as reflected in values and interests) will impact the workforce.

Notes

1. Judith E. Glaser, *The DNA of Leadership: Leverage Your Instincts to Communicate, Differentiate* (Avon, MA: Platinum Press, 2006), 108.
2. Jamie Notter, *Generational Diversity in the Workplace: Hype Won't Get You Results* (Gaithersburg, MD: Notter Consulting, 2007); available on the Internet at http://www.lulu.com/content/544094 (accessed 10 July 2008).
3. Chuck Underwood, *The Generational Imperative: Understanding Generational Differences in the Workplace, Marketplace, and Living Room* (Charleston, SC: BookSurge Publishing, 2007); available on the Internet at http://www.genimperative.com (accessed on 10 July 2008).
4. "Generation," Wikipedia article available on the Internet at http://en.wikipedia.org/wiki/Generation (accessed 10 July 2008).
5. Notter, *Generational Diversity in the Workplace.*
6. Melissa Dittman, "Generational Differences at Work," *Monitor on Psychology* 36, no. 6 (June 2005): 54; available on the Internet at http://www.apa.org/monitor/jun05/generational.html (accessed 10 July 2008).
7. Ibid.
8. Landon Y. Jones, "Swinging 60s?" *Smithsonian Magazine* 36, Issue 10 (January 2006), 102-107; available on the Internet at http://web.ebscohost.com/ehost/detail?vid=4&hid=105&sid=e0ab007e-fc74-43b8-9c6e-c783f6109d58%40sessionmgr102 (accessed 10 July 2008).
9. Morley Safer, as reported on the CBS network television program *60 Minutes*, November 2007.
10. Damien Oliver, "An Expectation of Continued Success: The Work Attitudes of Generation Y," *Labor & Industry* 17(1) 2006: 61-84.
11. Notter, *Generational Diversity in the Workplace.*
12. Ron Zemke, Claire Raines, and Bob Filipczak, *Generations at Work: Managing the Clash of Veterans, Boomers, Xers, and Nexters in the Workplace* (New York: AMACOM, 2000), 25-26.
13. Dittman, 54.
14. Zemke, Raines, and Filipczak, 154.
15. Art Fritzson, Lloyd W. Howell, Jr., and Dov S. Zakheim, "Military of Millennials," *Resilience Report* (10 March 2008), 1-8; available on the Internet at http://www.strategy-business.com/resiliencereport/resilience/rr00056 (accessed 10 July 2008).
16. Frank Giancola, "The Generation Gap: More Myth Than Reality," *Human Resource Planning* 29, no. 4 (1985): 32-37.

LEVERAGING
LEADER ASSETS

1. **Leadership via the Eyes of the Follower: Somebody's Watching You**
   Darrin Graham, Ed.D., Professor of Civilian Leader Development

2. **Core Values: The Essence of Leadership in the 21st Century**
   James Jarrett, Professor of Civilian Leader Development

3. **Mastering Teambuilding Principles**
   Kathy Strand, Professor of Civilian Leader Development

4. **Leadership and Emotional Intelligence**
   Constance Yelverton, Professor of Civilian Leader Development

5. **Women and Minority Leaders in the Federal Government**
   Angela Parham, Ph.D., Professor of Civilian Leader Development

6. **Distance Learning as an Enabler to Developing Army Leadership**
   Sidney Ricks, Professor of Civilian Leader Development

7. **Leveraging Self-Synchronization—A Leaders Art in Network Centric Warfare**
   Jim Geter, Technology and Operations Specialist

Darrin Graham, Ed.D.

Leadership via the Eyes of the Follower: Somebody's Watching You

Introduction

Many publications describe the skills and techniques of becoming an effective leader. However, there are few publications that illustrate how followers view leaders. It is said that leaders cannot be leaders if they have no followers.[1] With that said, it is safe to assume that one of the most overlooked elements in becoming a great leader is to understand how followers analyze leaders and the organization. The failure of leaders to understand how they are perceived by their followers could subsequently have an adverse effect on the future of the organization's mission.

There are many misconceptions that leaders may have about followers. For example, some leaders may view followers not as people, but rather as material to be molded.[2] Leaders solve complex, ill-structured problems daily, but many fail to understand their role through the eyes of their followers which, if handled incorrectly, could become a problem in itself. As leaders are educated in the school of leadership, it is the words of John Gardner that must remain forever embedded in their head, "That what you learn after you know it all is what really matters." [3] This chapter will attempt (in a realistic way) to depict what is expected of leaders through the eyes of followers.

In order to provide a clearer understanding of the supporting role in which followers are cast, this chapter will touch upon how followers not only understand their role in support of their leaders, but how they, themselves must be committed to this understanding. A lack of preparation on the part of leaders could turn some followers' first day of work into their last. The inability to unmask the leaders' fallacies of perfection will eventually destroy morale and lead to a lost of respect once rendered by the followers.

The inability of leaders to encourage their followers or give them the latitude to become critical thinkers has adverse effects the followers' emotions, perceptions, and motivation. Followers may know more about what is going on within the organization than the leaders could possibly imagine, and followers may be highly offended if they presume their leaders believed anything less. It is important to understand that followers expect their leaders to be structured, firm, consistent, and approachable. The followers' main desire is to make the organization successful. Followers yearn for guidance and the mentorship of great leaders. They (like most people) have difficulty dealing with change, but with continual guidance, clear (daily) communication, and a bit of patience, the average followers will prevail.

The Followers Role

Followers understand that there needs to be collaboration between them and their leaders.

> The most effective followers know that they cannot be fully effective unless they work in partnership, which requires both a commitment to high performance and a commitment to developing effective relationships with partners (including their boss), whose collaboration is essential to success in their own work. The followers, just as the leaders, are intent on high performance and recognize that they share the responsibility for the quality of the relationship they have with their leaders.[4]

Followers choose to be followers, just as leaders choose their role to lead. Leadership should be viewed as a relationship or a duality because there can be no successful leader without dedicated followers.[5] A fictional example might be:

Rich, owner of a small contracting company in Northern Virginia, was concerned when unexpected bad weather and a failing economy caused his business to decline. Rich had a small staff of five followers who never complained, were hard followers, were punctual, and left each day after the job was done. Rich really appreciated his staff, and he praised them at every opportunity. Rich's main role within the company was to market the business; he made the deals that put food on his team's table that (in return) made him successful and proud.

Around the same time that business slowed, Rich's secretary ran off to get married. Rich found himself without the resources to hire a new secretary and was forced to assume her administrative duties. Prevented from drumming up the much needed new business, Rich immediately held a meeting to inform his followers of the situation. He explained that he did not know how long the company could last if business did not pick up soon. He assured them that although the work might decrease, no one would lose their job—unless he lost his company.

As the weeks passed, Rich noticed that one of his roofers was coming into the changing room after working an 8 to10-hour shift and putting on a suit. At first Rich thought the man was going on job interviews, but each morning, the roofer would return to work on time and with a new work order. It started with one job here and two there, but quickly the company was getting more work than it could handle. Rich had to hire a new secretary and two new roofers. Amazed with the direction the company was headed (yet still puzzled with exactly how), Rich asked his roofer "How did you get all of these work orders?" The roofer replied, "I understand that you were unable to get out and make sales, so everyday after work I went out and knocked on doors and made telephone calls until I convinced people to allow our company to complete their construction needs."

Rich asked the roofer why he went beyond his duties as a roofer and dedicate his free time to save his diminishing company, taking time from his family and personal life. The roofer simply replied, "The Company was going under." Rich then replied, "That still doesn't make me understand why you made those sacrifices for this company. You could have easily taken the new customers and started your own business and put me out of business." The roofer looked at Rich and replied, "If this company fails, you fail; if you fail, we all fail."

Warren Bennie is emphasizes that "Exemplary leadership and organizational changes are impossible without the full inclusion, initiative, and cooperation of followers." Followers support leaders whom they feel will help them reach their fullest potential. Followers want to feel a sense of belonging and know that they are an important part of the organization's success. They want to feel comfortable in their workplace; they want to be recognized for their accomplishments; and they want to be kept informed, good or bad. In return, if followers view their leaders as loyal, they will also be loyal.

If followers view their leaders as dishonest, they may view the entire organization as being flawed. Followers believe in leaders who communicate with confidence, who display enthusiasm to inspire others, and who are firm in their convictions. They may avoid leaders who appear arrogant and make irrational decisions.[6] Followers feel comfortable with leaders who speak their language.[7] Leaders cannot expect their followers to understand their intentions unless they (the leaders) clearly define their expectations. When followers have input, they are more apt to remain engaged. Ken Blanchard in his book, *The Secret: What Great Leaders Know—and Do*, says,

> Another part of engagement has to do with the level of buy-in people have for a cause, their work, and a leader. You want to do more than enlist their hands; you want to engage their heads and hearts. With every pair of hands you hire, you get a free brain.[8]

The importance of follower buy-in is emphasized by Robert Vecchio when he stated that followers, "…have a responsibility to be conscientious and to expend energies for unit goals.[9]

One of the first policies that leaders of an organization should establish is a new follower welcoming program. The first day of work can be the make-or-break point for any new valued follower. Leaders should not look at new followers as people who need jobs; but rather look at them as people who have the skills and services that the organization needs. After all, the organization actively sought the highest qualified individuals to fill those slots, right? Right! Good leaders should ensure that new follower programs are adopted and functioning properly to assure the followers' longevity with the organization. According to Cheryl Mahaffey, Director of Consulting Services for Psychological Services, Inc., the first 30 days on the job are the most critical for new followers.[10]

This is evident with Southwest Airlines who aims to make their new followers realize how special they are and how their jobs are not just any job, from the moment they accept the position. Leaders immediately send out emails to team members announcing new followers. Leaders contact new followers at home prior to their start date to introduce themselves and to welcome the new members to the team.[11]

Upon arriving at the organization, new leaders should know some personal information about their followers, such as names of spouse and children, where they come from (last organization), and their interests. Leaders should be familiar with some of the answers to the same vital questions that were asked during the detailed interview. By doing these basic things, the organization ensures the followers feel as though they are part of a family. Imagine how you would feel if (upon entering your new organization) your new leader and team members greet you at the door calling you by your first name. If new followers, for example, receive a personal tour guide, they are more apt to feel comfortable and confident in the new organization.

What Followers See: Fallacies

Followers see blind spots; they can see the things that leaders try hard to camouflage, and they also see things that leaders do not know about themselves. Followers usually know most of the leaders' weaknesses. According to John C. Maxwell in the book *The 360 Degree Leader*, "One of the worst things leaders can do is to expend energy trying to makes others think they're perfect. That's true whether the leader is CEO or functioning in the middle of the organization." [12] Followers feel more comfortable with leaders who are concerned with the smooth running of the organization and who are not afraid to admit when they are wrong. Since no one is perfect, followers want leaders to quit pretending. [13]

Maxwell goes on to state, "One of the greatest mistakes leaders make is spending too much time in the office." [14] Followers want to see their leaders in places other than in meetings. They feel that leaders who walk through the halls and slow down to connect with people are more approachable. The followers look to see if their leaders are putting people first. Abraham Lincoln always wandered onto the battlefields to meet the troops and check the climate of his most valuable resources. Retired General Collin Powell, as a young lieutenant in Vietnam, used this fact-finding tactic to find out vital information the headquarters did not have. This is a prime opportunity for leaders to let their followers know that they (the leaders) are human and have a genuine concern for their (the followers) wellbeing and safety. It is also an opportunity to find out what's going on in the organization from the followers' points of view.

Research on How Followers View the Leader and the Organization

Research conducted by Teresa M. Amabile and Steven J. Kramer, in

Harvard Business Review, shows that people experience a constant stream of emotions, perceptions, and motivation as they react to and makes sense of the events of the workday.[15] Recent research in neuroscience found that emotion and cognition (which includes perception of events) are tightly intertwined. Areas of the brain associated with rational thought and decision making have direct connections to areas associated with feelings. [16]

When something happens at work, it immediately triggers cognitive, emotional, and motivational processes. The followers' minds start "sense-making." When this happens, they try to figure out why the event happened and what are its implications. For example, if they are happy and excited about it, they will easily complete the task and put great effort into it. The same goes for perception. If followers perceive the work (and themselves) as having high value to the organization, their motivation to complete the task will be high. When followers feel highly valued and certain about what needs to be accomplished, this too is translated into high performance. Not only does the team get the work done on time, but its high quality makes an immediate and measurable contribution to the company's success.

The research also showed that the greater the ability (or liberty) a person has to be creative and be a self thinker, the greater their mood and vise-versa. The people in the study were more creative when they interpreted the happenings in the organization as being positive—that is, when they saw their organization and leaders as collaborative, cooperative, open to new ideas, able to evaluate and develop new ideas fairly and clearly focused on an innovative vision, and willing to reward creative work. Followers were less creative when they perceived political infighting and internal competition among the leaders or aversion to new ideas. [17]

When leaders enable their followers to move forward, receive proper training, and do their work while treating them with respect, the followers are able to make progress and achieve their goals, accomplish tasks, and solve problems. Followers make more progress when the leadership clarifies where the work is heading and why it matters. During the research, leadership allowed their followers to set clear, individual goals as well as team goals. They allowed the followers to work freely towards those goals and (when necessary) make changes as a team.[18]

When second-line supervisors' actions impede progress, followers become angry, and their work slows down. Followers often wonder why first-line supervisors do not do more to facilitate the progress and feel that maybe their jobs are not important and their leaders are either willfully undermining them or are hopelessly incompetent.[19]

Followers Know More Than You Think

Leaders should be open to learning from their followers' vast pool of vital information that may save the organization money and time. [20] There was a young sergeant in the Army, arriving at a new organization and directed to lead people who may have been in the organization many years before her; she knew right off that she had one of two routes to take. She could pretend that she, a brand new sergeant, was Ms. Know-it-all and risk losing the respect and support of her team, or she could be honest with them and herself and reveal that she knew little about this new unit. She took the latter, and by taking the latter, she found her team to be very intelligent, dedicated, hard working Soldiers and Civilians. Because she was humble and honest, they accepted her, and they (as an organization) moved forward.

Consistency, Firm, Fair, and Structure

There will always be different perceptions of what leaders do, so leaders should always be consistent. Followers who believe in their leaders will sell their organization to whomever they may come in contact with because they also believe in the organization's mission, vision, goals, and values. They expect their leaders to be firm, structured, and (most of all) fair. If they believe in their leaders and feel those leaders have their best interests at heart, firm (but fair) is normally okay. [21]

This author witnessed a young private in basic training walk into the barracks room one Sunday afternoon to find one of his four roommates once again deeply engaged in a conversation about the drill sergeants. In their attempts to gain the private's support in what the private later deemed to be some type of jump ship tactic, his roommate said to him, "Private, the drill sergeants do not like you." He replied, "Really? Why do you say that?" The roommate said, "Because they are always yelling at you and making you drop to do push ups." The private said "Oh, I hadn't looked at it like that." He could see the look of amazement in their faces. The disgruntled group just knew that they were going to recruit the private in the plot that they were scheming up. So the roommate said to the private, "You do not think so, then, what is your take on it?"

The private said, "I come from a family of loud talkers, so, to me, they are not really yelling at me, they are just giving directions loudly, and didn't they say that we needed to pass a fitness test with one of the events being a push-up test before we could graduate?" The roommate replied with a yes, as his co-conspirators' heads went north and south. Then the private said, "Well they must really like me. In fact, I must be the drill sergeants' favorite!" said the private. His roommate looked at the private and turned to his partners in crime and said, "He's right; they favor him." The private smiled and walked away, and from that point forward, the private adopted that attitude and believed in his head that he was the favorite. From then on, the private quickly defended any negativity directed at his drill sergeant and his company.

In the story the drill sergeants, although very firm and sometimes aggressively demanding, had clearly showed the private that they had his welfare in mind. The private understood that it didn't matter if he liked the yelling or the constant demand to perform push ups; what mattered was that he understood their purpose. He understood that passing his physical fitness test was not only a requirement for graduation, it was also important to the drill sergeants, which the private computed as caring. His strong belief that the drill sergeants believed in him empowered him to support the drill sergeants and defend the organization. John Maxwell states, "Leaders should look at their follower as if they were tens."[22] The drill sergeants had a job to do; they made sure they were firm by giving direct, clear, and undisputable directions and by motivating the privates with push ups, while secretly enhancing their bodies to prepare them for the final fitness test. They were able to see the ten in the privates.

Followers seek Mentorship

Mentorship is defined by the Army as the voluntary developmental relationship that exists between a person of greater experience and a person of lesser experience that is characterized by mutual trust and respect.[23] Enthusiastic followers look for leaders who are willing to mentor. Followers may or may not ask their leaders to become their personal mentors; they may just secretly watch and mimic their every move. Some followers may direct their peers to seek mentorship from their leaders, especially if the followers think highly of and respect their leaders. When choosing mentors, followers look to see if the potential mentor has some of the qualities of a true leader. If the follower feels that the leader doesn't have those qualities, they may stay clear of them. [24]

Change: Leave the Old Job Behind

Followers want to understand and have input when changes occur within the organization. They take it personally when new leaders enter an organization and immediately implement change (in many instances) based on what took place in their previous organization. Followers feel that just because something worked in a previous organization does not mean it will work in their organization. Each and every organization is unique in its own way. Organizations may produce the same type of product and may even ship it to the same region or have the same name or logo; however, each is comprised of different people; the organization may sit on different blocks; or it may be located in different parts of the world. This means that it will face different challenges and situations.

People tend to resist change, especially if it is not clear from the beginning why that change needs to happen. Leaders who try to implement new rules or systems in an organization without first finding out why the people in the organization do what they do and the style with which they do it quickly risk the chance of losing good, loyal followers.[25] Followers may perceive the wrong message; they may feel that the new leader thinks that the organization is screwed up or they (the followers) are incompetent.

Len Fuchs states in his book, *The Greatest Mistake Leaders Make is Very Ego-Centered*, as a result, leaders are usually the last to recognize that there is anything wrong."[26] Followers do not think that just because certain leaders were chosen to lead that they know everything. The organization most likely was in existence before those leaders got there, and there is a great chance it will be there long after those leaders are gone. Leaders should not rudely ignore opinions and ideas of their followers. "The wasted human potential is incalculable." [27] Followers are motivated when their leaders work together with them to brainstorm and solve problems. Brainstorming is freethinking and is not what you do when you already know the answer. It is what leaders and followers do together when they are trying to decide the best route to take for the best possible solution. Leaders should accept that followers (in many cases) have been working there longer than they have, and the followers may just know the inner-workings of the organization. Leaders should not fall into the myth of thinking, "If followers have what it takes to be the leader, this organization wouldn't have hired me."[28]

Communication

Followers want to know where they stand in terms of their performance and job security, and they want to know in which direction the organization is heading. They want straightforward information (good or bad). When this information is not provided, they tend to feel that their leaders do not value them as part of the organization, and thus, become dissatisfied and feel that they cannot trust anything their leaders say. It is extremely important to followers that their leaders take time to communicate happenings within the organization.[29]

An effective illustration of this concept happened to this author a number of years ago. Followers of a medical company in Georgia heard rumors about the company downsizing. When the leadership was asked by the followers to clarify the rumors, a message was disseminated that what they (the followers) heard was just a rumor. After the downsizing actually happened, the leaders revealed that misinformation was given to them because (at the time) the organization was uncertain as to the number of followers affected in the downsizing. After the downsizing came to fruition, the organization lost more valued followers than it originally planned. Unbeknownst to the organization, misinformation caused the remaining followers to lose faith in the leadership and destroyed morale within the organization.

Some potential followers are inspired (or uninspired) by the nonverbal actions of leaders. Leaders are placed (not by choice) in a position to be viewed and followed by others; so it is vital that leaders are just as conscious of their nonverbal (messages) as they are of the verbal. Followers tend to do what their leaders model, just as much as they do what their leaders say. They view their leaders as role models and the epitome of trust.

Conclusion

"Without followers leadership is meaningless, and leaders do not exist."[31] So it is imperative that leaders recognize their role and what is expected of them through the eyes of their followers. Leaders should be firm and fair; they should have the ability to communicate, coach, mentor, and guide; they should have the humility to listen, respect, and trust. Leaders should give their followers the flexibility to be creative and the freedom to investigate all possibilities. Leaders should adopt the partnership concepts of their followers. Leaders must understand that their followers embrace the same goals, desires, and outcomes. If leaders fail, so do their followers. As Carl Jung said, "The true leader is always led."[32]

Notes

1. Robert Goffee and Gareth Jones, "Followership; It is Personal, Too," *Contemporary Issues in Leadership*, 6th ed. (Cambridge, MA: Westview Press, 2006), 127.
2. Earl H. Potter III and William E. Rosenbach, "Followers as Partners: The Spirit of Leadership," *Contemporary Issues in Leadership,* 6th ed. (Cambridge, MA: Westview Press, 2006), 143.
3. John Gardner's Writings, "Personal Renewal" Delivered to McKinsey & Company, Phoenix, AZ, November 10, 1990; Electronic article from the Public Broadcasting Service; (PBS), available on the Internet at http://www.pbs.org/johngardner/sections/writings_speech_1.html (assessed 1 June 2008).
4. Potter and Rosenbach, 146.

5. Robert Kelley, *The Power of Followership* (New York: Bantam Doubleday Publishing Group, Inc., 1992), 62.
6. Warren Bennis, "The End of Leadership: Exemplary Leadership is Impossible Without Full Inclusion, Initiatives, and Cooperation of Followers," *Contemporary Issues in Leadership*, 6th ed. (Cambridge, MA: Westview Press, 2006), 129
7. Warren Blank, *The 108 Skills of Natural Born Leaders* (New York: AMACOM, 2001), 204.
8. Ken Blanchard and Mark Miller, *The Secret: What Great Leaders Know—and Do* (San Francisco: Berrett-Koehler Publishers, Inc., 2004), 52.
9. Robert P. Vecchio, *Understanding the Dynamics of Power and Influence in Organizations* (Notre Dame, IN: University of Notre Dame Press, 1997), 115.
10. Cheryl Mahaffey, "The First 30 Days: The Most Critical Time To Influence Follower Success," *Employment Relations Today*, Summer (1999): 53.
11. Lorraine Grubbs-West, *Lessons in Loyalty: How Southwest Airlines Does It: An Insider's View* (Dallas: Conerstone Leadership Institute, 2005), 23.
12. John C. Maxwell, *The 360⁰ Leader* (Nashville: Thomas Nelson Publishers, 2005), 206.
13. Ibid.
14. Ibid.
15. Teresa M. Amabile and Steven J. Kramer, "Inner Work Life: Understanding the Student of Business Performance," *Harvard Business Review,* May (2007): 76.
16. Ibid.
17. Ibid.
18. Ibid.
19. Ibid.
20. Len Fuchs and John Nicholas, *You're a Leader Now What?: Knowing What To Do Next* (Gilbert, AZ: Real Leaders Institute, LLC, 2006), 26.
21. Maxwell, 221.
22. Ibid., 220.
23. *Army Leadership: Competent, Confident, and Agile* [Field Manual 6-22] (Washington, D.C.: Department of the Army, 12 October 2006), 8-14 and 8-84.
24. Ibid.
25. Frederick F. Reichheld, *Loyalty Rules: How Today's Leaders Build Lasting Relationships* (Boston: Harvard Business School Press, 2001), 173.
26. Fuchs and Nicholas, 24-25.
27. Fred Herrera, "Demystifying Hiring and Retention," *Employment Relations Today*, Vol. 28, issue 2 (2001): 87-95.
28. Amabile and Kramer, 80.
29. Robert Kelley, *The Power of Followership* (New York: Bantam Doubleday Publishing Group, Inc., 1992), 51.
30. Ibid., 62.
31. Ibid.
32. Larry E. Senn, *Leaders on Leading: Insights from the Field* (Long Beach, CA: Senn-Delaney Leadership Consulting Group, Inc., 1999), 93.

James Jarrett

Core Values: The Essence of Leadership in the 21st Century

Introduction

The United States of America began by establishing its core values in the Declaration of Independence, which reads, "We hold these truths to be self-evident, that all men are created equal; that they are endowed by their Creator with certain unalienable Rights, that among these are Life, Liberty, and the pursuit of Happiness."[1] The core values of equality, freedom, and opportunity were established for this Nation in the Declaration of Independence. These core values provided the focus by which this country moved towards greatness and created a source of contention from within to ensure that all citizens receive equal and fair treatment.

From the example of the United States establishing core values, leaders must determine their own core values. Identifying and establishing individual, as well as, organizational core values is a critical function if leaders are to bring their organization to high performance. Leaders' goals, decisions, and actions must be aligned with their core values to obtain personal and organizational success.

This chapter examines the importance of establishing core values and posits that the process for establishing them should be a vital part of individual goal setting and organizational goal- and vision-setting. In *On Becoming a*

Leader, Warren Bennis writes, "Until you truly know yourself, strengths and weaknesses, and know what you want to do and why you want to do it, you cannot succeed in any but the most superficial sense of the word."[2] Leaders who truly know themselves understand the importance that values have on motivating and inspiring others. By knowing and understanding the role that values have on our motivational system, leaders can appreciate the importance of aligning core values with goals and objectives. When this alignment is accomplished, leaders can easily achieve success for themselves and their organization.

What are Core Values?

Core values are the center of our being. The center as defined by *Webster's New World Dictionary* is "the point around which anything revolves; a point of origin, as of influence, ideas or action."[3] Our values provide a point of reference for all that we think, believe, and do. To illustrate how our values relate to a human's center, observe Figure 1. "The onion analogy depicts how our values are linked to our actions and responses. When interacting with another individual, the first noticeable observation is behavior. Behavior is the derivative of their attitude. Their attitude is generated from their beliefs."[4] According to Army Field Manual 6-22, *Army Leadership*, "beliefs are convictions that people hold as true, based on their experiences, and they provide a starting point for what to do in everyday situations. Values and beliefs are central to character."[5]

The further leaders analyze people, the better they will understand why people behave and think as they do, their motives, and the source of their energy. Values are at the core of all that people do, believe, and think.

Figure 1:
Onion Analogy

It is important that leaders identify their own core values. According to FM 6-22, "These values become an empowering set of personal guidelines that serve as anchor points for leading, coaching, and mentoring others for success. They provide the focus of what people do and why they do it. Values become the convictions that provide the internal stimulus towards a desired or preferred outcome."[6] A system of values defines purpose and motivation in life.

As values provide motivation in individuals for drive and determination, values in an organization provide the motivation for its continued existence. "Values are beacons that guide the pursuit of goals and objectives without losing its identity or its importance."[7] In *Core Values: The Precondition for Business Excellence*, Su Mi Park Dahlgaard states:

> Systematic leadership development for business excellence demands transformation of our mental models. This requires a profound understanding of so-called core values (intangibles) and their relation to the traditional tangibles (goals and core competencies). Often core values are not clearly identified, and they are seldom deployed with the same enthusiasm as the goals and core competencies needed for business excellence. It was assumed that if core values are neglected in the policy deployment process, it will never be possible to achieve business excellence.[8]

The process of goal setting and values determination is critical for individual leaders to obtain personal or organizational success. "Effective goals are best established after thoroughly thinking through your values and composing a personal mission statement." The process of goal setting and values determination must be conducted together to clearly understand the true purpose of a leader. Newberry states, "The best way to keep your commitment to reach a goal is to understand why you are striving for it. It is the "**why**" (or link to your values) that keeps you motivated."[9]

Where Values Come From

Personal experiences in earlier years helps form core values. Parents, siblings, role models, relatives, friends, and the institutions attended all are part of forming core values. Young children who participate in Boy or Girl Scouts are exposed to the Scout oath, laws, motto, and slogan. The scouting experience helps shape its members into whom they become.

In addition to developing values from scouting, parental teaching is paramount in developing values. Parents instill positive values such as a strong work ethic, resilience, honesty, integrity, and a sense of service. This learning is the foundation and support structure of individuals. The values that leaders and followers learned early in life become part of how they act and respond. Leaders and followers can determine or validate their own core values using the instructions at Figure 2 and the Personal Core Values Table at Figure 3.

Personal Core Values

Tiger Woods and Phil Mickelson, great golfers who are ranked number one and number two in the world respectively, demonstrate how parental teaching and professional role models provide the foundation for core values. Woods espouses the value of "service" to the community. This value was shared with him (from both parents) early as a child. The opportunity to serve the community is shown by the development of junior golf programs and the building of a multi-million dollar learning center.

Mickelson not only espouses the values of his parents, but he also adopted values from professional role models. As an amateur playing in his first Augusta National Masters Tournament, he observed the behaviors of Arnold Palmer and Jack Nicholas. He noticed how they respected the gallery and followers that supported the tournament. Today as a seasoned veteran, Mickelson always makes it a priority to respect the volunteers who support every tournament. His enthusiasm and energy can be observed as he greets spectators, volunteers, and opponents. This was a lesson learned from two excellent role models. As the top leaders in the golfing world, Woods and Mickelson continue to demonstrate their core values.

Leadership Defined

So what is leadership? This question is often asked; but the best definition can only come from within, reflecting the real meaning constructed by each person. To understand how values influence leadership, leaders must first know what it means. Army Field Manual 6-22 states, "Leadership is influencing people by providing purpose, direction, and motivation while operating to accomplish the mission and improving the organization." Army leadership consists of three levels: direct, organizational, and strategic. The following explanation provides a definition and examples of direct, organizational, and strategic leadership.

Direct leadership is face-to-face, first-line leadership where followers see their leaders at all times. Direct leaders' span of influence may range from a handful to several hundreds of people. Organizational leaders influence several hundred to several thousand people. Organizational leaders have staff that helps them lead their people and manage their organization's resources. Strategic leaders are responsible for large organizations, and they influence several thousand to hundreds of thousand of people. They establish force structure, allocate resources, communicate strategic vision, and prepare their organizations and America's Army as a whole for future roles.[10]

Individual Leadership Values

Leading others at any level, whether direct, organizational, or strategic requires leaders to know themselves first. A critical part of knowing themselves is to understand what motivates them and what they value. Leaders develop their orientation to their leadership style based on self-awareness and drive. It is from this understanding that leaders are able to provide critical influence and direction, whether at the direct, organizational, and strategic level.

Daniel Goleman states, "Leadership operates at its best through emotionally intelligent leaders who create resonance." Goleman believes that these leaders show strong leadership strengths in areas of self-awareness, self-management, social awareness, and relationship management. These emotionally intelligent skills are not innate talents, but are learned abilities that make these leaders effective.[11]

Leaders who are emotionally intelligent understand their strengths and weaknesses and are able to include their values in their leadership style. It is from these values, coupled with their drive and desire to succeed, that leaders draw the energy to motivate and lead their followers. When leaders incorporate the instincts that come with emotional intelligence with their personal value system, they become competent, agile leaders who can adapt in challenging situations.

The brain uses a hierarchy to prioritize beliefs from what is desired as most important to those things that are least important. For example, if the thought of mentoring high-performing followers appeals to leaders, they may find it highly inspirational, but if they must discipline low-performers, they might find it less motivating. When leaders identify their own values, they can visualize where they want to go and then make relationships with their followers that will help them get there.

To compare value-centered leadership with the character of a leader, Sankar states:

> The quest for leadership excellence is based more on character than charisma. The character of the leader is grounded in such core values as integrity, trust, truth, and human dignity, which influences the leader's vision, ethics, and behavior. The moral literacy of the leader and the essentials of an ethical culture are connected to the leader's character and not to a charismatic personality.[12]

Leaders of character are not born; they develop their character from their daily experiences and from those things that they consider as most important . . . their core values. In contrast, charisma focuses on style, image, self-confidence, admiration, and impression, but it is not grounded in core values. Charisma is self-serving versus character, which is firmly built on ethics and values. Lifelong learning together with emotional intelligence strengthens the self-awareness of leaders, which allows them the opportunity to lead their followers and their organization to success. "The result of value-centered leadership is building a ship of leaders."[13]

Values in Organizations

Leaders, in conjunction with their followers, establish the core values by which the organization will operate by developing a strategic plan. When all members have input into that which the organization deems important, they are more likely to accept and live by those values. "Values that come from properly modeled and reinforced founders can live on in organizations through many subsequent generations of leaders."[14]

An example of a company built on its founder's values is Hallmark Card Company. Joyce Hall built his organization around his personal values of quality, excellence, service, and caring for his followers and his customers. These values are still intact in the Hallmark Card Company today, 22 years after Hall's death. The followers know and live the values and vision of the company; they stay with this organization because they believe in and embrace those values; and they enjoy working there because of them. Hallmark followers say, "The values and the vision is the lifeblood of Hallmark."[15]

Organizational values are critical for any organization. Leaders who identify core values and incorporate them to the organization's vision, mission, and goals sanction those values and make it known that the organization will be accountable for its behavior. An organization's personality and culture are attached to its values and determine its success or failure. Leaders must not only espouse the values and behaviors by which their organization lives, but they also must emulate them in their everyday professional and personal lives because their followers are watching. If leaders fail to live by the values they themselves establish, their followers will not live by them either, and the organization will fall into disorder.

True effectiveness means using "leadership influences to unite the organization's efforts toward and beyond the bottom line. It means achieving goals and objectives in such a way that the team is still intact, morale is high, and people are lined up to be on the team."[16] Every organization and every person within it has a value system, but leaders must set the standard by demonstrating and supporting their followers through education, coaching, counseling, and mentoring them to succeed. The success of followers is directly related to the success of leaders and the success of the organization and the Army. Triumphant outcomes result in positive influence throughout the organization.

When leaders identify core values and keep them in mind, they build a solid foundation by which they can view their daily lives, their actions, and their decision-making when leading others. As they identify their own core values, they understand why some things bother them and other things do not, and why some things make them happy, satisfied, and fulfilled and why others do not.

Soldiers and Army Civilians take an oath to serve the Nation and the organization for which they work; they also agree to live and act by a new set of values—Army Values. However, taking an oath may not cause all who take it to embrace the Army Values because the core values they established in childhood and developed over many years of experiences also influence their behavior. It takes time, effort, and training to change core values.

The Army could use the process at Figure 2 and Figure 3 to help its members identify their personal core values and then follow up with education, coaching, counseling, and mentoring to integrate Army Values with personal core values. Once leaders and followers identify their core values, the process of aligning personal core values to Army Values can begin. Good leaders who emulate Army and strong, personal core values can have the most profound influence and impact on whether or not their followers accept and live by Army values.

Conclusion

Core values play a major role in the personal lives of leaders as they lead people and organizations. Their values shape their beliefs, attitudes, behaviors, and thinking. To be effective, leaders must be aware of the motivational factors that make people behave the way they do. Values provide the catalyst for actions, decisions, and behaviors. Therefore, it becomes important that leaders and followers identify their personal core values while establishing the goals and objectives of the organization.

The character of leaders is grounded in such core values as integrity, trust, truth, and human dignity, which influences their vision. Values help form an organization's identity and culture in conjunction with the mission and vision. Leaders must mirror their own core values in their professional and personal behaviors. When leaders integrate their personal core values with the goals, objectives, and values of the organization, they can achieve greatness for themselves, their followers, the organization, and the Army.

How to Determine Your Personal Core Values

The four steps of instruction below (using the personal values table at Figure 2 of this chapter) will help leaders identify their values.

Step 1	Go through the table the first time, and circle any and all of the values that you would risk your life for. Add values that aren't there, but are important to you.
Step 2	Go back through the items that you circled and narrow the list to only six. Which items are more important to you than the others? Place a star next to your top six values.
Step 3	From the six items that you identified, you can keep three. Which three will go? If all you have left in life are these three values, which would they be? Cross out three of the six so that your top three values remain.
Step 4	Rank-order your top three values. Of the three that remain, if you had to throw two away, which one would you throw away first? Label that, "No. 3." Which would you throw away second? Label that, "No. 2." So if all you had in life were one single value, which would it be? Label that, "No. 1."

Figure 2: Instructions for Determining Your Core Values

Accomplishment	Creativity	Integrity	Persistence
Accountability	Decisiveness	Leadership	Personal Growth
Accuracy	Duty	Learning	Positive Attitude
Achievement	Education	Leisure	Pride

Adventure	Efficiency	Loyalty	Respect
Authenticity	Empowerment	Meaning	Self-reliance
Authority	Excellence	Money	Service
Challenge	Faith	Nurturing	Simplicity
Change	Family	Openness	Skill
Cleanliness	Fitness	Opportunity	Speed
Commitment	Freedom	Optimism	Stability
Competence	Fun	Patriotism	Success
Competition	Hard work	Peace	Teamwork
Courage	Honesty	Perfection	Trust
Conviction	Humor	Performance	Well-being

Figure 3: Personal Core Values

Notes

1. John F. Kennedy, *A Nation of Immigrants* (New York: Harper and Row, 1964), 15-16; The great doctrine 'All men are created equal' incorporated into the Declaration of Independence by Thomas Jefferson, was paraphrased from the writing of Philip Mazzei, an Italian-born patriot and pamphleteer, who was a close friend of Jefferson;" available on the Internet at http://en.wikipedia.org/wiki/All_men_are_ created_equal (accessed 22 July 2008).

2. Warren Bennis, *On Becoming A Leader* (New York: The Perseus Books Group, 2003), 32.

3. Victoria Neufeldt, editor in chief, and David Guralnik, editor in chief emeritus, *Webster's New World Dictionary* (New York: Simon and Schuster, 1988), 227.

4. Michael Callahan and Fred Seeger, "Examine Individual Values and Army Values," *Intermediate Course Lesson Plan*, Army Management Staff College (Fort Belvoir, VA: February 2007), 4.

5. *Army Leadership: Competent, Confident, and Agile* [Field Manual 6-22] (Washington, D.C.: Department of the Army, 12 October 2006), 4-12.

6. Ibid.

7. Callahan and Seeger, 4.

8. Su Mi Park Dahlgaard, Jens J. Dahlgaard, and Rick L. Edgeman, "Core Values: The Precondition for Business Excellence," *Total Quality Management* 9, no. 4 (1 July 1998), 51-55.

9. Tommy Newberry, *Success is Not an Accident* (Carol Stream, IL: Tyndale House Publishers, Inc, 2007), 71.

10. *Army Leadership*, 3-7.

11. Daniel Goleman, Richard Boyatzis, and Annie McKee, *Primal Leadership: Realizing the Power of Emotional Intelligence* (Boston: Harvard Business School Press, 2002), 38-51.

12. Y. Sankar, "Character Not Charisma is the Critical Measure of Leadership Excellence," Journal of Leadership and Organizational Studies 9, no. 4 (Spring 2003): 45; available on the Internet at http://find.galegroup.com.lumen.cgsccarl.com/itx/printdoc.do?contentSet=IAC-Documents&docType=IAC.

13. Ibid.

14. Harvey Kaufman, "Values as Foundation: The Role of Values in Leadership and Organizations," from LeaderValues website, 2005; available on the Internet at http://www.leader-values.com/Content/ detail.asp?ContentDetailID=909 (accessed 2 May 2008).

15. Timothy Bostick, Shane Marriott, Susan Pattern, and Pat Gehringer, Executive Summary of interviews with Hallmark Card Company followers conducted by students from Intermediate Course, Class 08-4, Army Management Staff College, Fort Leavenworth, KS, March 2008.

16. Gene Klann, Building Character: Strengthening the Heart of Good Leadership (Hoboken, NJ: John Wiley and Sons, Inc., 2006), 6.

Kathy Strand

Mastering Teambuilding Principles

Introduction

This chapter investigates theories surrounding effective teambuilding using sports teams as a reference point for exploration. Using the culture of sports teams, it examines the process of building teams in the business environment by combining the development and communication of a comprehensive vision, the roles of team members in reference to the effectiveness of the overall team, and the motivation and evaluation of team performance. The sports analogy of Novice level of performance will serve as the baseline and will lead to further discussion of three of the five stages of knowledge acquisition in order to reveal the importance of individuals mastering their specific role on the team in regards to the overall effectiveness of teambuilding process[1].

The benefit of studying teambuilding within the context of sports teams provides a common frame of reference for development and application. Constantly testing and refining the basic teambuilding principles against a common sports analogy backdrop will enrich an understanding of the teambuilding process and enhance teambuilding to a higher level of skill acquisition. This analogy will provide a theoretical basis that demonstrates that as any skill is mastered, it allows participants to see reality more clearly.

Mastery

Personal mastery is a lifelong pursuit. The ability to influence results is dependant upon the level of skill mastery. Long-term vision and enhanced organizational success can be measured as a result of time invested in development of proficiency. As individual competency increases, the more likely team success can be predicted. For instance, a college football team is no match for a professional football team. The professional team has a much higher investment in resources (i.e., players, salaries, facilities, equipment, and prestige) and, as a result, is visibly different from the collegiate level.

Time and quality are directly related to competency level. Novices are only capable of applying the basic rules and can only achieve basic results.[2] To achieve a much greater impact, the level of proficiency must increase; advanced levels of proficiency lead to more precise calculations of impact. Sports novices are not able to accurately evaluate and assess the team's capabilities when faced with challenges. However, as they study the sport, its culture, vision, communication, and the roles and motivation of the team and its players, Competent team builders can begin to accurately anticipate how each team will react to challenges. It requires in-depth study to make accurate predictions about the outcome of a year of competitions and challenges.

Mastery as a teambuilding discipline is more than becoming aggressive against an external threat; it is a proactive approach to achieve desired results. A proactive stance enhances the ability to envision the impact of future events. It stems from individuals discovering how they contribute to their own problems.[3] It also follows that people with similar training and levels of experience, when placed in the same environment, will produce similar results.[4] In human systems, structure includes the decision making that translates perceptions, goals, rules, and norms into actions. People often have potential leverage that they do not exercise because they focus only on the visible effects and ignore the effects of distant relationships. Contrarily, failure to plan often places them in a reactive posture in relationship to the environment.[5]

Mastery as a discipline is achieved through the acquisition of knowledge and experience. It is a discipline, not a reactive posture, and mandates integration of a skill to the point that it becomes a subconscious activity.[6] Attaining the Expert level of proficiency requires individuals to augment the rules learned as a Novice with many individual experiences. Each trial, regardless of whether it was successful, provides greater knowledge, experience, and proficiency. As a task is mastered, the individuals proceed through the five stages of defined knowledge acquisition (Novice, Advanced Beginner, Competent, Proficient, and Expert).[7] To clearly distinguish the process of Mastery, this chapter concentrates on the Novice, Competent, and Expert stages of knowledge acquisition. Learning under the discipline of personal mastery is a continuous process of improving the ability to produce the results desired.[8]

Stages of Knowledge Acquisition

The first step in learning something new is looking at the fundamental qualities of the subject under investigation. What is it? What are the parts? What are the rules? Novice learners, at the foundation level, are limited to imitation and following the basic rules. They are developing an awareness of new principles and simple responses and reactions to those newly learned principles. Novices may not take responsibility for their actions and blame ignorance of the rules over their ability to apply the rules. Typically Novices are limited to poor performance when faced with challenges beyond the scope of the basic rules.[9]

To achieve proficiency under the discipline of personal mastery means continuous improvement of the ability to produce the desired results. As basketball Novices, the act of bouncing a ball is a very complex task that requires a great deal of focus and attention. As they gain experience in the game of basketball, bouncing the ball becomes natural and almost intuitive. When a level of competence is achieved, the focus shifts from the ball to visualizing the end state. As Experts visualize the end state, the activity of bouncing the ball shifts from the conscious to the subconscious level.[10] The dribbling experts are able to shift the dribbling to an element of the activity versus the entire activity and can take on additional activities to enhance their basketball performance. Without mastering dribbling, basketball players can never shift their focus beyond the ball to the other players or to winning the game.

Novice athletes learn the basic vocabulary of the sport and its players and the rules of the sport, its procedures, and its structure. They focus on the complexity of performing each individual task.[11] At the sub-varsity level, athletic skills are engaged at a level that allows skill development. Novice athletes in baseball learn to run the bases, for example, after hitting the ball off of a tee. Novice tennis players concentrate on engaging the ball and keeping it in play. Novice team leaders are able to apply the basic rules of teambuilding, but not much more. Team leader objectives at this stage are to manage the process in such a way as to maximize the talents of the members.

Competent athletes begin to test a variety of rules on their environment. They have developed a more robust understanding of the rules and how they work in multiple situations. They have learned a variety of rules and procedures and begin to determine which rule might work best in a given situation. Because of their enhanced development, Competent learners begin to feel responsible for poor choices and performance.[12] At this point, they see cause and effect relationships and can synthesize what they have learned in order to apply it to their environment. Even Competent athletes are only beginning to accurately evaluate their environment, and they begin to analyze beyond the short term immediate impact of their decisions.

The Competent athletes begin to see value in different alternatives, and can anticipate how they can influence the outcome. Because of their experience, Competent athletes can begin to deviate from the basic rules of the game, and they may begin to see the strengths and weaknesses of other players and plays. At this stage of learning, athletes begin to take responsibility for making the wrong decisions and think through decisions a little longer.[13] Competent baseball players may be able to determine whether to bunt the ball to get to first or smash it based on their experience and knowledge of the game and its players. Competent tennis players may be excited about being able to execute a planned strategy on their opponent. Competent team leaders may be excited about restructuring a team to increase efficiency and effectiveness.

Expert athletes' reliance on rules have been replaced by experiences, honed skills, and focus on the desired end-state. Experts are genuinely committed to clarity and have a grasp of the holistic situation.[14] As Experts develop their proficiency, decisions become intuitive; they can anticipate and impact the future without deliberate effort. Due to the disciplined nature of mastery, Experts are able to prevent being pigeonholed (tunnel vision) or easily influenced. Expert athletes no longer break plays down into rules or potential scenarios. They play from a natural response garnered from experience. Experts will often reveal that the play "felt right" or that everything seemed to "slow down" whereby they could visualize the environment with a heightened awareness. Experts appear truly gifted or even clairvoyant.[15] When Expert athletes play together, their combined skills cause a synergetic effect, where each inspires and encourages the other. The skills of a team of Expert athletes far outweigh those of Novice or even Competent teams.

The concepts (rules) are basic. The ability to increase the level of teambuilding proficiency beyond the level of Novice is dependant upon the desire to achieve a level of mastery of the rules through experience. Analyzing teambuilding concepts under the context of teams allows the athletes to develop skills combined with previous experience.

Teams

Teams give organizations a way to address the increasingly complex environment in which they operate. Teambuilding allows organizations to decentralize decision making and respond more quickly to challenges.[16] Implementation of any task with only a basic understanding can only produce Novice results. In order to get the most out of teambuilding, Novices must develop their understanding of effective teams in order to become Expert. A review of teambuilding begins with the basic principles of culture, vision, communication, roles, motivation, and evaluation. The discipline of mastery comes from continuously improving the ability to produce the results desired. The distinction of Expert is achieved through the exercise of applying rules to multiple cases in order to develop additional skills.[17]

Culture of teams

Culture is historically affiliated with diversity and conflict. Influencing culture can be time consuming, draining, and confusing. Due to the risk involved when organizations make cultural mistakes, most address it with mandated practices and an official approach. Examining culture is about understanding people and their interactions, beliefs, and values. Because few ideas are genuinely new, examining culture is the starting point at which to establish effective teambuilding. Culture can be examined by researching a team's technology, mannerisms, behaviors, documents, procedures, and structure.[18] Cultural features are influenced by personnel, resources, and systems.[19] The key elements of effective team culture are self-management, customer satisfaction, and information sharing.[20] It is imperative to understand the culture of existing teams, in order to effectively master and influence teams.

To master the differences in culture, Novices examine mannerisms, behaviors, documents, procedures, and structures. Understanding rules and processes is only the beginning of influencing team culture. Mastery is about taking a proactive approach to improving the ability to impact the future.[21] Expertise is gained through knowledge and practice; however, the mastery of one culture is not necessarily the mastery of all.

Shared Vision

Once the culture has been examined, the next step is to create a shared vision. Creating a vision is the act of conceptualizing something that may appear invisible to others.[22] Creating a team's vision is about creating a larger purpose that guides and directs the team as challenges develop. Visions are spread through the reinforcing process of communication, commitment, and enthusiasm. A truly shared vision will alter the relationships of the team members by creating a common identity. As team members align their personal visions with those of the team, they evolve into a generative role in which they strive to achieve the vision. Generative teams are possible only when members strive to accomplish something meaningful.[23]

Synergy is a capacity generated through relationships, communication, and a shared vision. A shared vision looks beyond, tasks, hierarchy, and control. It must address ideas fundamental to strong interpersonal relationships such as communication, diversity, empowerment, trust, and values. A shared vision encourages an environment in which followers love their work and capitalize on the synergy of alignment. Novices consider creation of the vision as a terminal activity. Novices' visions are characterized by short-term goals; a protecting, defending or defeating focus; or the resolution of a problem.[24] Team members who work to achieve an individual vision are characterized by compliant activity and adaptive learning designed to meet the minimum requirements. Experts, on the other hand, view the creation of a vision as the initiation of an activity. A vision becomes truly shared as team members become partners and co-creators of the vision and are characterized by commitment, energy, passion, and excitement.[25] A vision created out of experience connects with the personal views of its members and encourages on-going conversation, which inspires and fuels the vision. The ability to influence teams through creation, communication, and alignment of the vision is dependant on the level of mastery. The amount of time invested in developing the level of proficiency will determine the extent of the ability to predict success.

Team Communication

A vision is not effective unless you communicate it to others. Communication is the process by which teams transfer information and create a shared vision. Teams use communication to present ideas, gain understanding, interact/work together, analyze, and evaluate. It is through communication that team vision and roles are aligned and team cultures are established and encouraged. Trust, respect, and support promote open communication and active participation.[26] Effective communication is measured by its clarity and cumulative understanding. It is a continuous process of creating a shared understanding by revealing what the speaker knows and gaining an understanding of what the receiver knows. A shared vision must be consistent across all avenues of communication.

Feedback and active listening are necessary to ensure the system and the teams are sending congruent messages. Encouraging communication and feedback are necessary to diagnose any misunderstandings before they build into insurmountable actions and issues. An environment of trust, respect, and support encourages open communication. The task (initiation, discussion, summarizing, and consensus testing) and process roles (harmonizing, compromising, gate keeping, encouraging, and process leadership) of communication facilitate open dialogue and interaction. In this environment, communication and knowledge are treated not as power but rather as nourishment[27]. Communication barriers can take physical or psychological form. Team members may not always hear the verbal message, but they will interpret the behavior and adjust their actions. The cardinal rule in dealing with miscommunication is to address the issue and not the person.[28]

The Competent communicator has a fundamental understanding of communication—the history, its various forms, avenues, and roles. Competent communicators focus on communication channels and active engagement in effective communication practices. Communication Experts are aware of their impact on the team. They evaluate and address formal and informal communications simultaneously, foster an environment in which communication encourages and supports the goals of the team, realize that every element of the team affects the whole organization, and use alliances to endorse the team's vision. Experts do this seamlessly while the activity is invisible to Novices.

Individual and Collective Roles

There is a sense of comfort derived from affiliation with either groups or teams. Although the natural response is to create a team of like members, alignment of roles with personal strengths will enhance a team's effectiveness. Novices will react to their role with a more individual focus while Competent performers can see beyond their immediate role and focus on team performance. Experts focus on how their role will impact the environment.

A team is a group of people organized for a common purpose with complementary skills, and are affiliation and performance oriented.[29] Interdependent teams include members who specialize in different tasks and require assistance from complementary members. They are composed of members with the same tasks that may help one another; however, individual success is directly related to individual effort. The players are the building blocks of the team and work as an element of a total unit. Each individual player has the authority, responsibility, and accountability for their role[30] and has been adopted based on their mastery of those skills required for their role. All team members value and respect the team and their role as a member, and none of them can succeed alone. None have more value than another, and they must trust, respect, and support each another.

Roles within a team are built around structure and function. Dr. Meredith Belbin believes that people are most effective in a role that is natural to them.[31] His research demonstrates that balanced teams perform better. Under the concept of Personal Mastery, players are expected to know their role, study other players with similar roles, and develop their skills. In sports teams, for example, the roles are established and clearly defined. A natural response is to construct a team of like members. With like members, there is a mental model that allows for quicker responses in predetermined situations. This approach has an immediate benefit that is outweighed in the long-run. A team composed of all quarterbacks (even if they are the best quarterbacks in the business) will not beat a team that is more balanced with all positions filled. Experts are able to look beyond immediate benefits to long term advantages.

The most challenging aspect of teamwork is the "we." As a member of a sports team, the members give up their ability to control the details of the game in favor of enhancing the abilities of the team. Novice team members are mastering their role on the team and find it difficult to see beyond their individual contribution to the team. Competent team members have evolved beyond individual focus and now understand the roles of all team members more clearly. They understand their role and have experience adapting to the roles of the others on the team. They have developed a confidence in individual and team abilities and are confident in the skills of the other members. Experts focus on facilitating development of the team and players to a level that ensures team success.

Team Motivation and Evaluation

One critical element of teambuilding is team motivation and performance evaluation. A team reacts to outside influences as an organism would. The team retreats when threatened and is more productive when praised. A team, however, can be developed into a perfect fit as opposed to an individual who may not be perfect. Consider a sports team. Its goals, identity, ambition, rules, needs, products, network, skills, associations, resources, and voice are all distinct from the other teams. It reacts to wins and losses and to negative and positive public feedback. A team is as distinct and as recognizable as any individual member.

Evaluation systems do not usually reward or remove entire teams directly. When evaluation systems fail to recognize teamwork, they challenge team cooperation and create a sense of inequality and competition. In the presence of individual evaluation, the team is dependant upon the constant presence of communication and feedback to encourage an environment of trust, respect, and support. Evaluations must not treat members as followers or that is what they will become[32]. The desire is to have team members who lose sleep over achieving the team's vision[33].

Team motivation and evaluation are critically tied together. Evaluation (performance feedback) can serve to encourage or discourage team interaction. There are many theories in the realm of psychology and economics that support pay-for- performance systems. In order to get the most from a pay-for-performance system, users must have knowledge and experience with the system and the theories influencing follower motivation. Use of a pay-for-performance system is not sufficient to achieve an Expert level of influence of team motivation. The level of proficiency with the system dictates how well the system can be manipulated for success. The amount of time and energy allocated to mastering team motivation systems is indicative of the value placed on the system. To understand the pay-for-performance system, leaders must understand the systems that influence team motivation.[34] Basic knowledge of the following theories will yield Novice level results.

- **Expectancy Theory:** Team members believe that a certain level of performance will yield a desired outcome.[35]
- **Marginal Productivity Theory:** Followers' pay should be a reflection of their benefit to the organizations profit.[36]
- **Implicit Contract Theory:** Payment should be a reflection of individual effort. Performance ratings should be adjusted for

factors beyond the follower's control.[37]

- **Reinforcement Theory:** Team members believe that desirable behaviors will be rewarded.[38]
- **Equity Theory:** Team members believe that their compensation is fair in comparison to the efforts of others.[39]
- **Efficiency Wage Theory:** The level of effort is determined by the comparison to the efforts of others with equal wages.[40]
- **Goal Setting Theory:** Goals are motivating when they are specific, challenging. and accepted.[41]

Many organizations have multiple incentive programs available; different plans meet different needs. Merit pay is a strategy designed to compensate team members. Like any other strategy, in order to be effective, it must be properly communicated, taught, and applied. The capabilities are dependant on both the system and the users. Whether the system is used by Novices or Experts will determine the outcome and the team's perception of the importance of teamwork. Maximizing the affect of all systems will create the most productive environment.

Professional athletes' basic salary, for example, is based on contracts; however, in addition to contracts, athletes also have awards, bonuses, commissions, incentives, appearances, speaking engagements, and product endorsements. Professional athletes' compensation is tied directly to performance and constant observation. Football, in contrast to baseball and basketball, has little financial incentive to win due to the length of the typical career. Football careers average less than three years, and baseball and basketball average seven years. The result is that the long term incentive for football players is diminished in comparison to other sports.[42] Awareness of the strengths and weaknesses of the various systems is necessary to get the most out of the programs available.

Most team members believe their contributions to the organization are greater than those of their counterparts.[43] With this and the motivation theories in mind, the importance of the evaluation system and communication are paramount. The emphasis an organization places on evaluation systems is a reflection of the value that it places on follower performance. Systems can serve to encourage or discourage performance. When owners of athletic teams, for example, devote minimal time to pay and incentives, the response is diminished returns. The participants with more talent will seek out the employers that place more emphasis on benefits.[44] All avenues of communication must express the same message or teams will interpret the mixed messages and appear conflicted.

Conclusion

Planning is necessary for developing a proactive stance to address the issues faced by teams. Mastery is the discipline of continuously improving the ability to create the results desired. Planning and Mastery support the desire to create a successful and effective team. The level of Mastery achieved will determine the extent of successful teambuilding. The process of team development starts with examining the present culture of the team, proceeds through the development of a vision, and communicates it to others in order to create a shared vision. Determining the roles of the team members is essential to motivation and evaluation of the team. Team development starts and ends with evaluation . . . . first with team culture and then with team performance. The more competently leaders build their teams, the more likely they are able to accurately predict their teams' success. Regardless of the quality of the tools available to leaders, results are dependant on knowledge and experience. When teams are treated casually, only basic results at the Novice level are possible.

Notes

1. Peter M. Senge, *The Fifth Discipline: The Art and Practice of The Learning Organization* (New York: Doubleday, 1994), 63 and 114-272.
2. Stuart E. Dreyfus, "The Five-Stage Model of Adult Skill Acquisition," *Bulletin of Science, Technology & Society* (2004): 177-181.
3. Senge, 40.
4. Ibid., 42-43.
5. Ibid., 43.
6. Ibid., 163.
7. Dreyfus, 177-181.
8. Senge, 141.
9. Dreyfus, 177-181.
10. Senge, 163.
11. Dreyfus, 177-181.
12. Ibid.
13. Ibid.
14. Ibid.
15. Senge, 141.
16. David I. Cleland, *Strategic Management of Teams* (New York: John Wiley & Sons, Inc., 1996), 105.
17. Ibid.
18. Linda Ford, *The Fourth Factor: Managing Corporate Culture* (Indianapolis, IN: Dog Ear Publishing, 2008).
19. Cleland, 100.
20. Ibid., 105.
21. Senge, 141.

22. Senge, 205-232.
23. Ibid.
24. Ibid.
25. Ibid.
26. Ford, 100-106.
27. Margaret J. Wheatley, *Leadership and the New Science* (San Francisco: Berrett-Koehler Publishers, Inc, 2006), 101.
28. Cleland, 85.
29. Robert N. Lussier and Christopher F. Achua, *Leadership: Theory, Application, & Skill Development,* 3rd ed. (Mason, OH: Thomson South-Western, 2007), 81.
30. Cleland, 112.
31. David Marriott, "The Belbin Team Roles," Sabre Corporate Development, available on the Internet at http://www.sabrehq.com/team_building_articles/belbin-team-roles.htm (accessed 28 July 2008).
32. Dale Dauten, *The Gifted Boss* (New York: William Morrow and Company, Inc., 1999), 54.
33. Ibid., 14.
34. Robert L. Heneman and Courtney von Hippel, "Balancing Group and Individual Rewards: Rewarding Individual Contributions to the Team," *Compensation and Benefits Review* (1995): 63-68.
35. Robert L. Heneman, *Merit Pay: Linking Pay Increases to Performance Ratings* (New York: Addison-Wesley Publishing Company, 1992), 24.
36. Ibid., 35.
37. Ibid., 37.
38. Ibid., 28.
39. Ibid., 30.
40. Ibid., 39.
41. Ibid., 33.
42. Gerald W. Scully, "Views of Sport: Tackling the N.F.L Labor Impasse," *New York Times*; available on the Internet at http://query.nytimes.com (accessed May 16, 2008).
43. Jody Urquhart, "For the Good of the Group," *We Lead* (online magazine); available on the Internet at http://leadingtoday.org (accessed 17 May 2008).
44. Dauten, 47-58.

Constance Yelverton

Leadership and Emotional Intelligence

Introduction

Effective leadership skills are necessary to sustain the future of the Army as it transforms with adaptive leaders. Good leaders are intelligent, proficient, focused, and aware of how their emotions affect their leadership capabilities. They want intelligent followers who can function rationally in any situation and are emotionally intelligent. Emotional intelligence has been talked about loosely and researched for decades under a variety of names from character and personality to soft skills and competence. This chapter asserts that understanding and developing emotional intelligence in Army followers is a key factor for building essential leadership skills that are needed to meet the challenges in the Army's workforce.

What is Emotional Intelligence?

Author Daniel Goleman states, "Emotional intelligence is the ability to motivate oneself, persist in the face of frustrations, regulate one's moods, and keep distress from swamping the ability to think."[1] He believes that interdisciplinary research demonstrates the importance of emotional intelligence, emotional skills for career success, personal well-being, and leadership proficiency. According to Goleman, these research findings emphasize the necessity of including emotional skill development in programs designed to improve professional status. More precisely, emotional intelligence is the understanding of human talents.[2]

The application of knowledge with emotional intelligence and virtuous principles can create a framework to develop a positive work environment. It will increase productivity, job satisfaction, morale, profits, and the foremost functions of the organization. Leaders and followers want a quality work environment with the least amount of distractions from tasks, goals, and objectives to ensure the organization can accomplish its mission. This can also lead to a variety of other benefits. For instance, content followers normally use fewer sick leave hours due to stress-related health issues, and they also are more efficient and productive on the job.

Goleman found in his research with large global companies, that while the qualities traditionally associated with leadership (i.e., intelligence, toughness, determination, and vision) are required for success, they are insufficient. Most leaders need the ability to handle rapid and unpredictable changes, which is the difference between success and failure. They need "abilities such as being able to motivate and persist in the face of frustrations; to control impulse, and delay gratification; to regulate moods and keep distress from swamping the ability to think; to empathize, and to hope"[3] in order to lead effectively.

Why Emotional Intelligence is Important

The Army's workplace is ideal for promoting social and emotional competencies because it is such a diverse environment. When people realize that social and emotional skills hold the key to greater success, they become eager to develop those skills. As leaders recognize that their success depends on the emotional intelligence of their followers, they become amenable to programs that develop understanding and awareness of emotional intelligence.

There are several tools that can provide an Emotional Quotient so that leaders can identify the level of Emotional Intelligence in themselves and in their followers; a few are mentioned later in this chapter. Leaders and followers who are aware of their own emotional intelligence can improve their performance, make quality contributions to the organization, and improve the social skills that are needed to meet the challenges in a diverse workplace. We all know of someone who was promoted to a leadership position only to fail when presented with the emotional challenges of that position. An understanding of emotional intelligence would help explain why, despite equal intellectual capacity, training, or experience, some people excel while others of the same caliber lag behind. People with well-developed emotional skills are more likely to be content and effective in their lives because they master habits of the mind that fosters productivity. Those who cannot marshal some control over their emotional life fight inner-battles that sabotage their ability for focused work and clear thoughts.[4] This defines a need for leaders to address developing emotional intelligence skills in their followers.

Emotional Intelligence and Academic Intelligence

Emotional intelligence provides an understanding of what is learned through life experiences; while a high Intelligence Quotient (IQ) demonstrates an academic ability to learn. In broad terms, "Intelligence is what people use to solve problems, understand complex ideas, learn, remember, and deal with all the issues surrounding them through various forms of thought and reasoning."[5] While the primary focus of education is academic performance, leaders, as well as their followers, must emphasize learning and development of personal and emotional intelligence skills.

The IQ has been the standard qualifier for success, and it determined career success. A high IQ is what made Chief Executive Officers and high ranking Army Civilians successful through conventional wisdom or training. However, it seems that workplace skills are assessed by academic ability, and leaders must acknowledge that emotional performers are ineffective. Academic intelligence does not prepare leaders for the turmoil and emotional challenges that the workplace brings.[6] It is the academic record that gets people hired, but once there, performers must meet other expectations. Can they work as a team member? Can they work under pressure? Can they be patient? Can they communicate effectively?

Leaders must recognize the characteristics of emotional intelligence and understand how emotional intelligence and academic abilities impact the workplace. Research by Daniel Goleman, Robert K. Cooper, Ayman Sawaf, and Robert E. Kelley demonstrates that it is no "accident" that certain competencies are found repeatedly in high performers. Some of their research indicates that effective leaders must intentionally monitor themselves in order to maintain and improve their emotional intelligence.[7]

Information about emotional intelligence suggests that it can be as powerful as the IQ. Emotional development of adults does not come into focus unless workplace behavior becomes problematic (i.e., excessive absences, irritability, changes in behavior or attitude, violence, alcohol abuse, and lack of motivation). When severe problems become evident, leaders attempt to assist, but that help is often too little and too late. When potential problems are identified quickly, the information can be used productively to improve emotional intelligence, adapt to change, and learn new skills for a healthier outlook on life.[8]

Managing Emotional Intelligence

Managing emotions is the real key to developing emotional intelligence and mastering self-awareness and self-control. Leaders who are emotionally competent at self–awareness are fully aware of their values and core beliefs, and they know the impact and affect of compromising these core components. Self-control requires full mastery of being in control of emotions. Both positive and negative emotions are channeled most productively when leaders control their emotions versus having their emotions control them. When emotions can be mastered and controlled, leaders can anticipate and plan emotional reactions.[9] Self-awareness is a sense of inner control or the ability to modulate and control emotions and actions. In other words, leaders should not repress their feelings, but rather be able to recognize and understand their personal emotions. They must learn to excel in this area in order to achieve success in other areas of their lives. Army leaders and their followers can no longer rely solely on how smart they are or how proficient their technical skills may be; they must develop, maintain, and be able to apply emotional intelligence skills and techniques to be successful.

Emotional Intelligence Assessments

Proactive and systemic programs that identify and increase emotional intelligence skills are important to personal well-being (i.e., mental, physical, and emotional health) and are needed to prevent problematic behaviors. *The Emotional Intelligence Profile* is an example of one such program. The foundation and frameworks around this program are based on the research and work of Dr. Darwin Nelson and Dr. Gary Low. For over 25 years they have studied, researched, and worked with the emotional and personal skills essential for achievement, career success, healthy relationships, interpersonal communications, personal leadership skills, and a healthy orientation to life.[10]

The Army Junior Reserve Officer Training Corps (JROTC) currently measures the emotional intelligence of high school cadets during the first year they are enrolled. Each cadet is given an emotional intelligence assessment called the Personal Skills Map. It is the core assessment instrument in The

Success Profiler™, which is a systematic, research-based assessment and skill-building system designed for the following purposes: Adapt to change; develop leadership skills; enhance ability to learn; promote sensitivity/diversity; build teamwork skills; and prevent violent behavior. The Personal Skills Map is the missing link that allows each participant to "buy-in" to change and personal growth. This system focuses on the emotional intelligence needed for success in key areas. If barriers are identified, the system provides skill enhancement to remove those barriers. A major value of self-assessment with the Personal Skills Map is that the results allow users to identify clearly the personal skill areas in which they want or need to change. The Personal Skills Map provides a measure of the following:

1. Self-Esteem	2. Assertion
3. Interpersonal Awareness	4. Empathy
5. Drive Strength	6. Decision Making
7. Time Management	8. Sales Orientation
9. Commitment Ethic	10. Stress Management
11. Growth Motivation	

In addition, it provides a measure of Interpersonal Assertion, Interpersonal Aggression (Anger Management), Interpersonal Deference (Fear Management), and Change Orientation (Comfort Level). Practitioners in many fields have identified valuable uses for the Personal Skills Map, among which is "Predictable Tools for Personal Growth and Success" (Emotional Intelligence).[11]

Another example of emotional intelligence research was conducted in 2003 by Texas A&M University, Kingsville, Texas. The university completed extensive research to develop and implement a project (The Javelina Emotional Intelligence Program) in order to identify and understand the effects of emotional intelligence skills on achievement. This education-based model of emotional intelligence was planned and designed to help students identify, learn, and practice behaviors important to academic success in the first semester of college. The assessment model used The Emotional Skills Assessment Process, which is a 213-item self-assessment instrument that provides scale-specific measures of 10 emotional skills and three problematic indicators. The skills measured are assertion, comfort, empathy, decision-making, leadership, drive strength, time management, commitment ethic, stress management, and self esteem. The problematic indicators measured are aggression, deference, and change orientation.[12]

Why Emotional Intelligence is Important

Developing the ability to recognize and learn from mistakes is key to developing emotional intelligence, and this is parallel to the Army's review of lessons learned. Leaders should strive to develop a level of emotional intelligence that will increase their leadership capabilities and enhance their career potential. Intellectual and emotional growth weigh profoundly on lessons learned through experiences and relationships with others. Today's Army needs leaders who possess both high IQs and high EQs to be effective in daily challenges.

The ability to maintain a friendly work environment and friendships while accomplishing the mission is a difficult and challenging task, but managing relationships and building networks are key to establishing effective teams. Leading successfully requires social skills to articulate and expertise to build and lead teams. The simple greeting, "How are you?" takes on a much more complex meaning when employed by emotionally intelligent leaders.

The confidence and courage to rely on training, education, experience, and common sense prepare leaders to deal with the challenges that arise in any situation. According to authors Goleman and Bennett, to motivate, educate, and create a work environment that is both efficient and beneficial require confidence and courage on the part of leaders.[13] A "Can-Do" attitude is still contagious in any organization, and this concept is not new; positive thoughts and actions bring about positive results.

Many of the terms used in the works by Bennett, Goleman, and Walton provide guidance to the knowledge, skills, and abilities needed to perform as a leader at the top-levels of government.[15] Emotional Intelligence is being in tune with the work environment, followers, and resources, and it is beneficial to leaders and everyone throughout the organization.[14]

Developing followers is at the core of effective leadership. Leaders must ensure a healthy organizational structure; but there is more to being a leader than just conducting leadership. Leadership is a dynamic process of relationship-building between individuals and groups that develop trust, making emotional intelligence essential to effective leadership.

The Army strives to determine what makes effective leaders perform the way they do. Perhaps more efforts on developing emotional intelligence coupled with specific skill-building programs would identify strong, adaptable leaders who are equipped to lead effectively. The Army's workplace must have self-disciplined leaders who can handle frustration, have the empathy to sense stress, have the persistence to ensure quality, have the loyalty for longevity, and have the courage to make the hard decisions (especially now) while our country is involved in the Global War on Terrorism. Leaders have feelings and emotions, and emotions engender emotional intelligence; one attribute that defines leaders is passion. Development and awareness of leaders' levels of emotional intelligence improves their leadership capabilities.

Conclusion

Leaders have academic knowledge when they are assigned as leaders, but emotional intelligence is a dominant factor for a successful, harmonious work environment. So, as the Army transforms and the diversity of the workforce increase, leaders and followers must learn emotional intelligence skills. Leaders must identify and resolve challenging issues that relate to sustaining the future of the Army. Emotional intelligence and academic intelligence are essential for leaders and followers, and never has it been more apparent than in leadership practices of today. Developing knowledge, emotional intelligence, and leadership strategies are crucial for effective leadership. This chapter described emotional intelligent leaders as self-aware, persistent, self motivated, and intelligent. These qualities are key characteristics of adaptive Army leaders and followers. Understanding emotional intelligence is vital for leaders to meet the 21st Century challenges of an Army in transformation . . . an Army at war.

Notes

1. Daniel Goleman, *Emotional Intelligence: Why it Can Matter More Than IQ* (New York: Bantam Books, 1995)
2. Daniel Goleman, *Working with Emotional Intelligence* (New York: Bantam Books, 1998).
3. Goleman, *Emotional Intelligence: Why it Can Matter More Than IQ*, 34.
4. Ibid., 36.
5. Ibid.
6. Ibid.
7. Adele B. Lynn, *The Emotional Intelligence Activity Book* (New York: American Management Association, HRD Press, 2002), 1-4.
8. James Adams, "IQ and Intelligence," originally from http://brain.com/, reprinted in *Southern Connecticut Mensa* 9-8 (August 2000); available on the Internet at http://scm66.org/nl/Mensa%20Chronicle%202000_08.pdf (accessed 9 July 2008).
9. Gary Low and Nelson B. Darwin, *The Emotional Intelligence Profile*, available on

the Internet at http://www.conovercompany.com/products/eqprofilec/Index.html (accessed 10 July 2008).

10. James Adams, "IQ and Intelligence."

11. "The Conover Company, Success Profiler," available on the Internet at http://www. conovercompany.com/products/success/Index.html (accessed 10 july 2008)

12. Ibid.

13. Goleman, *Emotional Intelligence: Why it Can Matter More Than IQ*, 194.

14. Low and Darwin, *Emotional Intelligence Profile*.

15. Daniel Goleman, "What's Your Emotional Intelligence Quotient?" *Utne Reader* (November/December 1995), available on the Internet at http://www.utne.com/lens/bms/9bmseq.aspx (accessed 10 July 2008).

Angela Parham, Ph.D.

Women and Minority Leaders in the Federal Government

Introduction

Today in the Federal Government, one reason for underrepresentation of women and minorities in leadership positions is the "glass ceiling." The Department of Labor defines the term "glass ceiling" as "those artificial barriers based on attitudinal or organizational bias that prevents qualified individuals from advancing in their organization into upper management positions.[1] This term, first coined in 1986 in the *Wall Street Journal's* "Corporate Woman" column, was first associated with women's issues; however, it was quickly recognized that minorities were also being restricted in upward job mobility.[2]

The percentage of minorities employed with the Department of Army has only marginally increased since 1997 and continues to be below the Federal Government percentage as of fiscal year 2006. In fiscal year 2007, female representation in the Department of Army was 38.5 percent. This was a slight decrease from fiscal year 1997, when the representation was 40 percent.[3] This chapter focuses on the under-representation of women and minorities in middle and advanced leadership positions in the Federal Government.

Katherine Naff maintains that the Federal Government is experiencing a quiet crisis in regard to hiring and retaining federal followers. Women and minorities seem to be under-represented when it comes to advancement to middle- and upper-level management positions. Naff found that affirmative action programs (tools used to promote equal employment opportunity) are no longer enforced in many agencies. Leaders no longer feel the need to comply with equal employment guidelines, which reflects their personnel decisions.[4]

The "glass ceiling" provokes a serious economic problem for American businesses, both in the public and private sectors. The Merit System Protection Board concluded that in the private sector,

> The government is paying a cost for hindering women's advancement. It is under utilizing a major segment of its human resources and delaying attainment of an important goal . . . full representation of all segments of society at all grade levels in government.[5]

Mary Guy argues it will take a long time before women will hold leadership positions in proportion to their representation to the civil labor force and even longer for representation of their total population.[6] The Glass Ceiling Commission concluded that most female minority leaders do not work in the private-for-profit sector. As a result, they hold jobs in the public sector and "third sector"-non-governmental agencies in health, social welfare, education; legal service, professional service, membership organizations and associations; libraries, museums, and art organizations. Minorities and women are limited in their opportunity to obtain broad and varied experiences in most agencies. They usually are employed in supporting staff functional areas—personnel/human resources, communications, public relations, affirmative action, and customer relations. Movement between these positions and line positions is rare in most organizations.[7] Followers who hold line positions are the decision makers for their organization.

Women and minorities are faced with barriers that hinder them from achieving advanced leadership positions in the Federal Government. These barriers are believed to be invisible; therefore, it is problematic to identify them, and that continues to impede qualified women and minorities from advancement.

Paradigms

The manner in which different federal agencies attempt to meet equal opportunity goals as they relate to upward mobility for women and minorities will influence the effectiveness of the policy implementation process. Debra Stewart, in her chapter titled, "Women in Public Administration," in the book *Public Administration: The State of the Discipline* describes the paradigms—political, psychological, and sociological—for improving the status of women in public administration.

The political paradigm maintains that in order for women to achieve political equality, they must participate and possess the same political savvy as men. Women must organize in order to have a voice in the political process, which results in participation in political roles and (ultimately) access to and involvement in elite roles. The psychological paradigm maintained that women encounter problems due to inherent characteristics. In the 1950s and 1960s, it was argued that women, by nature and nurture, lacked motivation to compete in male-dominated occupations and resisted achievement. Women were believed to lack the necessary leadership traits, skills, and behaviors required to succeed in advanced leadership positions.[8]

Stewart's sociological paradigm contends that problems women encounter in organizations are from the composition of the organizational situation. These problems are not based on an follower's traits or the distribution of political participation.[9] The paradigm identifies problems that women experience in organizations based on its structural position, ratio of representation, power associated with position and role, and opportunity, which formulates the nature of the organization structures. Rosabeth Moss Kanter, in her seminal work, *Men and Women of the Corporation,* argues that behavior and attitudes can be used to determine who will be successful in their organization.[10] She contends that once an analysis is complete, the results facilitate the flow from structural positions within an organization to the intervening factors, which assist in modifying the existing structural conditions.

The sociological paradigm is related to the systematic theory. This theory argues that situations that women encounter are based on the composition of the organization. Literature supports this theory as it relates to the "glass ceiling." Many of the explanations of the systematic theory are based on Kanter's explanation of the structural positions within organizations: distribution of opportunity, distribution of power, and social composition of the group.[11] Kanter's explanation supports Stewart's argument concerning structural position.

Structural Position

Stewart maintains that structural position affects intervening factors, increasing information, training, and mentoring. Once these situations are analyzed, they are modified.[12] This modification leads to effective leadership behavior, which determines the success or failure of women.

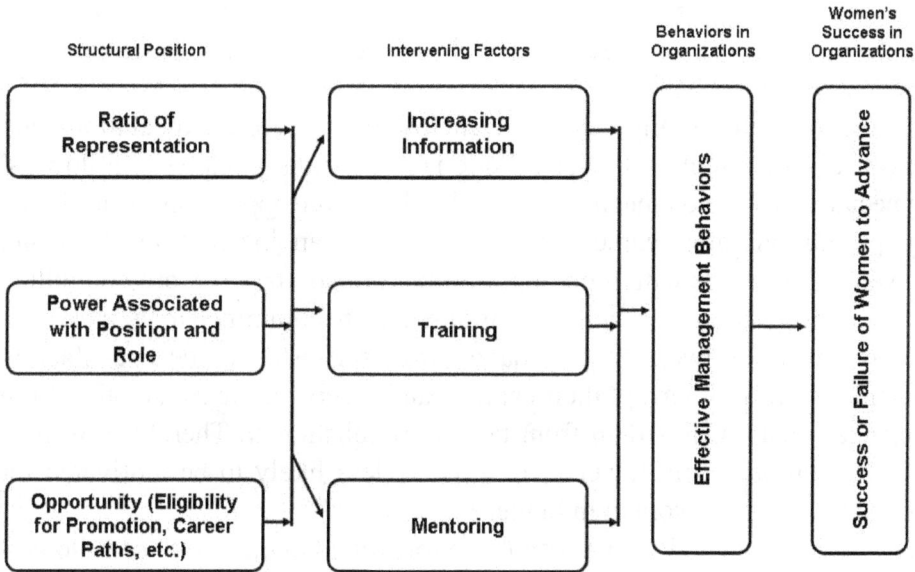

Figure 1: The Sociological Paradigm: A Conceptual Framework. Source: Debra W. Stewart, "Women in Public Administration," in *Public Administration: The State of the Discipline*, ed. Naomi B. Lynn and Aaron Wildavsky

Stewart's framework outlined three structural position elements—ratio of representation, opportunity, and power associated with position and role. First, ratio of representation in an organization refers to the number of people in an organization of like social type. A review of the literature supports the argument that an organization's composition affects its behavior, performance, and acceptance. Some organizations have the "cloning effect," and "those not fitting the desired mold are gradually excluded, resulting in an informal, sometimes preconscious form of discrimination."[13]

Social types that are represented in low numbers are more visible, more likely to be heavily scrutinized, lack credibility, are excluded from informal networks, and face more stress. Social types that are represented in high numbers tend to "fit in" and gain credibility. Members of this group are accepted into informal networks, establish peer alliances, are assisted by peers in learning the ropes, and are more likely to have a mentor.[14] Due to the low percentage of women and minorities compared to white males employed by the Federal Government, there may not be enough women and minorities in middle and advanced leadership positions to act as mentors. Madsen and Mabokela state in their article, "For leaders of color in managerial positions, they often reported having less job discretion and reported feeling less accepted than whites. Ethnic differences between leader and followers may result in exchanges that may be detrimental to the organization's goals."[15]

Second, opportunity relates to an follower's career expectations and advancement potential. The distribution of opportunity relates to followers' expectations and advancement potential. Follower opportunities are based on promotion rates, career advancement, and an increase in skills and rewards. Followers with high opportunities are competitive, are committed to the organization, have high aspirations, and are committed to their careers. Junior level followers usually have lower self-esteem, seek satisfaction outside of work, interrupt their careers, and receive more satisfaction from personal relationships than from task accomplishment. Therefore, women who are employed in lower level jobs are less likely to be motivated for advancement than women in higher level jobs.[16]

Power associated with position and role refers to the ability of followers to mobilize resources to accomplish their goals. Power is defined as being gender-neutral and incorporates ability, control, and privilege. Rosabeth Moss Kanter, in her research, concluded that followers who lack significant organizational power have low morale, are direct, act in an authoritarian manner, and use coercive power.[17] By contrast, followers who possess high levels of organizational power possess high morale, behave in a less rigid manner, and delegate more responsibilities.[18] Madsen and Mabokela contend "leaders of color face multiple challenges in how majority followers will respond to their authority. They have to understand the cultural variations among groups of followers and how that will influence their effectiveness."[19]

Intervening Factors

Training, mentoring, and increasing information are the three intervening factors that Stewart puts forth in her conceptual framework. Training (as defined by Stewart) refers to adequate training in areas such as objective rating scales and specific decision rules. Adequate training in these areas will modify the structural conditions. After training on rating scales, a rater's leniency is more likely to be reduced and evaluation more consistent. Benson Rosen and Thomas H. Jerdee contend that male raters are more lenient than female raters, despite additional training.

In addition, Rosen and Thomas maintain that specific decision rules, gender role stereotypes result in discrimination in personnel decisions involving promotion, development, and supervision. Women are more likely to be discriminated against in these situations. In administrative actions that are ambiguous or lack information, decision-makers are likely to rely on preconceived attitudes to make their decisions.[20]

In addition to Stewart's explanation of how training applies to leaders, it also applies to followers. Mark Van Vugt notes that there is a correlation between positions of leadership and education.[21] Training followers in essential skills will facilitate their development. By participating in training, they are investing in their careers, which is critical to advancement.

Mentors share knowledge, understand their protégés' needs, and take those protégés' under their wings for career guidance. Gerald Roche maintains that followers who have or have had a mentor are happier with their career progress and receive greater fulfillment from their jobs. Followers who benefited the most from their mentoring experience feel obligated to mentor others. Research shows that women are more likely to have a mentor than men, and women are more likely to form relationships in the workplace during the first 10 years of their careers. Those who attain feelings of achievement most often decide to pursue a career rather than simply work.[22] William Heery believes that corporate mentoring is an effective method to help qualified followers, (regardless of race or gender) advance in leadership positions.[23]

Increasing information is relevant to the amount of data available for decision-makers. There should be an increase in the amount of information available when decisions are being made. When the gender of an applicant is the only information provided, gender-role stereotypes could be a significant factor in the selection process. When additional data becomes available, the impact of gender-role stereotypes is reduced. Research indicates that males are preferred over females; however, a potential follower's scholastic achievement in the selection process is more influential than gender.[24] Stewart suggests that intervening factors such as mentoring, training, and increasing information influences the behavior in organizations, which leads to women's successes or failures.

It is important to consider the human capital factor, which enhances Stewart's model because it is among the most pivotal pertaining to career advancement. Education, ability, and experience are also included in the human capital theory intervening factors that Stewart does not recognize in her sociological paradigm. Scholars argue that education and experience are the two main qualities that account for the discrepancies of advancement between men and women (and whites and minorities).

Employment Barriers

The Glass Ceiling Commission, in its report, *Good for Business: Making Full Use of the Nation's Human Capital*, identified three levels of barriers that continue to hinder women and minorities from advancing. The three levels (Societal, Governmental, and Internal Structure) are linked with the sociological paradigm that Stewart describes for improving the status of women in public administration. These three levels of barriers are also associated with the human capital, sociopsychological, and systematic theories used to explain the discrimination that women encounter based on gender, which impedes them from obtaining upper management positions.

BARRIERS	CHARACTERISTICS
Societal	1. Pertains to educational opportunities and level of job attainment 2. Includes conscious and unconscious stereotyping and biases 3. Syndrome develops = those that do the hiring hire people who look like themselves
Governmental	1. Employment related data (at times) is difficult to collect and disaggregate 2. Collection of data related to the "glass ceiling" continues to be inadequate, as well as the information actually disseminated 3. Government needs to establish consistent enforcement and compliance of laws and policies related to equal employment opportunity
Internal Structure	1. Encompasses outreach opportunities and recruitment practices that are not being offered to women and minorities 2. An organization's climate can alienate and isolate one from advancing 3. Barriers can hinder advancement such as lack of training, inadequate mentoring, rating system, dysfunctional communication network, and lack of rotational assignments that lead to upper management positions

Table 1: Barriers That Hinder Minorities and Women from Career Advancement Source: Renee Redwood, "Giving Credit Where Credit is Due: The Work of the Federal Glass Ceiling Commission," *Credit World* (May/June 1996): 35-36.

The human capital theory is the level at which people are willing to invest in their own skill sets. Along with education, ability, and experience, human capital elements include training, hard work, overall effort, and productivity. These characteristics are used to explain the differences in individual achievement and career advancement. Human capital theorists argue that women invest in general skills. This theory focuses on voluntary choices and the choices that women make, which keeps them at the disadvantaged state. However, the literature does not explain why women are not succeeding at reaching advanced leadership positions.[25]

There are various factors that affect career advancement; however, the main factors are human capital, job choices, family responsibilities, and networking. One factor that impacts career advancement is job choices, which relates to the number of geographical moves an follower has made or is willing to make. Followers should be willing to move in order to receive a promotion. Research indicates that followers who have reached senior level positions have relocated more than those who have not. Women relocate less than men; the dual income scenario makes it more likely that women are not able to relocate.[26]

A second factor is family responsibilities. The number of absences that followers accrue could be viewed (by some) as a lack of commitment to the organization. These absences could be leave used for illness, education, or child and elderly. Some women with small children may not be able to have a flexible job schedule, which (in some organizations) is an informal requirement. Female followers are more likely than their male counterparts to be tasked with caring for children and the elderly. As a result, women are overlooked for career-enhancing assignments, developmental opportunities, and promotions. There is intentional discrimination when hiring women, because males believe that women have a lower career commitment due to family obligations. [27]

Critics of the "glass ceiling" believe that low numbers of women in advanced leadership positions does not prove discrimination; however, it does prove that women have made other choices, usually family choices, instead of being committed to their careers.[28] Some critics believe that women have not been in the pipeline as long as men; therefore, no action is necessary to eliminate barriers to advancement.

A third factor is networking. The representative theory maintains that "the power that position incumbents wield on behalf of individuals similar to themselves is an important factor in achieving a value-balance within the public sector."[29] Minorities and women are at a disadvantage due to the lack of power holders that are minority or female. Female role models are essential to female followers by serving as motivational reinforcements. Women and minorities are more likely to give other women and minorities challenging assignments, which could lead to career advancement. In the Federal Government, those who have worked the longest receive the promotions.[30]

Dennis Daley argues that the factors affecting women and minorities the most in career advancement are human capital, job choices, family responsibilities, networking, and development.[31] Most research related to career advancement in the Federal Government has focused on human capital factors and the attitudes and experiences of men and women.[32] Current literature suggests the theory does not completely explain why larger numbers of women are not advancing in their careers.[33] Katherine Naff supports the argument that women do face barriers that are not associated with their qualifications during career advancement; however, she does not identify those barriers. Regardless, in the Federal Government (Naff believes) the five factors that affect career advancement include experience, education, relocations, time devoted to the job, and children.[34]

The employment of women and minorities has increased in the last two decades, and projections show that this growth will continue in the new millennium. Mary Guy contends that there is little that can be done to increase women's chances to make it to the top.[35] This is a problem that will have to be attacked incrementally.

Conclusion

In the Department of Army, women and minorities have made significant gains in their advancement to leadership positions; however, both groups continue to be over-represented in lower General Schedule positions. As with minorities, the percentage of females in the Department of Army is lower than in the Federal Government. The Department of Army will need to continue its efforts (through such programs as the Department of Army Intern program) to move women and minorities through the pipeline to senior leadership positions.

Notes
1. *The Glass Ceiling Initiative: Are There Cracks in the Ceiling?* (Washington, D.C.: U.S. Department of Labor, June 1997), 7.
2. Carol Hymowitz and Timothy D. Schellhardt, "The Glass Ceiling: Why Women Cannot Seem to Break The Invisible Barrier that Blocks Them from the Top Jobs," *Wall Street Journal* (Eastern edition), 24 March 1986, 1.

3. "Civilian Human Resources: FY07 Annual Evaluation," Department of the Army publication; available on the Internet at http://www.cpol.army.mil/library/civplans/chr-eval/07eval/toc.html (accessed 15 July 2008).
4. Katherine C. Naff, "Progress toward Achieving a Representative Federal Bureaucracy: The Impact of Supervisors and Their Beliefs," *Public Personnel Management* 27 (1998): 137.
5. Carol Emert, "Survey Finds Federal Women Confronting Glass Ceiling" *States News Service* (7 December 1992).
6. Mary E. Guy, "Three Steps Forward, Two Steps Backward: The Status of Women," *Public Administration Review* (July/August 1993): 290.
7. *Good For Business: Making Full Use of the Nation's Human Capital* [A Fact-Finding Report] (Washington, D.C.: Glass Ceiling Commission, March 1995), 13-16.
8. Debra W. Stewart, "Women in Public Administration" in *Public Administration: The State of the Discipline*, Naomi B. Lynn and Aaron Wildavsky (Eds.) (New Jersey: Chatham House Publishers, Inc., 1990), 209.
9. Meredith Ann Newman, "Career Advancement: Does Gender Make a Difference?" *American Review of Public Administration* (December 1993): 363-364.
10. Ibid, 210-211.
11. Guy, 288.
12. Newman, 365.
13. Stewart, 212.
14. Newman, 363.
15. Guy, 288-289.
16. Jean A. Madsen and Reitumetse Obakeng Mabokela, "African American Leaders' Perceptions of Intergroup Conflict," *Peabody Journal of Education* 77, no. 1 (2002): 51.
17. Stewart, 210-211.
18. Guy, 288.
19. Madsen and Mabokela, 55.
20. Benson Rosen and Thomas H. Jerdee, "Influence of Gender Role Stereotypes on Personnel Decisions," *Journal of Applied Psychology* 59, no. 1 (1974): 12-13.
21. Mark Van Vugt, "Evolutionary Origin of Leadership and Followership", *Personality and Social Psychology Review* 10, no. 4 (2006): 357.
22. Gerard R. Roche, "Much Ado About Mentors," *Harvard Business Review* (January/February 1979): 15, 24.
23. William Heery, "Corporate Mentoring Can Break the Glass Ceiling," *HRFocus* (May 1994): 17.
24. Patricia Ann Renwick and Henry Tosi, "The Effects of Gender, Marital Status, and Educational Background on Selection Decisions," *Academy of Management Journal*, no. 1 (1978): 21, 24.
25. Newman, 363.
26. Naff, 510.
27. Ibid., 511.
28. Bob Adams, "The Issues," *CQ Researcher* (29 October 1993): 939.
29. Dennis Daley, "Paths of Glory and the Glass Ceiling: Differing Patterns of Career Advancement Among Women and Minority Federal Followers," *Public Administration Quarterly* (Summer 1996): 147.

30. Ibid.
31. Ibid., 145.
32. Naff, 508.
33. Newman, 363.
34. Naff, 510.
35. Guy, 290.

Sidney F. Ricks, Jr.

Distributed Learning: A Leadership Multiplier

Introduction

Leveraging technology is a key factor in the success of businesses and organizations today. Technology enhancements increase exponentially every day, and it is in the best interest of each organization and its leaders to embrace this technology wave and ride it to mission accomplishment. Sound, effective leadership is a requirement of any successful organization, but there is no organization where this is more critical than the U.S. Army. Training and developing leaders is a key concern for the Army and is an endeavor that demands an abundance of time and money. The Army has an absolute requirement for flexible, adaptive leaders who can lead under any circumstance. Distributed Learning (dL) that employs the latest technology can be an effective tool used by organizations to train and develop leaders.

The concept of dL in this chapter refers to learning whereby the instructor and the students are in physically separate locations. Leveraging dL is a cost-effective means of providing training and education that allows students in various locations worldwide to be in the same class and share in the same learning experiences. Before dL (in order to form a class of 100), students would travel from perhaps 100 locations to a single site. Utilizing the dL concept, 100 students from anywhere in the world can collaborate as part of the same class without any of them having to travel or leave their home station.

Whether on the battlefields of Iraq or at a depot in the United States, it is important for the Army to have a process of leader development that encourages and sustains a professional workforce. One of the Army's goals is to develop a workforce capable of more critical and creative thinking.

The Army (like most organizations) faces the challenge of developing a more efficient and effective way of doing business and resources are causing the Department of Defense (DoD) to examine smarter ways of doing its business. Force Redesign and Base Realignment and Closure are just two initiatives that have the entire Military in a perpetual state of change. The Army will need competent adaptive leaders to meet the many challenges it currently faces and will face in the future. Diminishing resources and additional requirements for the Global War on Terrorism will force the Army to look at different methods of training and developing leaders that are cost conscious and get maximum bang for the buck.

The Army can use dL to address the restraints of time and money confronting it today. Leader training that addresses critical thinking and problem solving is available through dL as evidenced in the new Civilian Education System (CES) curriculum. According to former Army Chief of Staff General Peter J. Schoomaker,

> We must continue to prepare Soldiers for the hardships, rigors, ambiguities, and ugliness of combat—by achieving a proper balance between training and education programs. *Training* prepares Soldiers and leaders to operate in relatively certain conditions, focusing on "what to think." Conversely, *education* prepares Soldiers and leaders to operate in uncertain conditions, focusing more on "how to think." In light of uncertain irregular environments in which we will operate, we must emphasize innovative educational experiences and shift our training-education balance accordingly.[1]

A well-developed dL program can provide a balance of education and training for leadership development around the world. Web-based training provides 24/7 access and can be tailored for almost any audience.

Developing Army Leaders

Army leadership development is time-tested and proven. The Army has a reputation of producing some of the greatest leaders in the world. It develops adaptive leaders who thrive not only in the Military environment, but also in private industry, business, and government. As noted by the Army Chief of Staff and others, the new challenges that face the Nation require an examination of how it does business. The Army needs to develop a new strategy that addresses these new challenges.

One of the most significant of the new challenges is the irregular nature of the enemy and the battlefield. The Army's challenge is to take a look at how leadership has been taught in the past and assess whether the same strategy will be effective for today and into the future. There appears to be a need for change, but the Army must proceed with caution in order to maintain the best and implement change only where needed.

Army training doctrine states that the Army's mission is to serve the Nation, defend enduring national interests, and engage and destroy the Nation's enemies. To accomplish this requires values-based leadership, impeccable character, and professional competence. Figure 1 shows the Army Leadership Requirements Model (ALRM), which provides a common basis for thinking and learning about leadership and associated doctrine.

Leadership Requirements Model	
Attributes What an Army Leader is:	**Core Leader Competencies** What an Army Leader does:
A Leader of character • Army Values • Empathy • Warrior Ethos **A Leader with presence** • Military Bearing • Physically Fit • Composed, Confident • Resilient **A Leader with intellectual capacity** • Mental Agility • Sound Judgment • Innovation • Interpersonal Tact • Domain Knowledge	**Leads** • Leads Others • Extends Influence Beyond The Chain of Command • Leads By Example • Communicates **Develops** • Creates A Positive Environment • Prepares Self • Develops Others **Achieves** • Gets Results

Figure 1

The ALRM outlines the attributes considered important to develop and train a leader; the components center on what a leader is and what a leader does. These leadership requirements enable leaders to create positive organizational climates and produce positive results.[2] The attributes in the ALRM have evolved over the 229-year history of the Army and have withstood the test of time. Throughout the Army's proud history, most of the emphasis was placed on Military leadership to support the battlefield. The Global War on Terrorism forces the Army to focus on Civilian leadership with the same intensity that it devotes to Military leadership. A significant number of Military positions are being converted to Civilian positions. More Civilians than ever in the Army's history are deployed into combat zones in support of Soldiers. The qualities and values the Army seeks to instill in its leadership core now, more then ever, include the Army Civilian Corps. This change is slowly gaining momentum in the ranks and files of the DoD.

Today both Military and Civilian leaders are expected to be strategic and critical thinkers who are capable of developing and sustaining teams to manage organizations in support of a wartime mission—any place; anytime. As a result of the current operational tempo, there is a greater number to train due to the inclusion of Civilians, and the prospective student pool is more geographically dispersed. Distributed Learning can serve as a leadership multiplier by addressing the time and resource implications of the current environment. The transition to dL is a change that has a direct impact on the learning culture. As an Army Command responsible for training, the U.S. Army Training and Doctrine Command (TRADOC) serves as the Army's champion to implement dL to every post, camp, and station around the world. The Army Management Staff College (AMSC), under TRADOC guidance, has deployed dL as a major component of CES.

Developing Distributed Learning

Any changes to leadership education and training must be carefully studied to ensure strategic alignment to current Army doctrine. One seemingly simple change may impact everything else. Distributed Learning is a major change not just for Army organizations, but also for most of the Army workforce. Decisions and plans must be developed to ensure acceptance of the process. As a result, the proponent of the initiative must align the strategy with the organization's goals and learning objectives.

How does one get started? Creative and critical thinking are needed to develop an action plan. Leaders must consult with internal customers, staff, faculty, technical support, and students (past and present) as well as external customers, managers, supervisors, and potential students to gather feedback on what people want to see in the program. If resources are going to be expended, people expect a return on their investment. What is the "value" to the organization for the time allowed for people to engage in the program? The feedback received from stakeholders will help determine individual goals, purpose, resources; needed skill sets, timelines, and many other important issues. Existing doctrine (along with input from stakeholders) are critical in determining strategic direction, and with change comes resistance. There will be loud voices of support, but others will come along more slowly, and there will be others who want to hold onto legacy courses and old methods of instruction.

Some of the barriers to change can be minimized by establishing structure to the planning process by selecting a project leader who is just that—a leader—a person who enjoys interacting with people and understands the power of developing high performance teams. They get the right people involved in the planning process and keep people informed on what is going on. They can balance risks as well as make decisions. A gap analysis will determine where individuals are and where they want to go. Those steps in between can be used as initiatives to arrive at the end state.

Another thing to consider is course adaptability to the dL format. For the Army to realize the promise of dL, there may be a need to change Army doctrine. Careful planning and implementation are required to ensure that the goals to develop leaders are the purpose of the dL process. This may call for courses in certain career fields, information, and training on a new threat, Family support, or even behavior issues that deal with a serious incident. According to the Army Research Division Arroyo Research Brief, "The Army must learn from the extensive experiences of industry and academe and take full advantage of emerging learning technologies."[3]

Courses should be designed to balance learning objectives and the mission of training and educating leaders. Many students involved in AMSC's Advanced Course, for example, are not allowed time to work on dL during work hours, even though policy stipulates that it is an on-duty education. Their organization's mission cannot afford the time away from mission requirements. Additionally, the system is web-based and there are a lot of technical issues (Army-wide) that make logging onto the course a real challenge.

In discussing change, it is imperative to look at some things that change will impact. An organization must ensure that dL courses are easy to access and navigate, that instructions are clear, easy to follow, and accurate for access. How many clicks will students make before they get to course modules? Are there any redundancies in the process? Who is going to be responsible for keeping information accurate and current? The information in the program must be constantly monitored and edited for valid and correct information. Inaccurate information diminishes the integrity of the dL and reflects poorly on the organization.

A very important element with any type of computer-based program is technical support. Who do those students/stakeholders call on a Saturday night at 11:30 p.m. when they can not connect to the course? The weekend is critical because that is the primary time that people have to devote to getting their dL work completed. How is the technical support set up? Reflecting on a situation when contacting a company with concerns about a product, how long are customers kept on hold? How many people do individuals have to speak to before they reach someone who is not just reading a manual? Is the support local? All these things are important issues to individuals whose technical expertise is limited to emails and PowerPoint presentations. This is very important to maintaining the requisite quality and effectiveness of training.

Leaders may have to make some tradeoffs between effectiveness and reduction in training time. With these concerns in mind, the Army should review current applications of dL and refocus it for optimum benefit to training and readiness. Time must be given to dL development to ensure the right courses are suited for the format in addition to time given to students to participate in the programs. Sometimes an organization's culture prevents timely attention to program details. It takes time to negotiate and deliver a contract on a dL product. This is the time that it takes to produce an idea until a student is actually online taking the course.

Leaders can maximize the dL program by developing complimentary programs that will interact with and increase the value of the existing system. The Army Management Staff College is in the process of developing a Learning Community that will be collaborative between faculty, current students, graduates, subject matter experts, and sources that reinforce dL goals and content. Students will be able to blog, chat, and engage ideas and concepts via a virtual community. A plan is also underway to introduce podcast to the learning community, delivering presentations, guest speakers, and other course material to enhance the learning environment. It is AMSC's goal to be on the cutting edge of learning technology in support of the Warfighter. The plan is to harness the technology today and in the future, either in-house or with vendors, to emphasize the principle of critical and creative thinking to leadership development. This is not to say that technology is the be-all, end- all; but technology enables leaders to be more proficient and effective with their time and resources.

Evaluating a Learning Management System

There must be an assessment tool to evaluate the dL program. What determines how effective the program is at developing future leaders? Exit surveys? Tracking upward mobility of the graduates? These issues must be examined as relevant and robust as the dL program is designed and developed. The program must be strong enough to service a global base—one that will meet the needs of users, developers, faculty, and potential students. It must be available to all these users at the same time. The program must be easy to use, friendly, and consistent with current training doctrine and policy. To keep pace with an ever-changing world, the program must have the capability of growing both in course content and student population to train the Army Civilian Corps. As Learning Communities, podcast, and other forms of technology are incorporated, the system must be able to support those efforts.

Technical support must be in place to support user population. People will resist using a program that is constantly down with inadequate technical support. The site must be secure. Use of proper security measures must be built into the program to ensure the integrity of course content, personal information, and the Army system. Last, but certainly not least, the program should be fun to engage and void of huge PowerPoint presentations with monotone voice-overs. Developing an interactive course that encourages users to learn makes the process interesting and challenging. Such a program may require outside assistance, but the investment may be well worth the return. To develop a program, sources should have previous dL experience. Time and resources spent on developing a sound plan can be the basis for resource allocation, training, vendor selection, and an array of other issues that evolve from the planning process.

According to the Army Distributed Learning System (DLS) website, hundreds of thousands of Soldiers around the world have been trained using DLS. From their experience, they share some of the benefits of the dL program. The Benefits of DLS include:

Efficiency. Provides the Army the ability to leverage technology to increase training efficiency and reduce costs. Significantly reduces the travel costs inherent in resident training, by bringing the training to the Soldier, rather than the Soldier to the training.

Flexibility. Increases the flexibility in scheduling training, since a significant portion of dL courses can be provided anywhere at anytime.

Increased Training Opportunities. Since individual training can be scheduled with increased flexibility, the options available to Soldiers and Civilians are greatly enhanced.

More Time at Home, Less Time Away from the Unit. Since Soldiers are able to take courses in their local DTF, at home, and in the office, this improves quality of life, morale, and increases the time available for duty and improves unit readiness.

Standardized Training. Courses are developed and often delivered by proponent school instructors, ensuring that the quality of training is standard across the Army, including Active, National Guard, and Reserve components.

Distributed Learning has changed the way the Army conducts its training today and will continue to do so well into the 21st Century.[4]

Conclusion

The Army must learn from the extensive experiences of industry and academia and take full advantage of emerging learning technologies for leadership development. Distributed Learning can be used to multiply the Army's ability to train and develop leaders. In order for dL to be effective, it must be aligned to organizational learning objectives and provide value to the provider, the students, their organizations, and the Army. Leader education provided in dL mode should reflect and account for the fact that individuals have various learning styles, and it must be flexible enough to react to the ever-changing conditions. The Army Management Staff College's dL program has improved the leadership management process without compromising the quality of training.

As the Army transitions and transforms, it will need a dL program that can support a cadre of Soldiers and Civilians. When Soldiers or Civilians deploy forward, the dL program must have the ability to reach them with current and relevant information. Synchronous and asynchronous approaches must be considered and deployed where needed; certain subjects are better suited to one or the other. However, some course content may not be suitable for the dL environment. The correct balance between dL and residential learning must be established and periodically reevaluated. Moreover, the time required for successful course completion must be realistically assessed, and students must be given the time they need to study and complete their coursework. The dL program must provide them with administrative support for scheduling, monitoring, and recording training results to help them reach their goals.

Finally, the Army must take care to ensure that dL maintains the requisite quality and effectiveness of training. Some studies of dL have found tradeoffs between effectiveness and the reductions in training time. With these concerns in mind, researchers recommend that the Army review current applications of dL and refocus it for optimum benefit to training and readiness.[5] The focus on training and educating future Army leaders should embrace and harness technology as an enabler to support a workforce that never sleeps and deter an enemy that is constantly watching. As Michael Allen states in his book, *Guide to E-Learning*,

> There is a reason for e-learning. It will allow us to learn what, where, and when we want to learn. It will provide choices in how we learn. It will make hard things easy and fun to learn. It will wrestle our intellectual laziness to the ground while helping each of us use more untapped capabilities.[6]

Success depends on the ability to design and develop programs that challenge tomorrow's leader to think and be creative, as well as learn and have fun. Using dL to train and educate Army leaders provides the education and training required and, at the same time, conserves resources of time and money that are becoming scarcer each year.

Notes

1. William Beck, "Developing Army Leaders through CGSOC/AMSP and BCTP" (2004); available on Internet at www.stormingmedia.us/4s/4547/A4547734.html (accessed 15 April 2008).
2. *Army Leadership: Competent, Confident, and Agile* [Field Manual 6-22] (Washington, D.C., Department of the Army, 12 October 2006), 2-4.
3. "Army Distance Learning Can Enhance Personnel Readiness," research brief from Army Research Division, Arroyo Center, (2002); available on the Internet at http://www.rand.org/pubs/research_briefs/RB3028/index1.html (accessed 15 April 2008).
4. Robert A. Bean (Lieutenant Colonel), "Product Manager, DLS," (electronic article from Distance Learning System); available on the Internet at http://www.dLs.army.mil/DLs_pm.html (accessed 5 May 2008).
5. "Army Distance Learning," Army Research Division, Arroyo Center.
6. Michael W. Allen, *Guide to E-Learning* (Hoboken, NJ: John Wiley & Sons, Inc., 2003), 3.

Jim Geter

Leveraging Self-Synchronization: A Leaders Art in Network Centric Warfare

Introduction

Leaders should explore the vast capability realized from self-synchronization in a network-centric Military organization and leverage the capability in Network Centric Warfare. Leaders need the ability to be networked with their resources to meet the mission, goals, and objectives of the organization. The resources include those things internal and external within the organization. It includes not only people, supplies, and funding but also a host of personal relationships. When placed together, it encompasses a mission capability package in a new sense.

Too often in some Military organizations, lengthy processes complicate getting things done quickly and precisely. Extra time is required to find what is needed due to massive storage media of information, extensive repositories, and archives. The best electronic computer search engines can find relevant and current information. A great deal of time is devoted to knowledge management in order to capture what some organizations term as corporate intelligence or continuity. Each of these efforts is important within their own right, but leaders need the ability to leverage self-synchronization in a network centric environment.

Data and technology continue to invoke change to existing leadership models in relationship to making decisions based on structural hierarchy, chains of command, and routing of organizational decision packages for coordination and approval. Individuals at all levels have access to the same information as commanders, and they can analyze information and act on decisions without traditional command and control.

Self-synchronization in a New Environment

Self-synchronization is the link between shared situational awareness and mission effectiveness[7] used to describe the absence of traditional hierarchy in command and control.[8] The original Greek meaning of synchronization translates as "shared or common" time. Blehkman et al. describes synchronization processes as either resulting from natural interaction or from intervention, forced or controlled.[9] Bezooijen refers to synchronization when applied to the Military as being either pre-planned synchronization (controlled) or self-synchronization (natural). Other research links human behavior influenced by personalization, synchronization, and difficulty.[10] "There is ample historical precedence for the co-evolution of organization, doctrine, and technology in the warfighting ecosystem,"[11] Simon Atkinson and James Moffatt said in the article, "The Agile Organization."

They feed information up the chain of command to distribute as they deem necessary. The evolution of technology has developed a computer-savvy generation due to modern entertainment electronics such as iPods and cellular technology. Leaders have the ability to interact directly with Soldiers on the battlefield. By flattening the chain of command, leaders can establish goals and objectives, interact with personnel at varying levels in an organization, and empower people to make quicker decisions at the lowest levels.[1] Network Centric Warfare (NCW) is derived from the effective linking or networking of knowledgeable entities that are geographically or hierarchically dispersed. The networking of knowledge entities enables them to share information and collaborate to develop shared awareness, and also to collaborate with one another to achieve a degree of self-synchronization.[2]

Self-synchronization puts leaders in a common and shared environment with those things needed to accomplish the mission. Leaders bring knowledge and skills with to the table. Traditional pyramid leadership is common in Military structures and organizations. Aside from the ability to search online or in traditional libraries for information, imagine tuning into a network of people to help leaders achieve effective results. Imagine there were no layers of processes, redundancies, and countless knowledge centers of information; imagine that leaders could get what they need for a quick decision without devoting extensive time. Leaders must have the ability to access a network of relationships and capitalize on accessing people with the knowledge.

Network Centric Warfare is a leader's art and should be embraced as leaders strive for self-synchronization. General William S. Wallace (as a lieutenant general) commanded the Army's V Corps that captured Baghdad and testified before a Congressional committee that:

> ... a digital divide currently exists between the operational and tactical levels of war. Despite our efforts to realize network-enhanced warfare since Desert Storm, the trigger puller on the ground still cannot tap into the network and realize its benefits. (And) despite all the incredible products at the disposal of my assault command post, we could not get relevant photos, imagery, or joint data down to the Soldier level in near real time. The opportunity to exploit intelligence to our advantage, to the advantage of the fire team in contact, was lost.[3]

The Global Information Grid provided Central Command and its allies the ability to tap into vital information during Operation Iraqi Freedom (OIF) and Operation Enduring Freedom (OEF). Watch Officers were able to make contributions to leadership and field units at various levels. InfoStructure platforms, integrated connectivity, alternative backups, and quick responses to network outages were transparent, yet effective for the capture of Baghdad. Daily defense collaboration tool suites aided Watch Officers meeting with organizations from different command levels, services, and allies to discuss tactical events, strategies, and execution while geographically separated. "Self-synchronization is achieving the goals of the organization without or with fewer leaders than in a hierarchical organization," Wallace said.[4] He emphasized the importance of sharing information prior to a situation and explained how prior knowledge gives leaders the ability to self-synchronize by having a shared situational awareness.

Familiarity and knowledge of communications units' areas of specialty, capability, and talent could have been leveraged and infused into OIF/OEF planning. The knowledge injected was transparent and allowed quick response by experiences achieved over the years. In his book, *American Soldier*, General Tommy Franks discusses utilization of the North Atlantic Treaty Organization's Warrior Preparation Center and highlighted General Gene Renuart's successes exercising the Commander's Concept at

Ramstein, Germany.[5] Lieutenant General Michael W. Peterson, now Chief of Warfighting Integration and Chief Information Officer for the Office of the Secretary of the Air Force, emphasizes the need for a Department of Defense (DoD)-wide strategy to manage data through the DoD Net-Centric Data Strategy Initiative, which seeks to expose various organizational levels to authoritative data.[6] The initiative stresses the importance of eliminating redundant and outdated information and the need for synchronization.

Synchronization is used in various doctrines to describe the process of coordinating units on the battlefield to create the necessary synergy. Both OIF and OEF provided a combination of automated air picture, ground picture, sea picture and reporting electromagnetic spectrum status to various levels of command. This collaboration of data collected from the field allowed interaction between commanders and their Soldiers on the front lines. The results were reflected early on in OIF/OEF. Ahvenainen[12] said,

> ... Organizations that are emerging as winners are those that can be described as being information-enabled. These organizations have found ways to leverage the available information and make the right decisions and products quickly and efficiently. [13]

Leaders in a Net-centric Environment

Successful leaders' entries into new organizations seek to establish relationships and leverage network-centricity and self-synchronization. They need to quickly understand the traditional structure by perhaps comparing it with one familiar to their past experiences. The next challenge for leaders is to find out which organizational players within the command would be part of the mission capability package. Leaders must understand the goals and objectives of an organization. Traditionally, the chain of command is clear, but leaders must figure out those resources to include in a customized and tailored mission capability package. Leaders establish who will be part of their network of resources and help them fulfill the overarching mission. Leaders need access to the private sector and external agencies as part of their network.

Linkage to professional career field organizations and functional units across a command structure and beyond Military service lines are important to benchmark successful best practices and lessons learned. Corporate knowledge on common equipment, processes, and policies provide a common platform for both technology and streamlining processes in search for efficiencies. Leaders must be able to get access to those people with the knowledge in order to respond quickly to meet mission needs.

Leaders must be networked together in order to share information and collaborate. It is important to conduct an initial analysis of available in-house resources are available. Leaders must be able to layer the transparencies and see where were the disconnects between those people they need to be networked with in order to achieve self-synchronization. Leaders can leverage self-synchronization by operating in a network-centric mindset. This approach allows for collaboration at various levels.

RAND National Defense Research Institute conducted a network-centric operations case study on the Stryker Brigade Combat Team on behalf of the Office of Force Transformation within the Office of the Secretary of Defense. The study looked at the operational concepts, the organizational structure, and the networking capabilities of the Stryker Brigade. The Stryker Brigade was equipped with state-of-the-art Army digital terrestrial and satellite communications capable of generating its own situational awareness data and generating exceptional overall awareness and understanding quickly.[14] The case study highlights the systems theory and the complexity theory, with an emphasis on the impact of a leader's capability by having greater situational awareness.

Based on the systems theory, complexity theory involves interactions, those things not explained in terms of linear cause and effect. Complex systems encompass sub-systems or agents that are open systems (that receive feedback from their interactions with other sub-systems and their environment). These sub-systems are irrelative to complex system behavior. Remnants of the complexity theory originated with astronomer Henri Poincare in 1892 when he discovered certain orbits of three or more interacting celestial bodies showed unstable and unpredictable behavior. Many recognize its origin in the 1984 foundation of the Santa Fe Institute for interdisciplinary study of complex systems. Complex systems have the ability to adapt based on feedback from various interactions.

This process of adaptation infused by feedback from interacting creates complexity, nonlinear effects or behaviors without orderly sequence. This in-turn creates a state of difficulty for making anticipations or predictions. This intense behavior doesn't produce a state of chaos–"it is specific, describable, and productive–it has visible purpose and direction."[15] Emergence is the overall system behavior that comes from the bottom up in typical organizational hierarchy, hard to predict and potentially difficult to control. A complex adaptive system, like an Army platoon, is now interconnected by a network within the overall complex adaptive system of a joint task force. It now has shared situational awareness of the interactions of all other complex adaptive systems within the Joint Task Force (JTF). It also now has access to the combat power of all the different complex adaptive systems (platforms, units) of the JTF available. Because of the network, a platoon has the same understanding of the commander's intent as every other unit/system within the JTF. Because of the network, the platoon also has the same situational awareness of the battlefield as every other unit/system/commander within the JTF. As a result, the platoon can quickly and effectively mass the effects of close air support, artillery and other systems of the JTF on a target within the bounds set by the JTF commander.[16]

Leaders must be savvy in knowing how to lead in a complex system and bring self-synchronization to fruition in an adaptive role, while infusing situational awareness by interacting with sub-systems or agents with necessary collaboration on demand.

As part of the Stryker Brigades' Military Capability Package (MCP), it included leader development that involved multi-echelon collaborative planning education and encompassed agility, confidence, and adaptability based on input received. It also included training that was a culmination of well-trained Soldiers, an inclusion of battle command systems, and familiarity with network-centric operations and complex operating environments. The MCP also included doctrine that combined network-centric concepts, the ability to build collaboration into the battle rhythm or synchronized operations tempo with mission orders, and the integration of reconnaissance, surveillance, and target acquisition. The Stryker Brigades' MCP consisted of an innovative organization of organic combined arms Brigade Combat Teams, cavalry squadrons, Military intelligence companies, and humanitarian intelligence teams. Finally, the MCP materials included a high-density Force XXI Brigade Command, Brigade, and Below System; Army Battle Command System; beyond line-of-sight satellite communications; increased mobility, protection, and firepower; and Stryker vehicles.

The study had an objective to analyze and understand the extent to which network-centric operations were a source of combat power and to determine if the hypothesis was realized by the Stryker Brigade. The study discussed the Stryker Brigades' ability to compile a variety of knowledge products from various staff elements and to obtain critical information source requirements. The brigade was successful at meshing together the mission and commander's intent, a synchronization matrix, and logs of significant events with real-time battlefield update briefings. The study highlights the

Stryker brigade's ability to achieve self-synchronization with its infantry battalions. "During the Shughart-Gordon attack, these network-centric warfare capabilities allowed the Stryker brigade to make, communicate, and implement better decisions faster than the enemy—the definition of decision superiority."[17] Self synchronization is a leader's art and can be leveraged in modern complex Military operations.

Additionally, private sector industry and government leaders work together to achieve self-synchronization. The Network Centric Operations Industry Consortium (NCOIC) emphasizes the importance of network centric environments as "... where all classes of information systems interoperate by integrating existing and emerging open standards into a common evolving global framework that employs a common set of principles and processes."[18] There are many legacy systems (databases with the same information) that are not linked together. Network-centricity leadership allows people to be connected on a common share whereby they can collaborate and gain relevant, current information by working better together. Self synchronization enables leaders to leverage an extended body of knowledge by enhancing inner abilities through a knowledge matrix interface with network resources.

David Alberts, John Garstka, and Frederick Stein say that virtual collaboration enables people to team up to accomplish a task in a virtual domain. It moves information instead of moving people and achieves a critical knowledge mass. Virtual integration enables leaders to be vertically integrated as one unit. The benefits of virtual collaboration are improved design, reduced response times, and increased operations tempo with lower risks and costs. It allows leaders to reduce their battlespace footprint and decrease planning time with operational flexibility.[19]

The Department of Defense is migrating to a new Internet protocol that will offer better connectivity to equipment in theater and global networks. Internet protocol version 6 can support an unlimited number of site addresses for wireless communications devices, vehicles, and precision-guided munitions and offers enhance administration and security. Advances in technology continue to allow greater opportunities for interoperability and remote connectivity as multimedia improves and the cost of bandwidth reduces. The InfoStructure along the Global Information Grid continues to provide greater opportunities for connecting leaders throughout the network to make decisions quickly based on greater situational awareness. Although technology enables leaders, trust relationships build on integrity and spark individual motivation, commitment, and impact on performance and leader effectiveness.

Conclusion

Leaders' ability to leverage self-synchronization is vast and is an important part of Civilian leader development in the future. Leaders can leverage the art of self-synchronization by gaining relevant knowledge quickly for necessary decision making, which creates greater situational awareness of the environment in preparation of future NCW. Network centric warfare continues to be a key component of DoD planning for transformation. As part of this transformation, leaders must embrace the concept and doctrine and adapt to the evolution of transforming people, processes, and systems by leveraging self-synchronization—a leader's art in Network Centric Warfare.

Notes

1. Barry Rosenberg, "Common Knowledge – Can leaders stay effective when troops have access to the same information?" *C4ISR – The Journal of Net-Centric Warfare* (2007); available on the Internet at Armed Services and Government News at http://www.newsbankMilitary.com/Military/index.cfm (accessed on 12 May 2008).

2. David S. Alberts, John J. Garstka, and Frederick P. Stein. *Net Centric Warfare: Developing and Leveraging Information Superiority*, 2nd Edition (Revised) (Washington, D.C.: DOD CRISR Cooperative Research Program, 1999).

3. Network Centric Operations Industry Consortium (2005); available on the Internet at www.ncoic.org (accessed on 12 May 2008).

4. Ibid.

5. Tommy Franks, with Malcolm McConnell, *American Soldier* (New York: Harper Collins Publishers Inc., 2004), Chapters 10 and 11.

6. Michael Peterson (Lieutenant General), "Data Transparency: Empowering Decisionmakers" *Joint Force Quarterly*, no. 49 (April 2008): 52-53; available on the Internet at infoweb.newsbank.com (accessed on 12 May 2008).

7. David S. Alberts, John J. Hayes, and Richard D Signori, *Understanding Information Age Warfare* (Washington, D.C.: Department of Defense Command and Control Research Program Publications, 2001).

8. B. Bezooijen, P. Essens, A. Vogelaar, *Military Self-Synchronization: An Exploration of the Concept* (The Netherlands: Tilburg University, 2006).

9. I. Blehkman, A. Fradkov, O. Tomchina, D. Bogdanovk, "Self-Synchronization and Controlled Synchronization," *Systems & Control Letters* 31 (2002): 299-305.

10. Harry C. Triandis, "The Self and Social Behavior in Differing Cultural Contexts," *Psychological Review* 96 (1989): 269-289.

11. Simon Reay Atkinson and James Moffat, "The Agile Organization," (2005); available on the Internet at www.dodccrp.org (accessed on 12 May 2008).

12. Sakari Ahvenainen, "Background and Principles of Network Centric Warfare," [Course of Network-Centric Warfare for Post-Graduate Students] (New Delhi, India: National Defence College, 2003).

13. Alberts, Garstka, and Stein; *Net Centric Warfare*.

14. Daniel Gonzales, Michael Johnson, Jimmie McEver, Dennis Leedom, Gina Kingston, Michael S. Tseng, *Network-Centric Operations Case Study: The Stryker*

Brigade Combat Team (Santa Monica, CA: RAND National Defense Research Institute, 2005).

15. James Greer (Colonel), "Operational Art for the Objective Force," *Military Review* (September-October 2002): 222-29.

16. Charles D. Costanza (Major), "Self-Synchronization, the Future Joint Force and the United States Army's Objective Force," [Monograph] (Fort Leavenworth, KS: School of Advanced Military Studies, United States Army Command and General Staff College, 2003).

17. Gonzalez et al., *Network-Centric Operations Case Study, The Stryker Brigade Combat Team.*

18. Network Centric Operations Industry Consortium.

19. Alberts et al., *Net Centric Warfare.*

STRENGTHENING

LEADERSHIP SKILLS

1. The Leader's Role in Increasing Ethical Reasoning Ability of Followers
    Pamela Raymer, Ed.D., Dean of Academics

2. The Role of Transformational Leadership: Lessons Learned
    from Visionary Leaders
    Deloris Willis and Judy Thompson-Moore, Professors of Civilian Leader
    Development

3. Redefining Army Leadership: Has the Be, Know, Do Model Been All that
    it Can Be?
    Fiona J. Burdick, Ph.D., Professor of Civilian Leader Development, and
    David S. Burdick, Professor of Installation Management

4. Civilians as Micro-Strategists
    Roy Eichhorn, Director of Research and Development

5. The Motivation Factor: The Invisible Barriers to Organizational
    Effectiveness
    Alton Dunham and Karen Spurgeon, Ed.D., Professor of Civilian Leader
    Development

6. Leading Change Through Investment
    John Plifka, Civilian Education System Basic Course Director;
    and Wayne Ditto, Professor of Civilian Leader Development

Pamela Raymer, Ed.D.

The Leader's Role in Increasing Ethical Reasoning Ability of Followers

Intruduction

Organizations need individuals with moral character in leadership positions and throughout all levels of followers. Gallup research indicates that only about one in six Americans describe the state of moral values in positive terms and that almost 50 percent rate moral values as "poor." When more than 80 percent of Americans believe morality is becoming worse (indicating a small increase in the last 3 years) and a decline in the percentage of Americans who say they hold "old-fashioned" values is down from 85 percent in 1997 to 76 percent in 2007,[1] the need to promote moral character is never more important.

If the prevailing view is one of moral relativism and situational ethics, as evidenced by Pew Research Center data showing only 39 percent of Americans "completely agree" that "there are clear guidelines about what's good and evil that apply to everyone regardless of their situation,"[2] leaders face a huge challenge to create an environment supportive of moral character. Leaders must not only establish a set of organizational values and live them, but must create a workplace that rewards ethical behavior. Additionally, leaders and followers must employ reasoning ability when confronted with ethical dilemmas, because people who can talk at a high moral development level may not behave accordingly. To translate a set of values, abstractly defined, to the ability to act ethically means moving those values across a chasm filled with multiple ambiguous, complex variables. The challenge for leaders is to find ways to enhance the ethical reasoning ability of followers to more successfully cross that chasm and, in so doing, personify moral character.

Character Defined
In her book, *Team of Rivals*, Doris Kearns Goodwin describes President Abraham Lincoln as a person of high moral character. Despite intense rivalry among three opponents in the Republican nomination for President, Lincoln brought these same rivals into top positions in his Cabinet - Edward Bates, William H. Seward, and Salmon P. Chase. He also offered positions to three former Democrats. Gideon Welles became Secretary of Navy, Montgomery Blair became Postmaster General, and Edwin M. Stanton became Secretary of War. His respect for the talent and attributes of these men enabled him to look beyond the animosity generated in the presidential race, and the result was a highly effective and loyal staff. The courage it took for Lincoln to bring these men—all of whom were more well-known, better educated, and more experienced politically than Lincoln—attest to his strong character.[3]

Warren Bennis, distinguished professor and author or editor of more than 25 books on leadership, says that of the multiple criteria organizations used to assess individuals, judgment and character are the least understood. Other criteria such as technical criteria and interpersonal and conceptual skills are much more easily evaluated. He adds that judgment—defined as the ability to make intelligent decisions under ambiguous circumstances and character—defined as the ability to do as you say—are much more difficult to quantify.[4]

Rushworth Kidder, a frequent writer on the subject of moral character, defines character with two components—values and behavior. To be a person of character, an individual must embrace a set of values but must also be able to act on them.[5] Kidder's view is that moral courage is what moves an individual from values to behavior,[6] but William Crain, author of *Theories of Development* believes that there is little correlation between moral (ethical) thinking and moral (ethical) action.[7] Believing in values such as honesty or fairness and acting on them are two different things—notwithstanding the courage it takes to act on those values.

Kidder's equation has a missing element—ethical reasoning. Having the courage to act on values is certainly necessary, but deriving the solution to an ethical dilemma must include reflection and analysis—reasoning. This ability is what will move values to ethical behavior.

Applying the highest levels of ethical reasoning will result in principled behavior—behavior exemplified in a person of character. Lincoln's character was surely enabled by his strong sense of values, his high level of reasoning ability, and his ability to persevere in difficult times. Thomas Reeves (biographer of John F. Kennedy) describes Kennedy as a man of serious intellect because he was willing to listen to alternate views and change his mind. [8] What makes leaders like Lincoln and Kennedy so exceptional is their ability to embrace advisors with very different opinions (however oppositional these opinions might be) and to alter their positions to do the right thing.

Values and Ethics

Establishing a set of values is a fairly routine activity for organizations. Whether determined by leadership or jointly agreed upon by followers, these values are then defined and posted with the expectation that all members will adhere to them.

Recent corporate scandals in companies such as Enron, Tyco, and Worldcom, and the cheating scandals in Military academies as well as the more serious ethics violations at Abu Ghraib Prison, serve to remind us of the difficulty of doing the right thing. These organizations—all of which had a published set of values—raise questions about the adequacy of this practice. Ethics classes (which most organizations mandate) are also inadequate to help followers solve ethical dilemmas. Ethics classes generally define what an individual shouldn't do and, consequently, do not contribute to increasing the ethical reasoning ability of an individual—the skill necessary when wrestling with the uncertainty and ambiguity associated with ethical dilemmas.

The 1982 Tylenol scare illustrates the complexity of solving an ethical dilemma. The Johnson and Johnson response to this situation is often cited as the classic example of a company that exemplified living its widely-published values-based credo of customers first and shareholders last. Laura Nash reports that Chairman James Burke and other senior leadership considered more than 200 decisions in the first 24 hours of the crisis, disputing the claim of some analysts who argued that Johnson and Johnson's decision was not based on ethics but simply a marketing strategy. Nash says this position fails to consider the complexity and number of decisions that company leadership had to make during a very brief period of time. [9] The reasoning ability this team brought to the situation resulted in the successful turn-around of Johnson and Johnson. Today Johnson and Johnson, along with Google, has the most positive image of 23 major corporations rated by the public in a recent Pew Research Center study.[10] Strict adherence to their organizational credo and acting on it by reasoning through ethical dilemmas is surely a major enabler to this positive image.

Moral Theory

To understand the complexity of the ethical reasoning exercises that organizations like Johnson and Johnson confront, an examination of moral theory is necessary. Some of the major moral theories identified by Robert Van Wyk include the natural law theory of St. Thomas Aquinas, the social contract ethics theory of Thomas Hobbes, and the duty-based ethics moral philosophy of Immanuel Kant.[11]

According to VanWyk, the natural law theory is grounded in the belief that a moral standard is not dependent on the customs or laws of a particular society—instead the moral standard is prescribed as it applies to the functions of human nature. For natural law to be plausible, defining "natural" and "unnatural" must be possible so that right and wrong can be determined. Defining what is natural and what is not natural is extremely problematic.[12]

The social contract theory is defined by VanWyk as one based on the belief that the moral standard is determined mutually by individuals through a set of rules that controls individual behavior with an expectation of reciprocal restraint from others. Changes in people's attitudes can alter the social contract and its rules—but this theory does not address the moral responsibility requisite for changing the rules for the common good. More importantly, no moral standards exist outside the rules by which they could be assessed.[13]

VanWyk describes the duty-based ethics theory as one premised on the belief that the difficulty facing an individual is not one of determining what one's duty is—instead it is performing one's duty when it conflicts with natural tendencies. Kant calls this "good will"—the will to fulfill one's responsibility. Kant also believed that reason supports morality by showing that to be immoral is in some way dissonant with standards of reason. According to VanWyk, this theory is accepted by many current moral philosophers as one that best describes the precepts of moral values—the idea of an individual who is concerned about morality—an individual who wants to be a person of high moral character.[14] This theory also provides support for the connection between values and behavior and the requirement to use reason.

John Gardner calls the natural tendencies that conflict with one's duty to be a person of goodwill "the old human difficulty" that keeps us from "honoring in our behavior the values we possess."[15] Michael Josephson labels these natural tendencies as self-righteousness, self-delusion and selfishness. He says that individuals often use virtuous behavior in other areas of their lives to justify an inflated view of their character, thereby exhibiting a self-righteous attitude and adds, an extremely "high self esteem creates a moral complacency that blinds us to our shortcomings."[16]

The second tendency identified by Josephson is self-delusion—rationalizing actions to fit what has already been done or what an individual really wants to do. The last human tendency is simply selfishness. When being ethical comes at a personal cost, it becomes difficult or impossible to act in a way that deprives an individual from getting what is desired. Josephson surveys report that 95 percent of people want to be viewed as highly ethical, and so it becomes all too easy to believe that individual character lives up to a personal belief rather than what might really be true. [17] Colin Greer says that "values can become self-righteous fortresses against others."[18] Deepak Malhortra et al reinforces these tenets with the following statement, "Research clearly demonstrates that we tend to overestimate how rational, careful, and logical we are. We are also prone to believe that others are more susceptible than we are to irrational decision making."[19]

Ethical Reasoning

Our ability to challenge ourselves continuously to be the person of character we should be, not the person of character we naively believe we are and to regard ethics as an unwavering principle, not a guideline we can arbitrate away, will help us obviate those human tendencies. Supportive of our ability to keep an open mind to resolve ethical dilemmas is the capacity to reason critically and ethically.

Lawrence Kohlberg, a leading researcher of moral development advocated that a high level of moral development is accompanied by a high level of reasoning. The significance of Kohlberg's work was in contributing to an awareness of the different moral development levels that individuals could advance through, supported by higher levels of reasoning ability. For a leader to appreciate the relationship between ethical reasoning and moral development, an understanding of Kohlberg's stage theory of moral development is useful. [20]

Kohlberg's Theory of Moral Development

As a developmental theory, Kohlberg did not believe that his stages were the product of maturation or socialization—instead the stages emerge from individual reflection on moral problems. Kohlberg, who taught at Harvard University from 1968 until his death in 1987, spent much of his career promoting the belief that the reasoning ability of individuals can be increased when placed in situations with others who have higher reasoning ability than their own.[21]

Kohlberg separated his six stages into three levels—the Preconventional Morality, the Conventional Morality, and the Postconventional Morality. The Preconventional Morality level encompasses the first two stages. For individuals in stage 1, adults with influence dictate what is right or wrong. Obedience and punishment are the primary driving factors. Failure to behave according to the expectations of the "authority" results in punishment. Adults at stage 1 relinquish their decision-making to another adult who then has the same power that influencers such as parents have over young children.[22] Adolf Eichmann, often referred to as the architect of the Holocaust, represents an adult who operated at stage 1 according to Kohlberg's ratings of statements Eichmann made at his 1961 trial in Israel. The following statements illustrate Eichmann's abdication of responsibility for his actions to Hitler or the German Reich:

> In actual fact, I was merely a little cog in the machinery that carried out the directives of the German Reich. I never met him personally, but his success alone proves to me that I should follower myself to this man. He was somehow so supremely capable that the people recognized him. And so with justification I recognized him joyfully and I still defend him.[23]

In stage 2, behavior is determined by what is in the best interests of the individual. Individuals operate in ways designed to meet their needs, even if the behavior fails to conform to rules set forth by "authority." Individualism is the operating factor at this stage, and issues begin to be "relative"—to depend upon the unique circumstances in a given situation.[24]

The second level, Conventional Morality, includes stages 3 and 4 where Kohlberg maintained the majority of individuals fall. He asserted that beliefs in these stages crossed cultures, i.e., that certain values such as lying, cheating, and stealing were universally accepted as wrong—although other researchers debated these findings. In stage 3, individuals begin to look beyond themselves and recognize a certain level of conformity is necessary to be accepted. Good interpersonal relationships, grounded in empathy and concern for others, drive behavior at this stage. In stage 4, individuals continue to look outward to society at-large. To achieve an orderly society, they recognize that rules and laws are necessary and are willing to forfeit the individualistic focus characterized by earlier stages.[25]

I. Preconventional Morality	1. Doing the right thing to avoid punishment AUTHORITY FOCUS	2. Doing what meets the individual's need, but recognizing that others may have different needs INDIVIDUAL FOCUS
II. Conventional Morality	3. Believing in the Golden Rule INTERPERSONAL CONFORMITY	4. Doing what's best for society SOCIAL CONFORMITY
III. Postconventional Morality	5. Recognizing diversity of values and opinions. Laws are social contracts that can be changed UTILITARIAN INDIVIDUAL RIGHTS	6. Following ethical principles that are believed to be of a higher, universal order UNIVERSAL RIGHTS

Table 1: Kohlberg's Model of Moral Development[28]

The third level, Postconventional Morality, includes the final two stages. In stage 5, individuals recognize and begin to value differences in opinion with others and with groups. Laws are considered to be social contracts—mutually agreed upon and subject to change—rather than rigid requirements. The greatest good for the greatest number of people is achieved through a majority rule and compromise. The social contract and individual rights are the driving factors at this stage. "Morality" and "rights" may take priority over laws. In stage 6, individuals are free to disobey unjust laws. Individuals recognize that laws must be based on justice, but believe that determining what is just or unjust can change and can be defined differently within society.[26]

The 1856 Dred Scott Supreme Court decision illustrates the changing views within society. In this 7-2 decision, the Supreme Court ruled that people of African descent whose ancestors were slaves could not become American citizens. Justice Scalia, commenting on the dissenting opinion written by Justice Benjamin Curtis, stated that it was very comforting to know that when history reflects a truly horrific Supreme Court decision such as this one, at least some justices recognized the injustice.[27]

As in the stage 5 description, whether laws are considered as social contracts subject to the will of the people and/or as in stage 6, a recognition that determining what is just or unjust is left to entities such as Congress and the United States Supreme Court—albeit an imperfect system as illustrated by the Dred Scott decision—there can be no denying that these are complex, difficult decisions. Moving individuals from lower to higher stages of moral reasoning may be a lofty goal for leaders, but has enormous potential. Equipping followers with skills needed to improve their ability to make ethical decisions in a world of moral and ethical relativism can only contribute to the effectiveness of an organization.

How do leaders increase the reasoning ability of followers? Kohlberg and Hersh advocated an active form of learning that required students to consider moral problems with complexities beyond their current level of reasoning ability.[29] Research on Kohlberg's theory provides evidence that individuals can prefer and even understand material one or two stages higher than the one in which they operate.[30]

Since reasoning ability is developmental (not a result of socialization or maturation and therefore subject to external influence) [31] leaders can be that external influence. They can place followers in exercises that require them to examine a perspective not yet considered to strengthen their reasoning ability that will push them toward higher levels of moral development. While Nash says that no textbook could possibly determine the exact number or even identify the decision-making processes that leaders in companies such as Johnson and Johnson followed to deal with a crisis, [32] all leaders can employ strategies to improve the decision-making ability of followers.

Ethics Programs for Leaders

Leaders can take their cue from educational institutions with character education programs that include ethics forums. An example of this type of program is one offered in the Hankamer School of Business at Baylor University. For the first time in 2007, the Hankamer School of Business initiated an MBA ethics case competition to coincide with their Dale P. Jones Business Ethics Forum. Teams are given a business scenario with an ethical dilemma and asked to recommend solutions to a panel of judges on how the company leadership should behave.[33] Colleges also widely participate in Ethics Bowls where teams of students consider ethical problems taken from the workplace. These competitions test students' abilities to present and defend solutions to complex, real-world ethical situations.

As part of an ethics program that extends beyond the rules-based "thou shalt not" classes, leaders in organizations can offer similar forums for followers. Requiring individuals to discuss, debate, and negotiate solutions to real-world ethical dilemmas gives them opportunities to become conversant with alternate views—not simply bent on pushing a personal agenda—and to test their critical thinking skills as preparation for addressing organizational ethical dilemmas they will surely encounter. Engaging in a moral dialogue on authentic, workplace examples intensifies the learning of participants and helps followers more easily translate a set of abstract values into behavior appropriate in unique types of situations. Even though the number of variables impacting workplace situations may be infinite, these forums serve to increase the technical competence and confidence of participants to assess the situations they will confront.

These forums are valuable in other ways. Followers can hear leaders' views on specific situations, even though leader opinions should be tendered only after followers have had opportunities to discuss and debate recommended solutions to specific dilemmas. The leader's expectations for follower behavior can be made explicit. Since leaders will not have an opportunity to model or regulate each and every possible variation of morally ambiguous situations, discussing them and listening to other's positions can be very useful. These exercises also afford leaders opportunities to hear the perspectives of followers to gain insight into the various levels of reasoning abilities. Leaders can take advantage of this knowledge to establish new or clarify existing organizational guidelines and policies where confusion or gaps exist.

Conclusion

Since ethical dilemmas confront individuals on a regular basis, promoting reasoning ability and moral development has enormous potential in today's environment of moral relativism and ethical dilemmas. These dilemmas range from routine decisions such as choosing to use duty time for personal activities rather than working a full, productive day; reporting unethical conduct of a colleague padding travel expenses; or recommending friends for jobs over more qualified candidates to larger issues dealing with contract awards. Kidder says that "ethical thinkers are catalysts" and that "ethical fitness makes ethical thinkers."[34] Ethics forums in the workplace are ethical fitness opportunities to develop ethical catalysts.

Alfred Nobel had a unique opportunity to change the world's view of him. When his brother died, the obituary of Alfred Nobel was mistakenly printed. Even though the article portrayed Nobel as a brilliant chemist and extremely wealthy as the inventor of dynamite, he did not want to be remembered this way. To change his legacy, he used his fortune to establish the Nobel Prizes.[35]

Even though most leaders will not have the same opportunity as Nobel to change their legacy in as dramatic or global scale, they can enhance their legacy within their own organization by promoting "ethical fitness" for all. Leaders may have a greater responsibility to promote ethical behavior, but all levels of influence, both followers and leaders, must advocate for an environment in which every member within the organization employs ethical reasoning. A high level of moral development will contribute to every individual's ability to guard against the natural tendency of self-interest to select the ethical choice—to exemplify a person of character. Both leaders and followers with high moral character can only enrich the quality within— and ultimately the overall effectiveness of the organization.

Notes
1. Joseph Carroll, "Americans Remain Negative on State of Nation's Moral Values" (electronic article from Gallup News Service, June 2007); available on the Internet at http://www.gallup.com/2011/27754 (accessed 23 May 2008).
2. Pew Research Center, "Trends in Political Values and Core Attitudes: 1987-2007," (Washington, D.C.: 22 March 2007), 36; available on the internet at http://www. people-org/reports/pdf/312.pdf
3. Doris Kearns Goodwin, *A Team of Rivals: The Political Genius of Abraham Lincoln* (New York: Simon & Schuster, 2005), xv-xvii.
4. Warren Bennis, "The Character of Hardship," Michael S. Josephson and Wes Hanson (Eds.), *The Power of Character* (San Francisco, CA: Jossey-Bass, 1998), 143-149.
5. Rushworth M. Kidder, "The Eagle and the Knapsack," In M.S. Josephson and Wes Henson (Eds.), *The Power of Character* (San Francisco, CA: Jossey-Bass, 1998), 181-189.
6. Rushworth M. Kidder, *Moral Courage* (New York, NY: W. Morrow, 2005), 64.
7. William C. Crain, *Theories of Development,* 5th ed. (New Jersey: Prentice-Hall, 2004), 166.
8. Thomas C. Reeves "John F. Kennedy" in *Character Above All: Ten Presidents for FDR to George Bush,* Robert A. Wilson (Ed), (New York, NY: Simon & Schuster, 1995), 102.
9. Laura Nash, *Good Intentions Aside: A Manager's Guide to Resolving Ethical*

Problems (Boston: Harvard Business School Press, 1990), 38-43.

10. Pew Research Center, "Trends in Political Values and Core Attitudes: 1987-2007;" (Washington, D.C.: 22 March 2007); available on the Internet at http://www.people-press.org/reports/pdf/312

11. Robert N. Van Wyk, *Introduction to Ethics* (New York: St. Martin's Press, 1990), 55-97.

12. Ibid., 55-69.

13. Ibid., 70-78.

14. Ibid., 79-97.

15. John W. Gardner, *On Leadership* (New York: Free Press, 1990), 77.

16. Michael S. Josephson and Wes Hanson, *The Power of Character: Prominent Americans Talk About Life, Family, Work, Values and More* (San Francisco: Jossey-Bass, 1998), 12.

17. Ibid., 8.

18. Colin Greer, "Awakening on Moral Imagination," *The Power of Character*, Michael Josephson and Wes Hanson, (Eds.) (San Francisco: Jossey-Bass, 1998), 231.

19. Deepak Malhotra, Gillian Ku and J. Keith Murnighan, "When Winning is Everything" (Boston: Harvard Business Review, May 2008), 78-86.

20. Lawrence Kohlberg, *The Psychology of Moral Development: The Nature and Validity of Moral Stage, Vol. 2* (San Francisco: Harper & Row, 1984), 170-211.

21. William C. Crain, *Theories of Development, 5th Ed.* (New Jersey: Prentice-Hall, 2004), 159-173.

22. Ibid., 155-157.

23. Kohlberg, *The Psychology of Moral Development: The Nature and Validity of Moral Stage, Vol. 2.* 54-55.

24. Crain, *Theories of Development, 5th Ed.* 154-155.

25. Ibid., 155-157.

26. Ibid., 157-159.

27. Ruth Bader Ginsburg, "The Role of Dissenting Opinions: Address U.S.," *Vital Speeches of the Day* 74, no. 4 (April 2008): 157-160.

28. Lawrence Kohlberg, *The Psychology of Moral Development: The Nature and Validity of Moral Stage, Vol. 2* (San Francisco, CA: Harper & Row), 174-176.

29. Lawrence Kohlberg and Richard H. Hersh, "Moral Development: A Review of the Theory," *Theory into Practice* 16, no. 2 (1977): 53-59.

30. James J. Rest, Elliot Turiel and Lawrence Kohlberg, "Level of Moral Development as a Determinant of Preference and Comprehension of Moral Judgment Made By Others," *Journal of Personality 37*, no. 2 (1969): 237.

31. William C. Crain, *Theories of Development, 5th Ed.* 160.

32. Nash, 39.

33. Jeff Brown, "Ethics in Action" *Baylor Magazine* 6, no. 2 (2007): 28-31.

34. Rushworth Kidder, *How Good People Make Tough Choices* (New York, NY: William Morrow, 1995), 210-211.

35. Josephson and Hanson, "Being Good: Easier Said Than Done" (1998), 7-15.

Deloris Willis and Judy Thompson-Moore

The Role of Transformational Leadership: Lessons Learned from Visionary Leaders

There are 288 million Americans, and we've tried for several decades to get along without leaders. It hasn't worked very well. So let's admit it: we cannot function without leaders. Our quality of life depends on the quality of our leaders. And since no one else seems to be volunteering, it is up to you. If you've ever had dreams of leadership, now is the time, this is the place, and you're it. We need you.[1]

Warren Bennis

Introduction

The Army needs strong leaders—leaders who have the courage to look forward into the future rather than taking steps back into the past. It needs leaders who have the ability to guide future generations with passion, enthusiasm, and hope. Leaders of the future must be transformational and resilient. The transformational style of leadership guides followers to achieve performance at levels that exceed the expectations of the organization. This style emphasizes charismatic and transformational approaches with vision-related goals. Transformational leaders have the ability to influence followers' lives and possess high levels of ethical and moral responsibility.

It has been 30 years since James MacGregor Burns published his seminal work introducing the concepts of transformational and transactional leadership.[2] Bernard Bass, a distinguished professor emeritus in the School of Management at Binghamton University and a member of the Academy of Senior Professionals at Eckerd College, further developed Burns' work by advancing the theories of transformational leadership.[3] Bass says that the attributes of transformational leaders center on a leader's ability to generate a purpose of mission and uplift the morale, motivation, and morals of their followers.[4] Accordingly, Bass says that transformational leaders emphasize what they can do for the country, whereas transactional leaders focus on what the country can do for them.[5] The attributes of transformational leaders provide the capability to lead organizations through constant change. Leaders who are more transformational and less transactional are effective and particularly suited for promoting both internal and external organizational change.

The authors conducted interviews with four visionary leaders in May 2008. In conducting the interviews, an open-ended questionnaire was designed to provide opportunities for the leaders to elaborate on their leadership experiences. The following Army leaders: Steve Wilberger, Deputy Commandant and Dean of Operations at the Army Management Staff College; Army (Ret.) General William G. T. Tuttle, Jr.; and corporate America leaders Carol Pearson, Director of The James MacGregor Burns Academy of Leadership, and Bob Stone, Faculty of the Ukleja Center for Ethical Leadership at California State University, provided information based on the questionnaire. These leaders provided insight on their leadership experiences and emphasized their perspectives of the transformational qualities they believe are inherent to leader effectiveness.

In this chapter, the authors examine the theories and dimensions of transformational and transactional leadership and provide content analysis of interview transcripts pertaining to the attributes of transformational leadership from the perspectives of the Army and corporate America leaders. These leaders provided candid lessons learned and specific examples of how they have used attributes and characteristics of transformational leadership effectively during times of turbulent change. Leaders who use a transformational leadership style enhance organizational effectiveness by creating a compelling vision, an environment where risk-taking becomes safe, and a culture where innovative ideas can be shared.[6]

Transformational and Transactional Leadership Theory

Transformational leadership theory is new in the area of management initiatives. In recent years, management theorists have given considerable thought and attention to this form of leadership.[7] Burns was the first author to contrast transformational and transactional leadership. He said, "In transactional leadership, followers receive offers of rewards or penalties in exchange for compliance or non-compliance with the leaders' wishes."[8] In contrast, transformational leaders motivate followers to a higher standard than that of self-interest. They also guide followers to achieve performance well beyond expectations by transforming their attitudes, beliefs, and values as opposed to the process of only gaining compliance.[9]

The transformational style of leadership (as opposed to transactional leadership) is sometimes referred to as transforming leadership, which focuses on lifting an organization to higher levels of expectations.[10] Burns says:

> Such leadership occurs when one or more persons engage with others in such a way that leaders and followers raise one another to higher levels of motivation and morality. Their purposes, which might have started out as separate but related, as in the case of transactional leadership, become fused. Power bases are linked not as counterweights but as mutual support for common purpose . . . the relationship can be moralistic, of course. But transforming leadership ultimately becomes moral in that it raises the level of human conduct and ethical aspiration of both leader and led, and thus it has a transforming effect on both.[11]

Transactional leader behavior is the leadership model used most often in organizations today.[12] This style offers contingent rewards in exchange for performance. However, transformational leader behavior originates in the personal values and beliefs of the leader and does not constitute an exchange of rewards for performance. Bass claims that in this context, transformational leaders operate out of deeply held personal value systems of justice and integrity.[13] By expressing these values, leaders are able to influence their followers by having the ability to change their goals and beliefs. These leaders are considered more transformational and less transactional.[14] Transformational leadership results in achievement of higher levels of performance from followers than previously believed.[15] This higher level of achievement has a direct impact on organizational effectiveness and the leader's ability to sustain improved performance.

Yukl, Howell, and Avolio argue that ineffective leadership has an impact on unit and organization performance.[16] Consequently, Howell and Avolio conducted a study of one of the largest and most successful financial institutions in Canada over a 1-year period to examine the relationship of transactional leadership to unit performance. This study used measures of leadership to examine the locus of control and support for innovation to predict the consolidated unit performance of 78 managers.[17] The findings revealed that the more positive contributions associated with effective behaviors came from those associated with transformational leadership.

The uncertainty of the environment studied by Howell and Avolio provided a setting more conducive to the emergence of transformational leadership rather than transactional leadership.[18] The findings indicated that leaders who displayed more individualized consideration, intellectual stimulation, and charisma and less management by exception and contingent reward, contributed to a more positive level in the achievement of business unit performance. The findings concluded that the more positive contributions associated with effective leadership came from those associated with transformational leadership behaviors.[19]

This is just one example of the many studies that began to shift the thinking previously held of organizational leadership theories. Hosfstede et al. assert that a paradigm shift has occurred in new organizational leadership theories such as transformational, charismatic, and transactional. This shift has become a focus of empirical research.[20] Bass contributed to this paradigm shift by characterizing the four dimensions of leadership to include individualized consideration, inspirational motivation, intellectual stimulation and idealized influence as key characteristics of organizational effectiveness.[21]

The first dimension is individualized consideration. Bass asserts that attaining charisma in the eyes of followers is a critical behavior in becoming a transformational leader.[22] Like Bass, Robert J. House also has a strong belief in the value of charisma as part of transformational leadership.[23] House asserts that charismatic leaders are those who are capable of having a discerning effect on their followers. These individuals are able to motivate others and have the feeling of self-efficacy, which in turn makes them believe they are capable of being effective leaders.[24] Charismatic leaders are confident leaders with the drive and ability to influence followers to think beyond individual interests and broaden their focus along the interests and overall well-being of the organization.

The second dimension is inspiration (often referred to as inspirational motivation) and is usually found in conjunction with charisma. Transformational leaders have the ability to inspire their followers to do great things. If leaders are able to communicate their vision, they will gain the confidence and trust of their followers to help them achieve their vision.[25] Charisma and inspirational motivation are displayed when leaders envision a desirable future, communicate that future to their followers, and show determination and confidence in achieving it.[26] It is at this point that followers are able to envision the future and build support for their leader in order to make the vision become a reality.

Intellectual stimulation is the third dimension associated with transformational leadership. Bass characterizes this as leaders promoting intelligence, rationality, logical thinking, and problem-solving.[27] Leaders who want their followers to succeed are intent on encouraging them to seek new and innovative ways to solve problems. An example of a leader who promotes creative thinking and problem-solving is Army Colonel Leonard Wong. In the Iraq War, he saw the Army encouraging "reactive instead of proactive thinking." Colonel Wong began working with junior officers to be creative and take more risks.[28] Leaders must be willing to allow their followers the opportunity to examine their own assumptions, make mistakes, and test new ideas. In essence, these leaders are teaching their followers to turn their mistakes into learning opportunities.

The last dimension is idealized influence. Bass states that leaders show respect for others by building confidence and trust in their ability to accomplish the overall mission. When followers observe their leader showing positive results, they more likely want to emulate those same behaviors.[29] Leaders act as coaches and mentors by focusing on the developmental needs of followers and showing them that they can accomplish objectives they felt were impossible. These leaders are able to convince followers to perform to their fullest potential.

Each of these four dimensions is significant in becoming a transformational leader. When used effectively, they have the ability to elevate followers' achievements, ideas, and contributions to the organization and society beyond expectations. Bass summed up the relevance of transformational leadership by stating:

One of the ways to achieve the needed alignment of individual soldier interests with the interests of one's unit, organization, and the Army as a whole is through leadership at all levels. Whereas commitment and involvement of the better educated, more intelligent, more fully trained, diverse, technologically tuned-in, and more skeptical about the ideals of just causes and patriotic duty personnel may be maintained to some degree by the "carrot and stick" contingent reinforcement of transactional leadership, it is argued that much more will be achieved if transformational leadership is added.[30]

Consistent with Bass's evaluation of transformational leadership, organizations should have a balance of both transformational and transactional leadership styles. While an organization can be said to be purely transformational or transactional, it is more effective if it moves in the direction of transformational qualities.[31] Bass argues that transactional leaders work within their organization to follow established rules, procedures, and norms whereas transformational leaders work to change their culture by first understanding it. Through understanding the organization's culture, transformational leaders can work to realign the culture with a new vision and a revision of its shared assumptions, values, and norms.[32] A leader who builds such cultures and is able to articulate a vision and purpose to followers successfully empowers them to take responsibility for achieving the organization's vision.[33]

Lessons Learned from Visionary Leaders

As mentioned earlier, an open-ended questionnaire was used with selected visionary leaders. The elements addressed in the questionnaire were leadership style, human potential in organizations, vision, measuring accountability, and lessons learned. These leaders shared experiences and specific examples of how they have inspired others and what leaders can do to steer individuals into being champions in their own organizations.

Steve Wilberger, Deputy Commandant and Dean of Operations at the Army Management Staff College, provided insight into his philosophy of transformational leadership.[34] He stated that transformational leadership is participative leadership. He believes this style builds consensus as it holds people accountable, with an expectation to meet milestones toward goal accomplishment. Wilberger said that he believes in building a team and improving morale. He believes that you must engage followers in the solutions business. For example, "If you are a leader and a follower comes to you with a problem, the follower should also come with a suggestion." Wilberger believes that leaders should be risk-takers.

Wilberger believes that he truly depicts a "leader by example" in being able to motivate and uplift the morale of followers. He said that he is demanding and personally engages his people, but he also expects results. He discussed how he helped design his own organizational appreciation certificates, and then shamelessly recognized his followers for their contributions to those organizations.

He moved on to discuss the importance of challenging people. Wilberger stated, "You should challenge your people, and they will come up with ingenious ways to improve organizational processes." He emphasized that "Leaders must stay engaged, like Abraham Lincoln's Management by Walking Around (MBWA)." Hopkins-Doerr asserts that the main purpose of MBWA is for managers to use it as a high priority of their own ability to affect the organizational climate.[35] Leaders should not use MBWA as an inspection of the workplace and followers must trust management and feel comfortable in sharing information on organizational processes. Organizations like to see their leaders get out of their offices and be visible in the workplace. Wilberger offered some sound advice on leader roles and responsibilities. He stated:

> As you rise up in leadership roles and responsibilities, you have to realize that you must stay out of the weeds. You have the responsibility to guide, order, and direct. Leaders should not only look ahead but also guide their followers toward the organizational vision. Without micromanaging, leaders must be able to strategically guide people in order to avoid pitfalls and problems.

Wilberger added, "Effective leaders are also approachable leaders. People who see this characteristic will come to you because they see that you are approachable." In addition to being approachable, he believes leaders must be engaged and decisive. He offers the following steps for leadership and decision-making:

- Make a decision and do not sit on things hoping for change to happen.
- Do not shoot the messenger when there is bad news, otherwise, your people won't come to you with good ideas.
- Be accessible, caring, visible in the workplace, and inspirational, and hold your followers accountable for results.

When it comes to people skills, Wilberger added:

Competence and people skills are the two most vital skills for leaders. A person in a leadership role can be technically competent, but must also be able to engage people. Leaders hire their key people for applicable talent and for the passion they display within their functional lanes. At the strategic level, he believes that absolute control and micro-management do not work. Leaders should let their people handle day-to-day tasks, leaving the leaders somewhat less encumbered to focus on the bigger picture. As hectic as the Army can be, especially in our current persistent conflict, we do not always take time to think about the bigger picture and whether or not collectively we are heading in the right direction.

Wilberger's leadership philosophy is "People first, mission will follow." He said that if you take actions with your people's best interests at heart, they will bend over backwards to accomplish the mission, and they will not let the organization fail." He recommends that leaders read, *"Good to Great: Why Some Companies Make the Leap and Why Others Do not* by Jim Collins.[36] Wilberger stated, "This book discusses getting the 'right' people on the bus, and then getting the right people in the right seats on the bus, which goes back to hiring the right talent in your organization."

He further stated, "You are building your team for success. In a way, leadership is like parenting. To succeed, you need compassion and discipline, and not necessarily in that order." Some of the lessons learned that Wilberger extends to leaders are: be accountable for your actions, be mobile, take charge, take difficult jobs, and become a subject matter expert in whatever you do.

While transactional leadership is generally easier because it does not require a sense of value in order to motivate followers, leaders can gather from Wilberger's leadership insights that he believes transformational leadership is an effective form of leadership. When compliance to standards, rather than commitment to ideals, is required to accomplish certain tasks or missions, transactional leadership may be more appropriate. Military leaders typically exhibit a complementary mix of both transactional and transformational leadership styles. The determination of how to mix the two styles is largely affected by factors such as "organizational climate, unit mission, and the leader's own experience and comfort zone."[37] Wilberger's interview captured the true essence of a transformational leader. While being in a key position with the Army Management Staff College, he has seen how the Civilian Education System is helping to shape future leaders. He has a balanced blend of Bass's four dimensions of transformational leadership.

The next Army leader interviewed was General (Ret.) William G. T. Tuttle, Jr., author of *"Defense Logistics for the 21st Century."*[38] When asked which style of leadership he prefers . . . transformational, transactional, or another. Tuttle replied, "Transformational and transactional leadership styles are too confining." He believes behaviors can be learned, and his leadership style initially in his Military career was dysfunctional. He contends that everyone needs to test behavior.

During the interview, Tuttle provided a briefing that he had presented titled *"One Old Soldier's Perspective on Leading Units."* His briefing addressed character traits that are critical to relationships. Tuttle stated, "Character traits (such as integrity and honesty) are critical because they are the bedrock for the condition of character." He discussed his leadership responsibility of having to relieve some people as a result of "integrity" issues. He believes that a lack of integrity can destroy an organization. In essence, people cannot lead effectively if they do not have integrity. Tuttle said that he believes in several other attributes of character such as courage. The courage he advocates is less physical (which certainly is important) and more moral (doing the right thing because it is right). He added the trait of kindness. He smiled and shared a quote, "Be kind to people; you do not have to demean them as persons; you criticize behavior, not the person."

Tuttle said that leaders should know what counts and what is important. They need to understand other people's viewpoints. This will allow both to be on the same page. Another important factor of leadership is to have the ability to define the area of expectations. Leaders need to embrace the reality that uncertainty exists. You never have all of the available evidence needed when decisions must be made, as there is always some form of ambiguity for which a leader should have a high tolerance. Tuttle added, "Even though we cannot forecast the future, we can make mid-course adjustments to respond to changing situations."

Being customer-focused is also a key characteristic to successful leadership of service organizations. Tuttle stated, "They have customers, their reason for existence." He added that he would visit customers both to solicit their feedback on the quality of logistics support and to set an example of healthy customer relations for organizational members. An important dimension of customer relations is to manage customer expectations at an achievable level of performance. Overreaching breeds dissatisfaction when performance lags and is unfair to the supporting organization's followers. Leaders should make agreements with their customers on the standards of expectations.

Leaders of high performing organizations build a culture of commitment to support continuous improvement of all its members. There is always room for continuous improvement—nothing is as good as it could be. Leaders should constantly nourish the culture in search of improvements, which can require significant changes of strategy necessary to meet the changing needs of customers or to adapt to environmental changes

The evaluation process is critical to organizational performance. Tuttle stated:

> Leaders must review the performance of their followers in meeting mutually understood objectives. Each individual's objectives should relate directly to the organization's objectives, and performance metrics should be agreed upon between leader and followers. Supervisors generally do not like face-to-face discussions with people, but they are critical and should occur during evaluation periods as well as at the end so there is a continuing, mutual understanding about the follower's performance in meeting objectives.

Tuttle said that he believes that effective leaders must focus on relationships as well as task performance. He recommends that leaders visualize a two-dimensional matrix with commitment to task performance rated from 0 to 10 on the horizontal scale and relationship skills rated the same way on the vertical scale (Figure 1). He stated, "If your leadership style is at level 10 (task-oriented) and 0 (relationship-oriented), the organization will suffer in the long run." He added that while a score of 10-10 probably is not achievable, a high focus on task with a commensurately high focus on relationships by leaders will likely enable the organization to be high achieving. Leaders must balance task and relationship skills. Leadership is about the ability to influence people to achieve the organization's mission. Leaders influence by their behavior and their accessibility.

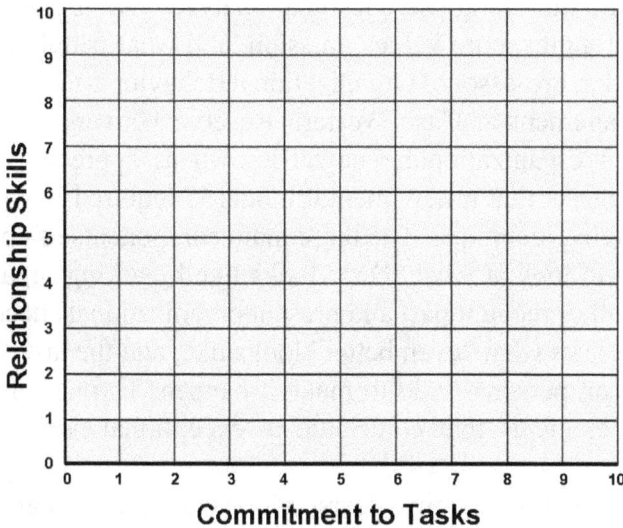

Figure 1

Finally, Tuttle summed up his leadership approach as he had often explained it to newly appointed staff members when he was President and Chief Executive Officer of the Logistics Management Institute (LMI). He said:

> They were almost all professionals, and I showed them an organization diagram of an inverted pyramid. The people at the top of the inverted pyramid were researchers who did the organization's work for clients. My and the other leaders' and support staff's jobs were to support the research staff in doing their jobs for the client-customers. That included everything from developing LMI's strategic plan and managing its resources to ensuring a pleasant cafeteria for the staff.

Leaders (like Tuttle and Wilberger) who use transformational attributes are exceptional change agents. They have the ability to inspire and motivate followers to superior performance. These leaders are able to articulate effective visions that spur followers forward with optimism while embracing the future.[39]

Carol Pearson, Director of The James MacGregor Burns Academy of Leadership, said she believes that she is a transformational leader, as she is always trying to bring out the best potential in people, organizations, and situations.[40] When asked how she deals with issues in the workplace, she explained that the first thing she does is to analyze what is right about the situation—its strengths, core values, mission, and what people care about. David Cooperrider, Professor of Organizational Behavior at the Weatherhead School of Management at Case Western Reserve University, coined the methodology for organizational renewal known as appreciative inquiry. Cooperrider suggests that a new mental model is required beyond that of the problem-solving technique. The three main components of appreciative inquiry propose to look at what "best" looks like by asking organizational members to recall or recount past and present organizational successes. The next component asks what "even better" looks like, and the last component asks what you can personally do to make it happen. Through this process of inquiry, the elements that contribute to exceptional performance are reinforced.[41]

Through appreciative inquiry, Pearson looks at a problem and analyzes what is going wrong and why. She said that sometimes the problem is in the structure and the systems that need to be redesigned. Sometimes the issue is that people think about processes using the wrong frame or narrative, and they need to re-frame and re-imagine how to view the situation. Sometimes the situation cannot be changed, but they can accept it and determine how to make the best of it and succeed at their work, even with its limitations and frustrations.

Pearson discussed the opportunities she has had to design or redesign positions in her organization to add more meaning and challenge. She said that she came to the Academy when her work group moved from the College of Behavioral and Social Sciences to the School of Public Policy. As a result, she needed to shift some of the staff's duties to be relevant to the new environment, both in what they do now (oriented to the public domain) and in how they do it (less autonomous, more networked). When asked how she passes down her vision to her leaders for implementation, she said that she does not just pass down her vision, but rather works with her senior team and her entire staff to develop a vision they can all embrace. The staff goes through a branding exercise to gain consensus on key issues, and they agree to collectively live with (and deliver on) those issues.

Pearson said she measures her leaders buy-in to support the vision and holds them accountable for implementing it. When she issues an annual contract to each follower, she identifies the requirements and expectations. She reviews the follower's performance at midpoint of the contract and again at the end of the contract year to ensure expectations are met. When unforeseen events happen, she and her staff appropriately revise the expectations.

Pearson shared some lessons learned. She said:

Communicate honestly, but kindly. It is not kindness to let people get away with things. The whole team needs accountability. I specialize in thinking about leadership and understanding the archetypal stories that we live and the mental frames that define how we make meaning of what is happening. Changing the frame or mental model can change everything.

The last interview was with Bob Stone, better known as the "Energizer-in-Chief."[42] Stone worked as a civil servant for 30 years. He started a quality revolution at the Pentagon (and later in the White House) where he led the campaign to reinvent the U.S. Government. He worked as a project leader for Vice President Al Gore's National Performance Review. Stone currently consults and teaches ethical leadership and leading change and is a member of the governing council and faculty of the Ukleja Center for Ethical Leadership at California State University.

When asked what type of leadership style he prefers, Stone said that he admires the general concept of servant leadership. He said that he has been refining his style for several years, and he now thinks his formula is "A-B-C." The three essential elements are **Authenticity**, which is the determination to be seen as you really are; **Buoyancy**, the ability and determination to keep lifting people up; and **Control,** the ability to adhere to core principles and not allow deviations from them.

When asked about passing down his vision, Stone said that he communicates with people throughout the organization. He described the two audiences he had when he worked for Vice President Al Gore; one audience was the National Performance Review (NPR) staff, which for 6 months was 350 people; and the other audience consisted of millions of people who worked for the Federal Government. According to Stone, it was important to pass down the vision to both groups, and his formula was different with the NPR staff because he dealt with them one-on-one. He spent his time energizing people and mentoring many on an informal basis, which earned him the title "Energizer-in Chief."

Stone said the Military does an exceptional job on leadership development and that Civil Service could use some improvement. He likes the idea of the Army Management Staff College's Civilian Education System Program. He said there are millions of prospective leaders in the government, but most of them never get help developing to their full leadership potential.

The Civilian Education System is leading the initiative in developing Army leaders for higher levels of responsibility.

Stone had a tremendous influence in his role as Energizer-in-Chief and intellectually stimulated millions within the Federal Government. In his book *Confessions of a Civil Servant*, Stone lists the following ten leadership lessons that easily relate to the characteristics and attributes of a transformational leader.[43]

Be Pleasant	If you're going to be a leader, you're going to need a lot of help.
Be Trusting	People who are trusted are happier and more productive in their work.
Be Bold	Leadership is about movement and causing others to go somewhere different.
Be Uplifting	People want purpose in their work.
Be Positive	Look for things that went right and try to build on them.
Be Enabling	People want to be in charge of their part of the world.
Be Controlling	The leader must guard the core principles of the enterprise, that is, the leader's own core principles.
Be Unreasonable	George Bernard Shaw wrote, "The reasonable man adapts himself to the world; the unreasonable one persists in trying to adapt the world to himself. Therefore, all progress depends on the unreasonable man."
Be Clear	When you're perfectly clear and the message has gotten through, wonderful things start to happen.
Think Three	The rule of three is flexible. For you: be pleasant, be trusting, be bold. For others: be uplifting, be positive, be enabling. For your principles: be controlling, be unreasonable, be clear.

Stone's 10 leadership lessons serve as words of wisdom on how leaders can be victors within their own organizations. His focus is on putting customers first, empowering people, and inspiring leaders to view problems as opportunities. Transformational leaders are interested in expanding their followers' and their own conceptualizations to help move people from concerns of remaining with the status quo towards higher-level concerns associated with achievement, change, and growth.[44]

Based on the content analysis of the interviews with the four leaders, six characteristics of transformational leadership (along with the associated behavioral attributes) emerged; those characteristics are positive moral character, strong interpersonal skills, willingness to take risks, relationship building and teamwork, the ability to communicate, and leadership execution (Figure 2).

Characteristics	Behavioral Attributes
Positive Moral Character	• Shows a high sense of integrity and honesty • Seeks to gain trust and confidence of others • Exercises discipline and fairness in the treatment of others • Gives back to the community
Strong Interpersonal Skills	• Believes in being visible • Is approachable and accessible • Puts people first
Willingness to take Risks	• Embraces tolerance and ambiguity • Is open to other points of view
Relationship Building and Teamwork	• Shows empathy and concern for others • Is always kind to others • Focuses on the customer • Supports the mission of the organization • Is a team player
Ability to Communicate	• Meets with followers between evaluation periods • Communicates performance objectives and work performance expectations clearly • Articulates vision clearly
Leadership Execution	• Is a mentor • Is a visionary leader • Is a catalyst for change • Inspires and motivates followers for superior performance • Has the ability to influence others • Strives to balance task and relationship oriented leader skills

Figure 2: Key Characteristics and Behavioral Attributes

The key characteristics and behavioral attributes build upon the dimensions of transformational leadership as an integral part of organizational success. In a changing environment, an organization depends on its leaders to motivate, inspire, and develop their followers for superior performance. Their positive moral character is a testament to their ability to show empathy, care, and fairness in the treatment of others. They are willing to take risks while embracing tolerance and ambiguity. They trust their followers by empowering them to be innovative and to seek new ways to improve organizational success. Through leadership execution, they are catalysts for change and have the ability to transform a culture dedicated to supporting an organization's vision.

Leadership involves people, and interpersonal skills or "people skills" is at the top of the list of what an Army leader must possess.[45] These leaders have the attributes of interpersonal skills such as effective communication, supervision, mentoring, and counseling as skills that leaders must perform. These core interpersonal skills are what the Army needs leaders to have in order for them to be effective at leading organizations.[46] The antecedents of transformational leadership do not happen arbitrarily.[47] Certain conditions, such as individual experiences that leaders have with early role models and learning from experiences of their predecessors, set the stage for personal development.[48]

Conclusion

Transformational leadership is a positive style of leadership that Army leaders can emulate to improve their organizational climate. Leaders who use this style can broaden their followers' interests, and as a result, increase their effectiveness and interpersonal skills. They also have the ability to articulate a vision that will convince followers to develop creative and innovative ideas to make major changes. The dimensions of transformational leadership include individualized consideration, inspirational motivation, intellectual stimulation, and idealized influence. These dimensions constitute transformational leadership and help guide leaders to motivate their followers to appeal to higher goals that go beyond organizational expectations. The characteristics of transformational leadership provide Army leaders with effective communication skills and efficient leadership and decision-making concepts.[49]

The interviews in this chapter provided lessons learned from these visionary leaders, with an emphasis on transformational qualities that are essential for leader effectiveness. These words of wisdom describe how Army leaders can propose and communicate a compelling vision in their own organizations.

Notes

1. Warren Bennis, *On Becoming a Leader* (New York: Basic Books, 2003), 3.
2. James MacGregor Burns, as cited in Bernard M. Bass, "Two Decades of Research and Development in Transformational Leadership," *European Journal of Work and Organizational Psychology* 8, no. 1 (1999): 9-32.
3. Bernard M. Bass, "Two Decades of Research and Development in Transformational Leadership," *European Journal of Work and Organizational Psychology* 8, no. 1 (1999): 9-32.
4. Ibid., 9.
5. Ibid.
6. Richard L. Daft, *Organization Theory and Design*, (Mason, OH: Thomson South-Western, 2007), 425.
7. John H. Humphreys and Walter O. Einstein, "Nothing New Under the Sun: Transformational Leadership from a Historical Perspective," *Management Decision London* 41 (2003), 85.
8. James MacGregor Burns, as cited in Alannah E. Rafferty and Mark A. Griffin, "Dimensions of Transformational Leadership: Conceptual and Empirical Extensions," *The Leadership Quarterly* 15, no. 3 (2004) 329-354; available on the Internet at htttp://www.sciencedirect.com.ezprozy.umuc.edu/ sciene?_ob=ArticleURL&_udiB6W5N (accessed 5 June 2008).
9. Ibid., 329; and Gary Yukl, "An Evaluation of Conceptual Weaknesses in Transformational and Charismatic Leadership," *The Leadership Quarterly* 10, no. 2 (1999), 285-305.
10. James MacGregor Burns, *Leadership* (New York: Harper, 1978), 19.
11. Ibid.
12. Humphreys and Einstein, 85.
13. Burns, *Leadership*, 19.
14. Bass, "Two Decades of Research and Development in Transformational Leadership," 11.
15. Bernard M Bass, "From Transactional to Transformational Leadership: Learning to Share the Vision," *Organizational Dynamics* 18, no. 3 (1990), 19-31.
16. Gary Yukl, as cited in Jon Yean-Sub Lim, "Transformational Leadership Organizational Culture and Organizational Effectiveness Sport," *United States Sports Academy* 4, no 2 (2001) available on the Internet at http://www.thesportjournal.org/article/transformational-leadership-organizational-culture-and-organizational-effectiveness-sport-or (accessed 15 May 2008), and Jane M. Howell and Bruce J. Avolio, "Transformational Leadership, Transactional Leadership, Locus of Control, and Support for Innovation: Key Predictors of Consolidated-Business-Unit Performance," *Journal of Applied Psychology* 78, no. 6 (1993), 891-902.
17. Howell and Avolio, "Transformational Leadership, 891-902; and Bruce J. Avolio, David A. Waldman and Francis J. Yammarino, "Leading in the 1990s: The Four I's of Transformational Leadership," *Journal of European Industrial Training* 15, no. 4 (1991), 9-15.
18. Howell and Avolio, "Transformational Leadership," 894.
19. Ibid., 899.
20. Geert Hofstede, Bram Neuijen, Denise Daval Ohayv and Geert Sanders, "Measuring Organizational Cultures: A Qualitative and Quantitative Study Across Twenty Cases," *Administrative Science Quarterly* 35, no. 2 (1990), 286-316.
21. Avolio et al., "Leading in the 1990s," 13.
22. Bass, "Transactional to Transformational Leadership," 19-31.
23. Robert J. House, as cited in John R. Schermerhorn, Jr., James G. Hunt and Richard N. Osborn, *Organizational Behavior* (New York: John Wiley & Sons, 2000), 299-300.
24. Ibid., 299.

25. Humphreys and Einstein, 86.
26. Bernard Bass as cited in Alannah E. Rafferty and Mark A. Griffin, "Dimensions of Transformational Leadership," 6.
27. Avolio et al., "Leading in the 1990s," 15.
28. Stephen P. Robbins and Timothy A. Judge, *Organizational Behavior* (Upper Saddle River, NJ: Pearson Prentice Hall, 2007), 439.
29. Avolio et al., "Leading in the 1990s," 13-15.
30. Bernard M. Bass, as cited in David E. Chesser, "Transformational Leadership: An Imperative for Army Reserve Readiness in the 21st Century," *USAWC Strategy Research Project* (Carlisle Barracks, PA: U.S. Army War College, 15 March 2006), 8; available on the Internet at http://stinet.dtic.mil/oai/oai?verb=getRecord&metadataPrefix=html&identifier=A DA449818 (accessed 5 June 2008).
31. Bernard M. Bass and Bruce J. Avolio. "Transformational Leadership and Organizational Culture," *Public Administration Quarterly* 17, no. 1 (1993), 112-121.
32. Ibid., 112.
33. Ibid.
34. Steve Wilberger, interview with Judy Thompson-Moore, May 15, 2008.
35. Mike Hopkins-Doerr, "Getting More out of MBWA," *Supervisory Management, Marketing Management* 34, no. 2 (Sept/Oct 2007), 17; available on the Internet at ABI/INFORM Global database (Document ID: 813206), (accessed 29 June 2008).37.
36. Jim Collins, *Good to Great: Why Some Companies Make the Leap and Others Do Not*, (New York: Harper Collins Publishers, Inc., 2001), 13.
37. Chesser, 8.
38. William G. T. Tuttle, interview with Judy Thompson-Moore, 19 May 2008.
39. Paul Kirkbride, "Developing Transformational Leaders: The Full Range Leadership Model in Action." *Industrial and Commercial Training 38,* no. 1 (2006), 23-32.
40. Carol Pearson, interview with Judy Thompson-Moore (written correspondence), 29 May 2008.
41. William B. Locander and David L. Luechauer, "Leader as Inquirer; Change Your Approach to Inquiry" *Leadership Journey* 16, no. 5, 46.
42. Bob Stone, interview with Judy Thompson-Moore (telephone), 13 May 2008.
43. Bob Stone, *Confessions of a Civil Servant* (New York: Rowman & Littlefield, 2003), 167-175.
44. Avolio et al., "Leading in the 1990s," 9-15.
45. Frances Hesselbein and Eric K. Shinseki (General, USA, Ret.), *Be-Know-Do: Leadership the Army Way* (San Francisco: Jossey-Bass, 2004), 48.
46. Ibid.
47. Avolio et al., "Leading in the 1990s," 9-15.
48. Ibid., 11.
49. Shelley Dionne, Francis Yammarion, Leanne Atwater and Walter Spangler. "Transformational Leadership and Team Performance," *Journal of Organizational Change Management 17*, no. 2 (2004), 177-193.

Fiona J. Burdick, Ph.D. and David S. Burdick

Redefining Army Leadership: Has the BE, KNOW, DO Model Been All that it Can Be?

During [military] funerals, we typically read the tributes offered at the [memorial] services conducted [earlier] in theater. Nothing speaks to the families like the words of buddies and commanders. These people knew him or lived with her; fought beside and loved them. When a tank commander writes about the loss of his driver, you realize that a tank crew is a single entity—a living, breathing organism. It, too, has lost an integral piece that made it whole.... I've learned that war most often claims the lives of young kids who go out on patrol day after day, night after night. They go because they are good soldiers led by good sergeants. *They go with a singular purpose: to not let their buddies down*[1] (emphasis added).

Major General William Troy

Introduction

In July 2003, Dr. Leonard Wong and his associates at the Army War College Strategic Studies Institute published a paper entitled, "Why They Fight: Combat Motivation in Iraq." Their findings documented what General Troy later observed first hand—the most frequent response given for combat motivation was fighting for "my buddies." The Wong study echoed findings from World War II sociologist Samuel Stouffer in 1949, and military historian S.L.A. Marshall in 1942, who concluded:

> I hold it to be of the simplest truths of war that the thing which enables an infantry soldier to keep going with his weapons is the near presence or the presumed presence of a comrade… He is sustained by his fellows primarily and by his weapons secondarily.[2]

How well individuals develop and maintain effective relationships with one another is a key measurement of how successful leadership is within organizations, especially in organizations like military units, police departments, or fire departments, that call upon their members to operate under the most stressful of conditions to include, at times, making the ultimate sacrifice. Developing and sustaining successful relationships within organizations are said to be soft skills, so do they have a place in military leadership? Over 20 years ago, James Kouzes and Barry Posner, in their seminal work, *The Leadership Challenge*,[3] introduced the notion of "leadership as a relationship" to the corporate world, and since then the idea has spread to, or more accurately been discovered to exist in diverse fields including politics, academics, and religious institutions. Within *in extremis* organizations, those organizations whose members operate under extreme or life-threatening conditions (e.g., police, firefighting, or military units), a common thread woven throughout anecdotal and documented stories of successful leadership is that the soft skills of relationship building and maintenance are of critical importance, perhaps more so than other traditional leadership traits of decisiveness, authority, or control. In this chapter, the authors offer that Army leadership is much more than occupying a position of influence, power, and responsibility over others—rather, it is the quality of the relationships developed and sustained among unit members that contributes most significantly to an Army unit's success.

Army Leadership Doctrine

Army leadership doctrine is leader-centric, describing leadership primarily in terms of the leader—what he or she must BE, KNOW, and DO. Emphasis is placed on the values and attributes that shape a leader's character; the knowledge, skills, and abilities that shape a leader's identity; and the actions and influence applied to followers that shape a leader's effectiveness. Field Manual 6-22, the Army's doctrinal publication on leadership, defines leadership as "the process of [leaders] influencing people [followers] by providing purpose, direction, and motivation while operating to accomplish the mission and improving the organization."[4] The Wong Study would seem to suggest that perhaps Army leadership doctrine should be expanded to include a greater emphasis on the relationship between leaders and followers as members of teams, collaborating to achieve mission accomplishment. Dr. Carl Brungardt, Chair of the Leadership Studies Department, and Dr. Larry Gould, Provost and Chief Academic Officer at Fort Hays State University in Hays, Kansas suggest:

> Contemporary definitions [of leadership] most often reject the idea that leadership revolves around the leader's ability [KNOW], behaviors [DO], styles or charisma [BE]. Today, scholars discuss the basic nature of leadership in terms of the "interaction" among the people involved in the process: both leaders and followers. Thus, leadership is not the work of a single person; rather it can be explained and defined as a "collaborative endeavor" among group members. Therefore, the essence of leadership is not the leader, but the relationship.[5]

Anticipating this shift in defining leadership, Dr. Joseph C. Rost, Professor Emeritus of Leadership Studies at the University of San Diego, asserted that the industrial paradigm of leadership in the 20th century must give way to a new paradigm for the post-industrial thinking of the 21st century.[6] He defined leadership under the old century's industrial paradigm as "...great men and women [KNOW] with certain preferred traits [BE] influencing followers to do what the leaders wish [DO] in order to achieve group/organizational goals that reflect excellence defined as some kind of higher-level effectiveness."[7] In short, Rost views the old paradigm as simply, "leadership is good management."[8]

While considering Rost's 20th century definition of leadership, it is worth noting that Dr. Peter G. Northouse, Professor of Communication at Western Michigan University, argues that leadership and management have many similarities in that they are both focused on influencing people to accomplish organizational goals; however, management is primarily concerned with providing order and consistency within organizations, while leadership is primarily concerned with the production of change and movement in organizations.[9] Northouse's thoughts on leadership and management square nicely with what we'll call the Army leadership paradox. That paradox is the fact that for an organization that trains its leaders to exercise their leadership under *in extremis* conditions, its approach is primarily managerial in nature—maintain order and consistency amidst the chaos and confusion of war. Many Army leaders, especially at the lower echelons of the Army hierarchy, are risk averse and happy to maintain the status quo during their tenures of command, as long as the next assignment and promotion come on time.

Visionary leaders in the Army are not as welcomed by the masses, as two recent cases demonstrate. The first case is former Army Chief of Staff General Eric Shinseki's decision to change the Army's headgear from the utility cap (i.e., baseball cap) to the Rangers' black beret to enhance Soldier morale and esprit de corps, causing the Rangers to adopt a tan beret as their new distinctive headgear. This decision was viewed by many as unnecessary and it caused much resentment of him as a leader at a time when his views on Iraq policy might have been given more consideration by the defense establishment and Bush Administration. Now retired, Shinseki is remembered more as the one who advocated employing more troops in the Iraq War than were finally used, as opposed to the one who changed the headgear.

The second case is former Defense Secretary Donald Rumsfeld's transformation of the military, wherein he recommended a new round of Base Realignment and Closure (BRAC) decisions to the President and Congress, as well as a massive restationing of military units from overseas to the U.S. homeland. Although Rumsfeld is currently viewed by many as the personification of the failures of the Bush Administration's Iraq policies, he, in fact, may be remembered as the visionary who successfully (we hope) transformed the military from its Cold War posture into an expeditionary force capable of worldwide deployment and engagement in support of the nation's foreign policy goals.

A New Paradigm of Leadership

Rost's 21st century post-industrial paradigm turns old definitions of leadership on their heads. He offers that, "Leadership is an influence relationship among leaders and collaborators (those he formerly called followers) who intend real changes that reflect the purposes mutually held by both leaders and collaborators."[10] In contrast to Northouse, Rost distinguishes leadership from management as follows: "Leadership is a multidirectional influence relationship, whereas management is a unidirectional authority relationship."[11]

Rost outlines four essential elements of leadership as a relationship. First, the relationship is based on influence. While the FM 6-22 definition also describes leadership as an influence process, Rost's new paradigm implies that this influence is multidirectional. Rost clarifies, "Influence can go any which way, not just from the top down. It is non-coercive because the relationship would turn into an authority, power, or dictatorial relationship."[12] Similarly, his second premise is that leaders and collaborators are the actors in this relationship. "If leadership is what the relationship is, then both collaborators and leaders are all doing leadership."[13] Army researchers have described "strategic" leadership as the vision of the future. The Wong study stated, "It is not uncommon to hear of the 'strategic Captain' or 'strategic Corporal.' This use of strategic broadens the definition to such a degree that ALL soldiers should be strategic."[14] With the latest in modern weaponry, battle practices, and coalition building, it would follow that a strategic soldier would be far preferable to one that is not. Virtually anywhere in today's Army, company-grade officers could regale their peers with stories of incidents where platoon sergeants and other non-commissioned officers exerted bottom-driven influence.

The third essential element outlined by Rost in the relationship called leadership is that both leaders and collaborators intend real changes.[15] The changes they promote are purposeful, substantive, and transforming. It is important to acknowledge that sometimes these changes do not happen, however, the intent is present. Finally, the fourth essential element of leadership as a relationship is that any changes that leaders and collaborators intend reflect their mutual purposes. While the FM 6-22 definition of leadership addresses the need for leaders to provide purpose and direction to others, the intent of this definition is that leadership is clearly top-initiated and driven mainly by mission dictates rather than altruistic mutual purposes.

Although Rost promotes leadership as a relationship as the paradigm for the 21st century, this is not the first time that leadership as a relationship has been examined by the military. A 1976 study conducted by Utecht and Heier considered whether business and management psychologist Fred Fiedler's contingency theory (i.e., effective leadership is just as dependent on the group situation as it is on the leader) could be used to predict the effectiveness of task-oriented versus relationship-oriented military leaders. Utecht and Heier hypothesized that successful military leaders previously held positions favorable to their leadership style—in other words, they were the right person, in the right place, at the right time throughout their careers.

Although their data did not support this "luck o' the Irish" hypothesis, they did discover that for both task-oriented and relationship-oriented leaders in military organizations, "good leader-member relations may be the predominant factor needed for successful job performance."[16]

Much of the research of the past years as it relates to military leadership as a relationship has focused on cohesion. Robert P. Vecchio and Donna M. Brazil explain that, "Cohesion refers to feelings of unit and togetherness that are based on interpersonal relations within a primary group."[17] They acknowledge that in workgroups that are in highly stressful and competitive circumstances (i.e. military units) cohesion is a critical element to achieving unit objectives. Military historian Victor Davis Hanson observed, "The lethality of the military is not just organizational or a dividend of high-technology. Moral and group cohesion explain more still."[18]   The Wong study echoed the importance of cohesion and affirmed its relevance in the current Army policy arena. In the current Iraq War, Wong et al. showed that while the U.S. Army certainly has the best equipment and training, a human dimension is often overlooked. The Wong study identified two roles served by social cohesion in a war-time setting. First, Soldiers individually felt responsible to achieve group success and protect their respective units from harm and second, cohesion provided the assurance and confidence that trustworthy soldiers were watching their backs. Posner identified that the all-volunteer Army was "compelled to transform itself into an institution that people would respect and trust. Bonds forged by trust replaced bonds forged by fear of punishment."[19] Contrasting their study of American forces with the Iraqi regular army, Wong et al. observed that,

> The Iraqi Regular Army appeared to be a poorly trained, poorly led, disparate group of conscripts who were more concerned with self-preservation and family ties than defending their country. It provided a good case study of what happens to a unit when social cohesion and leadership are absent.[20]

Similarly, in his study of leadership under *in extremis* conditions, West Point professor Colonel Thomas Kolditz concludes that most effective teams or organizations value trust, based on competence, as the primary factor contributing to their success in any endeavor.[21] In his book, *The Five Dysfunctions of a Team*, Peter Lencioni offers that the first and most foundational dysfunction is the absence of trust.[22] In the Wong study, a soldier describes this aspect of leadership succinctly: "If you are going to war, you want to be able to trust the person who is beside you. If you are his friend, you know he is not going to let you down."[23] How is this trust formed? Wong et al. surmise that soldiers develop this trust relationship by spending large amounts of time together, usually in austere conditions. Weeks of training prior to deployment also helps build relationships between soldiers. This collaboration speaks directly to the importance of both moral and social cohesion. In the Foreword to the Wong study, Douglas Lovelace summarized, "Today's soldiers trust each other; they trust their leaders; they trust the Army."[24]

Leadership in Complex Adaptive Systems

One study, conducted by Christopher Paparone, Ruth Anderson, and Reuben McDaniel in 2008, contributes to this new thinking on military leadership by comparing the old-school view of the military as both a professional organization and vast government bureaucracy, with a new view of the military as a complex adaptive system (CAS). This view is instructive and worthy of closer examination. Paparone et al. suggest that traditional strategic leadership as practiced by the military is not suitable for today's turbulent environment because it cannot respond to change in a timely manner. Whereas in the current hierarchical design of the military, formal position authority is most valued, under a CAS design knowledge sharing, individual and team competence, and ethical reasoning are most valued.

While the Army as a whole is a CAS, it is the dynamic, nonlinear interactions occurring locally among subordinate units that demonstrate the usefulness of this view. Put another way, the Army is like a large molecule composed of many different atoms interacting continuously in a nonlinear fashion. The most important interactions, however, are occurring within the atoms themselves as electrons, protons, and neurons interact within that smaller group, much like the interactions occurring day-to-day among members of an infantry squad, tank crew, or artillery section.

There are three separate properties that identify a CAS and distinguish it from traditional linear systems normally associated with organizational structure. The first is that "CASs are *recursive* systems, defined in terms of connections and patterns of relationships among members"[25] [emphasis in original]. Again, these relationships are those local ones among the collaborators of a squad, crew, section, or other small work unit. These individuals are often not aware of the happenings of the larger organization, nor are they expected to be, as the larger organization (in this case the Army as a whole) is too large for almost anyone to understand completely.

The next property is that of synergy, i.e., the whole is greater than the sum of its parts. "This means that order emerges without the need for hierarchical systems of command and control."[26] Instead, interaction causes the CAS organization to emerge on its own, much like the friction among subatomic particles forms the atom, and friction among atoms forms the molecule. The final property of CASs is that their course over time is unknowable. The nonlinear interactions and relationships are unpredictable, although they may lie within certain broad boundaries. "Even in the face of CAS uncertainty and unpredictability, armies may share many characteristics, companies and platoons often look alike, and one military installation is often very much like another."[27]

Looking at military leadership through a CAS prism requires a set of new leadership tasks as the old ones are not sufficient to explain system characteristics (Figure 1). *Role Defining* under the traditional notion of military leadership becomes *Relationship Building* under CAS, with "attention to the management of relationships (becoming) more important than the management of roles."[28] *Standardization* makes way for *Loose Coupling,* which "enhances adaptability because it allows more degrees of freedom at the local level."[29] *Simplifying* becomes *Complicating* as studies of organizations operating in volatile, uncertain, complex, and ambiguous environments (e.g., the Army) "found that the most successful ones were those in which the strategy was diverse, emergent, and complicated."[30] Managing complicated information networks and remaining agile amid constant change are preferred over the checklist mentality of traditional approaches.

Traditional Notions of the Military	Notions of the Military as a Complex Adaptive System
Role Defining	Relationship Building
Standardization	Loose Coupling
Simplifying	Complicating
Socializing	Diversifying
Decision-making	Sensemaking
Knowing	Learning
Commanding & Controlling	Improvising
Planning based on Estimates	Emergent Thinking

Figure 1: Key Leadership Tasks for Complex Adaptive Systems[31]

The traditional leadership task of *Socializing* becomes *Diversifying* in the CAS model:

> Because of the dependence on patterns of interactions, CASs must have diversity in both the members and, even more importantly, the interactions among members…. When the complexity of problems explode…administrators need all the different points of view they can muster."[32]

Traditional military *Decision-making* is less important than *Sensemaking* in a CAS organization where the trajectory of the system is unknowable. "Sense making is a social activity that requires interaction and development of a collective mind. A collective mind is not groupthink but a shared sense of meaning in the situation."[33] This leads to the next traditional task of *Knowing*, which is quite essential in a hierarchical organization where subordinates wait for knowing leaders to tell them what is going on and what they need to do. In a CAS environment, knowing is not as important as *Learning*, because one can hardly know everything in an organization that is constantly changing. The goal in a CAS organization "is to create a learning organization that values knowledge sharing, individual and team competence, and ethical reasoning."[34]

The traditional leadership task of *Commanding and Controlling* must give way to *Improvising* in a CAS organization. This is not to say that CAS organizations are disorderly, but instead suggest that CAS organizations rely on highly-trained and proficient professionals to develop relationships among one another that lead to mutual trust and confidence. These relationships allow them to react to and learn from events and unanticipated circumstances that occur in organizations that operate in volatile, uncertain, complex, and ambiguous environments:

> As in the jazz band, improvisation happens when individuals play off the strength of others. "Improvisation begets skill, which affords more choice, which in turn affects the complexity of improvised activity."[35]

Finally, the traditional leadership task of *Planning Based on Estimates* becomes *Emergent Thinking* in a CAS organization:

> Formal planning, with its reliance on forecasting and estimating events and clear understanding of cause-effect relationships, is [not as] useful...[as] developing skills at *bricolage*—the ability to create what is needed at the moment out of whatever materials are at hand.[36]

CAS leaders foster a climate or culture within their organizations that encourages members to "think about what they can do with what they have rather than what they might do if they only had something else."[37]

Conclusion

Viewing the military as a complex adaptive system provides a solid framework for adopting a new definition of military leadership. These notions link closely with those Dr. Joseph Rost sets forth in his premise of leadership as a relationship where the two primary criteria are influence and mutuality. The Wong study similarly described the emerging strategic leader as one who shares power with his/her subordinates, peers, and constituents. "They must have the willingness and ability to involve others and elicit their participation . . . [They] rely less on fiat, asking others to join in rather than telling them."[38] Conversely, Taiwanese researchers have argued, "The behavior of an authoritarian leader will hurt the two-way communications and interactions with subordinates."[39] However, Colonel Thomas Kolditz points out that in most effective teams or organizations, "relationships are placed before perquisites or status."[40]

Dr. Shanan Gibson asserts that "the U.S. military has a long and illustrious history of providing a framework for learning about leadership."[41] While this framework may have been sufficient for the Army of the Cold War, it will not suffice for the expeditionary Army of the 21st century. The Wong study reminds us that future strategic leaders must be able to drop outmoded perspectives, methods, or assumptions in a world of uncertainty. Paparone et al. affirm, "The fundamental importance of relationship building must be acknowledged."[42] Perhaps it is time for the Army to retire the decades-old, leader-centric model of BE, KNOW, DO, and replace it with one that acknowledges openly that leadership is a relationship—a BE, LEARN, COLLABORATE model, if you will, where all collaborators are leaders with strong character and values (BE), that are continually learning and growing in a volatile, uncertain, complex, and ambiguous environment (LEARN), to accomplish together the goals and tasks that are before them (COLLABORATE).

Notes

1. William Troy, "Funeral Duty," *Washington Post*, 26 May 2008, A17; available on the Internet at http://www.washingtonpost.com/wp-dyn/content/article/2008/05/25/AR2008052502283.html (accessed 11 June 2008).
2. S. L. A. Marshall, as quoted in Leonard Wong, Thomas A. Kolditz, Raymond A. Millen, and Terrence M. Potter, *Why they fight: Combat Motivation in the Iraq War* (Carlisle, PA: U.S. Army War College Strategic Studies Institute, 2003), 2; available on the Internet at http://www.strategicstudiesinstitute.army.mil/pdffiles/PUB179.pdf (accessed 11 June 2008).
3. James M. Kouzes and Barry Z. Posner, *The Leadership Challenge* (San Francisco: Jossey-Bass, 1987).
4. *Army Leadership: Competent, Confident, and Agile* [Field Manual 6-22] (Washington, D.C.: Department of the Army, 12 October 2006), 1-2; available on the Internet at https://akocomm.us.army.mil/usapa/doctrine/ DR_pubs/dr_aa/pdf/fm6_22.pdf (accessed 11 June 2008).
5. Curt Brungardt and Larry Gould, "Making the Case for Leadership Studies" (electronic article from Fort Hays State University (Hays, Kansas), Department of Leadership Studies, 2001); available on the Internet at http://www.fhsu.edu/leadership/making_the_case.shtml (accessed 23 May 2008).
6. Joseph C. Rost, "Leadership: A Discussion about Ethics," *Business Ethics Quarterly* 5, no. 1 (1995): 130-142.
7. Joseph C. Rost, *Leadership for the Twenty-First Century* (New York: Praeger,1991), 180.
8. Ibid., 94.
9. Peter G. Northouse, *Leadership Theory and Practice* (Thousand Oaks, CA: Sage, 2007), 1-14.
10. Rost, Leadership for the Twenty-First Century, 102.
11. Rost, "Leadership: A Discussion about Ethics," 135.
12. Ibid., 133.
13. Ibid.
14. Leonard Wong, Thomas A. Kolditz, Raymond A. Millen, and Terrence M. Potter, *Why They Fight: Combat Motivation in the Iraq War* (Carlisle, PA: U.S. Army War College Strategic Studies Institute, 2003), 1; available on the Internet at http://www.strategicstudiesinstitute.army.mil/pdffiles/PUB179.pdf (accessed 11 June 2008).
15. Rost, "Leadership: A Discussion About Ethics," 133.
16. R. E. Utecht and W. D. Heier, "The Contingency Model and Successful Military Leadership," *Academy of Management Journal* (December 1976): 615.
17. Robert P. Vecchio and Donna M. Brazil, "Leadership and Sex-Similarity: A Comparison in a Military Setting," *Personnel Psychology* 60, no. 2 (2007): 305.
18. Victor Davis Hanson, "Anatomy of the Three-Week War," *National Review Online*, April 17, 2003; available on the Internet at http://www.nationalreview.com/hanson/hanson041703.asp (accessed 12 June 2008).

19. Wong et al., 9.
20. Richard A. Posner, "An Army of the Willing," *New Republic*, May 19, 2003, 27.
21. Thomas A. Kolditz, "In Extremis Leadership: Learning to Lead as if Lives Depend on It" (keynote address at Army Management Staff College's 3rd Annual Leadership Symposium, Fort Belvoir, VA, January 29-31, 2008).
22. Peter Lencioni, *The Five Dysfunctions of a Team* (San Francisco: Jossey-Bass, 2003).
23. Wong et al., 11.
24. Ibid., iii.
25. Christopher R. Paparone, Ruth A. Anderson, and Reuben R. McDaniel, Jr., "Where Military Professionalism Meets Complexity Science" *Armed Forces and Society* 34, no. 3 (2008): 439.
26. Ibid.
27. Ibid., 440.
28. Ibid., 442.
29. Ibid.
30. Ibid., 443.
31. Ibid., 441.
32. Ibid.
33. Ibid., 444.
34. Ibid.
35. Ibid., 445.
36. Ibid.
37. Ibid.
38. Wong et al., 8.
39. Shing-Ko Liang, Hsiao-Chi Ling, and Sung-Yi Hsieh, "The Mediating Effects of Leader-member Exchange Quality to Influence the Relationships Between Paternalistic Leadership and Organizational Citizenship Behaviors," *Journal of American Academy of Business*, 10, no. 2 (March 2007): 127-137.
40. Kolditz, "In Extremis Leadership."
41. Shanan G. Gibson, "Perceptions of U.S. Military Leadership: Are all Leaders Created Equally?" *Equal Opportunities International,* 24, no. 2: 10.
42. Paparone et al., 442.

Roy Eichhorn

Civilians as Micro-Strategists

Introduction

When we think of the Army and strategy, we tend to evoke pictures of generals hunched over maps of the world, making plans country by country. But is that all the strategy making that goes on in the Army?

According to Army Doctrine,

> The Army has roughly 600 authorized Military and Civilian positions classified as senior strategic leaders. Strategic leaders are responsible for large organizations and influence several thousands to hundreds of thousands of people. They establish force structure, allocate resources, communicate strategic vision, and prepare their commands and the Army as a whole for their future roles.

To summarize the doctrinal statement, strategic leaders build the capabilities of their organizations to conform to their vision of a future environmental context and need.

Note that the Field Manual says "senior" strategic leaders. By implication, there must be junior strategic leaders as well. These are people included under the term "micro-strategists."[1] They are doing the same kinds of things the senior strategic leaders are doing in terms of building capability, but in smaller scopes, with narrower bands of influence, and with fewer variables and resources. They may or may not be in formal leadership positions, but they are making the strategies for their world. Where are they? What do they do? Where does the Army get the people with those skills? While much has been written about building strategists for the Military side of the Army, this chapter will address these questions as they relate to the Army Civilian Corps and the Army's Generating Force.

Concepts of Strategy

A traditional definition of strategy is that it is the combination of ends-ways-means; ends are objectives, means are resources, and ways are methods, processes, or applications. In many ways, the Ends-Ways-Means model for strategy mirrors Wasilly Leontief's Input-Process-Output systems model, which has been applied in Military strategic modeling[2] and has also been adapted as a model for use in the generating force in the Operations Systems Management Model.[3] The Ends-Ways-Means model became a standard during the Cold War. It was easy to use as a descriptive model when the national objectives were fairly stable (as were the competitors) and has the virtue of being relatively easy to get students to understand, but:

> The foundation of our shortfall is our linear definition of strategy: The calculated relationship between ends, ways, and means. . . this often resorts to a mechanical process where material resources dominate the intellectual effort, instead of the more subtle human dimension of strategy.[4]

The ends-ways-means model doesn't necessarily get at the thinking behind the model and can lead to the trap that Marcella and Fought referred to in education when they talked about schools teaching *about* strategy rather than teaching how to develop strategy.[5]

Business models of strategy may talk about strategy as the overarching concept of how an organization will achieve objectives, but tend to shift quickly to discussions about exploiting environmental opportunities to achieve competitive advantage.[6] In this way, business strategies can start to look much like mechanistic Military strategies and also share the danger of thinking about strategy rather than thinking strategically.

Gabriel Marcella and Steve Fought proposed an alternate definition to strategy as, "Strategy is a (sometimes exponential) multiplier that adds value to the relationship between (and among) ends and means in and of itself."[7] This model of strategy is probably also appropriate for the Army Civilian Corps, since Civilians primarily operate in the generating force of the Army that deals with shifting ends and apportioning shortages among the means. The art form of maneuvering within these elements is about recognizing the right combinations of factors at the right moment to optimize the end result while at the same time building capability for the future.

The strategies that Army Civilian leaders most typically use fall into the realm of "micro-strategies." This usage of the term shares some of the characteristics from Edward DeBono's definition of micro-strategies as," forming complex strategies that evolve in order to cope with particular situations."[8] Strategies within the Army generating force are probably more like self-contained strategies for working within particular functional areas. To someone making strategy at the enterprise level, the work of follower layers probably looks like operational or tactical work.[9] But one has to understand what the leaders below are actually doing before that call can be made accurately. For example, in the training environment it is tactical if the training managers or school heads manipulate given resources on a repetitive basis to "train the load." It is, in effect, doing the same thing over and over, and one cannot reasonably expect different results.

That same school of leadership, however, can be operating strategically if it looks to the future objectives of what the Army needs for its graduates and builds (and continually adapts) a curriculum that deliberately develops critical thinking skills that set the graduate up to do relevant self-directed lifelong learning. In this case, the school is teaching for thinking skills that will be a critical capability in the future environment and not just for content that will sooner or later be obsolete. In the former case, the student still gets the content but also knows how he or she can replace that content as needed.

The ideas in this chapter crystallized after two events. The first event took place in 2006 while Army Management Staff College (AMSC) faculty worked on the curriculum design and development for the Army's new Civilian Education System (CES).[10] The curriculum teams were building outlines for the different segments of the CES Advanced Course, which is designed for managers and managers of managers at the GS-13-15 level.

The critical task list for the course included the following tasks for Civilian managers:[11]

1. Advise the Commander on the impact of internal and external political factors.
2. Advise the Commander on the impact of the national security environment and its demands on the Army as a partner in joint or multi-national scenarios.
3. Advise the Commander of the impact on the organization of operations and the inter-relationships of the major Department of Defense and Department of Army decision support systems.
4. Apply long-term perspective in analyzing policy issues, setting priorities, and developing objectives.
5. Develop strategic and other long-term plans.

The tasks above suggested to the AMSC faculty that Advanced Course students needed education in developing strategies, but strategy was not included in the final pilot design on the assumption that Army Civilians do not do strategy. This suggests either an incomplete understanding of what Civilian leaders do or a conceptual difficulty seeing how Civilians operating below the national level could be acting strategically. At first it seemed as if the problem was the first part of this issue—people didn't understand what Army Civilian leaders really do. It would take another event to clarify the deeper issue; we were not dealing with the idea of what strategy is, in and of itself, we were only considering the topic in light of published national level documents like the National Security Strategy of the United States.

The second event that crystallized the ideas here came immediately after the XIX Annual Strategy Conference at the U.S. Army War College on April 11, 2008. A separate workshop on teaching strategy was conducted by Gabriel Marcella, Steve Fought,[12] Robert Gray,[13] Ross Harrison,[14] Michael Pillsbury, and Tomaz Gueres DaCosta. In that workshop, the panel proposed both some new ideas about strategy in the 21st Century and how we ought to view it with an eye toward new ways of developing strategists. Although the panelists were primarily addressing developing Military strategists and senior strategic leaders, the principles they collectively presented are equally applicable to Civilians.

Strategy in the Current Environment
The 21st Century started with a series of events that caused the United

States and the Army to face different environments from what they had been used to for the 4 1/2 decades of the Cold War. Since others have written about this in depth (and will presumably continue to write about it), the following is a summary of some of the key points that affect this discussion.

The first change the Army and the Nation had to deal with in the 21st Century was a major change of focus from single state-based competitors to a series of smaller, more diffused, interconnected, and predominantly ideologically-based competitors. The change in competition was reflected in changes in operational modes, doctrines, and force structure. The Army deployed greater portions of its forces, used the Guard and Reserve forces much more heavily, and deployed large numbers of Army Civilians and contractors. Although Military units ramp up and down as they prepare to deploy, then deploy, and return, the mostly Civilian generating forces (which were built for the Cold War) have been at or near peak operations since 2001.

The Army deployments into Iraq and Afghanistan were initial tactical successes, but soon had to transition to a post-conflict environment that cut across the traditional spectrum from peace to major conflict. The new operational reality was captured in the Army's central doctrinal document, Field Manual 3-0, *Army Operations*, which was released Spring 2008.[15] Part of where the current version of the manual differs from its predecessors is the increased need for stability and support types of operations. These include developmental and aid operations; they tend to be multi-agency and can also involve non-governmental agencies. The shift to a broad spectrum approach to operations means that strategies will have to be generated at multiple levels for the ends and means that different players bring and that Army Officers, Army Civilians, and members of other services and agencies will have to coordinate their individual strategies to form a holistic approach. Without coordination of strategies, it is possible that one partner in an interagency endeavor can pursue ends in a way that undercuts the efforts of another.

As the nature of Army operations changed, so did resources of all kinds—from money to materiel, to availability of personnel. At the time of this writing, the Army is confronted with a large series of Base Realignment and Closure activities. All these factors have greatly changed "business as usual" for the Civilian Corps and require new solutions. The generating force needs to reinvent itself from a Cold War model to something that fits better with the changes facing the operational force, it has to keep operating in a war environment while building new capability for the future environment, and it has to do all this with increasing reliance on leaders within the generating force.

The Need for Strategic Thinking

While the Army is engaged in war, there is a natural tendency within the service to look at operational and tactical problems rather than strategic ones. As AMSC faculty members go out to other organizations and engage in collaborative research, they sometimes hear that expressed as, "We aren't interested in the strategic view." They also hear, "You are talking about something that's too far away;" or "For us, 6 months is a long time, and 1 year is the outside."

Faced with all the changes noted above, the Army has a great need for someone to look forward and formulate strategies to get us to the objectives we want to achieve. The skills that are needed can be summed up in the acronym FEE:

- Formulate a strategy
- Execute a strategy
- Evaluate and adapt a strategy

In the generating force, the strategies will primarily be micro-strategies, and the people making and executing them will probably be members of the Army Civilian Corps.

Developing Critical and Strategic Thinkers

If one accepts the proposition that leaders in the Civilian Corps should envision future states and conditions that do not yet exist, analyze these conditions, prioritize, and make decisions now that will set a course to the future, then it follows that leaders in the Civilian Corps need to be able to think and act analytically, critically, and strategically. The follow-on question is, "How does the Army get these leaders?" The answer comes down to one of two alternatives, buy the skills or make the skills.

Buying higher-order thinking skills is one solution that is currently popular. The Army Review of Education, Training and Leader Development of 2005 indicated that the Army was filling at least 50 percent of the leader positions in the Civilian Corps with newly retired Military officers.[16] The senior service graduates among these are generally regarded as having the finest education in strategy. One question that should be asked though is whether the knowledge of strategy is about strategy and how to execute within an already established one or do the people coming directly from active duty have real expertise and experience in the creation of strategy? Marcella and Fought have raised this as a significant question.[17] If the newly retired officers are experienced in strategy creation, do they understand the generating force sufficiently to be able to work effectively with the environmental constraints and opportunities that go with it, and can they execute all the aspects of FEE within the constraints of the generating force?

A follow-on method of buying skills is contracting out. Sometimes this is used to augment the practice of buying the skills from retired Military, but it only goes so far. Contractors excel in strategy execution, but somebody, at some point, needs to be able to see the whole environment and make the analyses and the decisions. To do this they have to accurately understand the contextual environment. Where contractors are asked to develop strategies, they question people in the requiring organization closely and assemble the strategy from what they got from the government personnel. Essentially, they feed our own knowledge back to us.

If the Army is to cope with the strategic challenges within the sustaining base, we need leaders who can (first of all) understand the context of the generating force and then think critically about the questions and problems that present themselves. There are several models of critical thinking, but what we at the Army Management Staff College have found is that the model by Richard Paul and Linda Elder[18] works very well for our environment.[19] The Paul and Elder model puts an emphasis on both the structured approach to the thinking and the universal intellectual standards for the thinking. These elements are important for strategic thinking, and the universal intellectual standards of clarity, accuracy, precision, depth, breadth, logic, and support[20] are particularly useful as a first cut tool for evaluating any strategy. For example, if a strategy is not clear, is it useful? Is it precise enough for the task? What use is it if it is not logical? Does it look deeply enough to consider the environment that the strategy will have to work within, etc.

Another model for critical thinking is that proposed by Lynch and Wolcott.[21] Their emphasis is on the underlying levels of cognitive development that must be met before it is practical to expect someone to reason critically, and Lion Gardiner[22] has made a similar proposal. The following restatement of both Lynch and Wolcott's and Gardiner's argument illustrates the point. The cognitive development level of most undergraduate college students is a duality—every question has one right answer and all answers that do not match the right answer are wrong.[23] For a person at that level of cognitive development, the idea of being able to think through a strategy and look at it from both your perspective and the perspective of someone who may oppose you is unlikely.

Taken together, Paul and Elder, Lynch and Wolcott, and Gardiner provide a composite of the base that is needed in terms of cognitive development and critical thinking before strategic thinking is likely to operate. Marcella and Fought proposed a similar structure for teaching strategy; they argue that at levels far below grand strategy, Army Captains think they are operating strategically and may not be far off.[24] What makes the strategies of Captains different from those of Generals is that they have:

1. Shorter time horizons
2. Fewer variables to factor in at any one time
3. Less ambiguity or different types of ambiguity that can be coped with short-term

The three factors above increase in complexity as one moves up in position. If that holds (as it should for leaders in the Civilian Corps) then the way to develop strategists is to start sequentially and progressively from the lower levels. Development of strategists can be asked as two contrasting questions.

- Does it make more sense to expect someone in a leadership position to suddenly start thinking strategically when they become part of the identified group of 600 Army senior strategic leaders,[25] or...
- Should we make strategists by starting development in a problem-based educational format?

The approach to development that both the Officer Corps and the Civilian Corps are taking is sequential and progressive. That argues for a very specific approach to developing strategic thinking skills in the Civilian Corps, but is still within the specific contexts of the generating force and not the Military.[26]

The progressive and sequential developmental approach for Civilians is learner-centered and should have two main elements. First, it must have a methodology that specifically teaches for and not just about critical and strategic thinking. The model is similar to what Swartz and Parks recommended[27] with the idea of an infusion model, where one teaches for the thinking using the context and content. This approach is in contrast to teaching straight content and can be achieved through well-crafted active learning methodologies like problem-based learning, inquiry-guided learning or inquiry-based learning.

What all these methods have in common is having students build their own learning, but in a carefully scaffolded and supported environment. Marcella, Fought, and Harrison have all proposed this for the senior service colleges and AMSC is currently doing it in its CES Basic, Intermediate, and Advanced Courses. The problem-or inquiry-based approach is not to suggest having students go into pure discovery learning with no scaffolding and no standard, because they need to learn to develop strategy and get feedback on their activities in progressive stages in order to actually learn.

Second, educators must recognize the cognitive developmental level of the student and the types of problems and contexts to which they can relate. Fought proposes that we can start teaching strategic thinking with Captains by giving them problems with well-defined ends and means and known limits. As we progress to higher levels, we can leave the ends undefined.[28]

The same things can be done for Army Civilians. Starting at the CES Basic Course level, for example, using inquiry-based methodology, AMSC can build for thinking within this limited variable set and with only limited ambiguity. Part of what students will learn as they become more self-aware is tolerance for ambiguity and the ability to flex approaches rather than staying wedded to only one course of action. A model for developing both strategic and critical thinking for Army Civilians is shown in Figure 1. (next page)

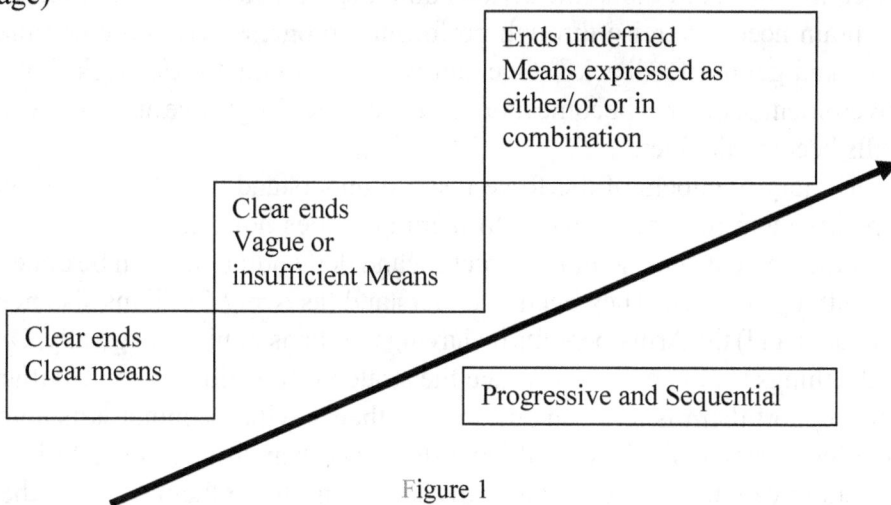

Figure 1

Conclusion—Moving from Theory to Practice

The first thing that has to happen in developing micro-strategists who can think strategically and critically is consciousness-raising and changing the culture to accept the method. Army Civilians need to understand what strategy is and be able to distinguish between simply executing orders and actually taking the initiative and responsibility for what they do and look toward building the capability in their organizations to meet the future. The National Security Personnel System can support the development of Civilians as strategic leaders because it rewards for performance. Objectives can be written to distinguish between competent executors and Civilian leaders who execute the full FEE cycle.

Two-part objectives that reward strategic thinking can conceivably be carried down to individual Civilians who have no followers but who manage programs that cut across areas and have larger affects. For example, an objective for a safety officer can be written such that full performance comes from operating successfully and meeting all the requirements of the position. If the safety officer wants to move beyond a 3 rating, there has to be a clear demonstration that he or she built additional capability that the organization will need in a reasonable future context.

Another issue regards the use of contractors. How does one maintain a strategic focus and continue with lifelong learning if the smart work is being done by someone else? Contractors are very useful when they can be directed to do specific tasks with identifiable outputs. Contractors are less useful when government personnel become dependent on them, and the contractors start doing the serious thinking. Just as in physical exercise, the brain needs exercise through performing progressively more complex tasks and getting feedback.[29] One can watch a contractor do work, but as government personnel become more detached, their cognitive and contextual skills become flabbier.

Military members of the force need to understand that the system that supports them may be invisible to them and does not run like a mindless machine; there is only so much directing and demanding that can be done to make things happen. They need to understand (as Army Civilians also need to understand) the Army benefits by having Civilians think strategically. One of the things they can do to advance the strategic capability of the Civilians who support them is to teach and mentor their Civilian counterparts about thinking strategically. This will have the added benefit of forcing Military leaders to examine what they actually know and force them to make their knowledge more explicit.

Ultimately, we have to build a Civilian force that is expert in the way the world is, and will be, not in the way it was. We must implement sound developmental strategies to develop our strategists for the future.

Notes

1. Edward DeBono, "Micro-strategies: Forming Complex Strategies which Evolve in Order to Cope with Particular Situations;" available on the Internet at http://www.thinkingmanagers.com/management/micro-strategies.php (accessed 2 July 2008).
2. Anthony W. Snodgrass, "Leontief Metamodeling for Military Strategic Affects." Defense Technical Information Center ADA378344; Available on the Internet at http://handle.dtic.mil/100.2/ ADA378344 (accessed 26 June 2008).
3. Roy Eichhorn, "Tactical Proficiency for the Civilian Leader;" article for the Sustaining Base Leadership and Management Program, (Fort Belvoir, VA: Army Management Staff College, 1996).
4. Ibid., 3.
5. Ibid., 2.
6. Robert N. Lussier and Christopher F. Achua, *Leadership, Theory, Application, Skill Development, 2nd Edition*. (Eagan, MN: South-Western/Thomson, 2004), 380.
7. Ibid., 4.
8. DeBono, "Micro-strategies: Forming Complex Strategies which Evolve in Order to Cope with Particular Situations."
9. Gabriel Marcella and Steven O. Fought, "The Strategy of Teaching Strategy in the Twenty First Century," (23 February 2008); paper presented at the XIX Annual Strategy Conference at the U.S. Army War College on 11 April 2008. See pg. 7 for the Military equivalent of this statement.
10. The CES has eight courses. The Foundation Course which is for new entries into the Army Civilian Corps, the Basic Course, which is predominantly for people who exercise direct leadership, the Intermediate Course, which is for people who are transitioning from direct to indirect leadership, the Advanced Course, which is for managers of other managers and supervisors, the Continuing Education for Senior Leaders course which is a plateau course for senior leaders to keep current, and Action Officers Development Course, Supervisors Development Course and Managers Development Course.
11. This was from the initial U.S. Army Training and Doctrine Command task list for the Advanced Course. The task list was revised in 2007.
12. Marcella and Fought, "The Strategy of Teaching Strategy in the Twenty First Century."
13. Robert C. Gray, "The Challenge of Teaching Strategy;" Paper presented at the XIX Annual Strategy Conference at the U.S. Army War College on 11 April 2008.
14. Ross Harrison, "Are strategists Born or Made?" Paper presented at the XIX Annual Strategy Conference at the U.S. Army War College on 11 April 2008.
15. *Army Operations* [Field Manual 3-0] (Washington, D.C.: Department of the Army, 2008).
16. U.S. Army, Review of Training Education and Army Leadership 2007 [Report], (Washington, D.C: Department of Army, 2007). "Managing the Civilian Workforce as an Army Enterprise Asset." "Since the abolishment of statutory limitations on

dual compensation for retired Military in 1999 the number of retired Military hired for senior leadership positions in the civilian workforce has dramatically increased. Currently 50 percent or more of positions at the GS-13 -15 and SES are being filled with retired Military, in most cases retired Colonels."

17. Marcella and Fought, "The Strategy of Teaching Strategy in the Twenty First Century," 2.

18. Richard Paul and Linda Elder, *The Miniature Guide to Critical Thinking,* 4th Ed. (Dillon Beach, CA: The Foundation for Critical Thinking, 2001), 2-8.

19. Roy Eichhorn, "Developing Thinking Skills: Critical Thinking at the Army Management Staff College," (Fort Belvoir, VA: Army Management Staff College, 2002); Available on the Internet at http://www.amsc.belvoir.army.mil/roy.html)

20. Ibid., 7-8.

21. Cindy L. Lynch and Susan K. Wolcott, "Helping Your Students Develop Critical Thinking Skills;" Available on the Internet at http://www.idea.ksu.edu/papers/Idea_ Paper_37.pdf (accessed 2 July 2008).

22. Lion F. Gardiner, "Redesigning Higher Education: Producing Dramatic Gains in Student Learning," *ASHE-ERIC Higher Education Report 23*, no 7 (Washington D.C.: The George Washington University, Graduate School of Education and Human Development). Lion Gardiner, personal communication. Gardiner was a professor at Rutgers University and a consultant on Educational Leadership for the Army Management Staff College in 2000-2001. His monograph in ASHE-ERIC is a good discussion on stages of cognitive development

23. Lynch and Wolcott, "Helping Your Students Develop Critical Thinking Skills." This is what they refer to as stage zero in cognitive development. Gardiner refers to this same stage as the dualistic learner.

24. Marcella and Fought, "The Strategy of Teaching Strategy in the Twenty First Century," 7.

25. *Army Leadership: Competent, Confident, and Agile* [Field Manual 6-22] (Washington, DC: Department of the Army, 12 October 2006), 3-42.

26. Harrison, "Are Strategists Born or Made?" 2.

27. Robert J. Swartz and Sandra Parks, Infusing the *Teaching of Critical and Creative Thinking into Elementary Instruction*, (Pacific Grove, CA: Critical Thinking Press and Software, 1994), 3-10.

28. Fought proposed this in session at the U.S. Army War College 11 April 2008.

29. Linda Elder and Richard Paul, *The Thinker's Guide to the Art of Strategic Thinking – 25 Weeks to Better Thinking and Better Living- First Steps to Becoming a Critical Thinker*. (Dillon Beach, CA: The Foundation for Critical Thinking, 2004), 9.

Alton Dunham and Karen Spurgeon, Ed.D.

The Motivation Factor: The Invisible Barriers to Organizational Effectiveness

Introduction

The field of motivation theory has been traditionally dominated by a focus on influencing decisions and purposeful rationalization. Both approaches ignore the complexity and ambiguity of real-world organizations. This chapter is a common sense look at how the real meaning of motivation becomes obvious when people look below the surface at underlying de-motivators, and then recognize the significance these elements play in organizational failure. It will provoke thinking about achieving organizational success, either in spite of (or because of) the explicit and implicit barriers faced by organizations in their quest to excel. It is this ability to negotiate through the maze of organizational and cultural norms that is key. It sounds easy, but in reality, it may not be so. Whether an asset or a stumbling block, recognizing barriers provides people in organizations an opportunity to engage in further analysis.

Literature on motivational theory suggests that successful organizations are fueled by people who are empowered to perform with trust and confidence—those who possess a "can-do" attitude that embraces personal responsibility and new ideas. These organizations are usually characterized as agile and innovative. How does motivation contribute to these qualities?

Leadership and Motivation

Leadership is the art of influencing an organization positively to change from its present state toward a common goal or objective. In order for this to happen, a leader must effectively articulate this vision to all members within the organization. Motivation theory is the study of "the how"— how followers positively support the transformation of an organization's vision into the desired end state. Leaders study human behavior in order to influence factors that motivate followers to increase productivity. Classic theorists such as Maslow, MacGregor, and Argyris have presented an excellent grounding in basic motivation theory and fundamentally altered the perception of followers' roles within organizations.

Research in leadership invariably discusses the similarities and differences between transactional and transformational leadership. A transformational leader is a modern day superhero with the ability to persuade followers to embrace a common vision. Additionally, a transformational leader is a skilled communicator, is able to challenge the status quo, is a master motivator, is authentic, and most importantly, always delivers spectacular results. Transformational leadership, while highly effective, can only succeed under a certain set of conditions (normally precipitated by an external event). A crisis drives the need for the transformation, and the leader must have the authority to implement unilateral change. Once the transformation is complete (or has failed), and the normalization takes place, the leader usually leaves the organization. A prime example in the fleeting power of transformational leadership is demonstrated during the British general election of 1945. It was then that the popular Winston Churchill was unexpectedly defeated. The superhero of World War II was rebuffed and denied re-election by the British citizenry. The same characteristics that distinctively suited Churchill to wartime leadership were not qualities that combined to make him attractive to Britons in peacetime.[1]

Most leaders are transactional leaders as opposed to transformational leaders. While transactional leaders increase efficiencies and improve morale, they generally lack the inherent authority to transform the organization. Transactional leaders are usually not in charge of an entire organization. Consequently, leaders and followers generate a mutually benefiting pact of relational reciprocity that is based on the leader exchanging a positive remuneration in return for increased follower performance.

Self-Interest

The core principle critical to follower motivation is the concept of self-interest. While self-interest and organization objectives are normally compatible and mutually advantageous, it is uncertain whether the follower would engage in the task that provides the greatest potential for personal satisfaction if the organization finds no value in the act. In the book, *Warrior Politics: Why Leadership Demands a Pagan Ethos*, Robert Kaplan discusses an interesting conclusion of the Athenian historian Thucydides. He writes:

> Thucydides' Military history leads him to the following conclusion: Whatever we may think or profess, human behavior is guided by fear (*phobos*), self-interest (*kerdos*), and honor (*doxa*). These aspects of human nature cause war and instability, accounting for *antropinon*, the 'human condition.' The human condition, in turn, leads to political crises: when *physis* (pure instinct) triumphs over *noimoi* (laws), politics fails and is replaced by anarchy. The solution to anarchy is not to deny fear, self-interest, and honor but to manage them for the sake of outcome.[2]

Stoic philosopher Epictetus believed that self-interest is a central element of a person's character. He writes:

> Be not deceived: nothing is so dear to any creature as its own profit. Whatsoever may seem to hinder this, be it father or child or friend or lover, this he will hate and abuse and curse. For Nature hath never so made anything as to love aught but its own profit: this is father and brother and kin and country and God. When, then, the Gods appear to hinder us in this, we revile even them, and overthrow their images and burn their temples; as Alexander, when his friend died, commanded to burn the temples of Esculapius.[3]

A review of current leadership literature suggests that several motivation and leadership theories are built around this concept of self-interest. Expectancy theory states that a follower's motivation is based on the belief of the probability that effort will lead to performance (expectancy), multiplied by the probability that performance will lead to reward (instrumentality), and multiplied by the perceived value of the reward (valence).[4] In other words, self-interest is a principal factor in a follower's willingness to contribute to an organization.

Transactional leadership theory is another example of how a leader can motivate an follower by influencing the follower's self-interest. Basically, this theory suggests that an follower will perform task(s) in exchange for compensation and states that transactional leadership is based on an economic and social exchange process in which the leader provides rewards in return for the follower's effort and performance.[5] Bass, Avolio, Jung, and Berson argue that two leadership styles frequently employed by transactional leaders are contingent reward leadership and management-by-exception (active and passive) leadership.[6]

The motivation concept of self-interest is significant to contemporary organizational leadership. Followers may believe in the "vision" of an organization and be committed to work towards achieving the goals set out by the organization's leadership, but followers still must feel their contributions are appreciated and believe that they will receive positive benefits for their efforts. An effective leader understands that followers may work harder for an organization that rewards their contributions while best serving the interest of the follower. The symbiotic relationship must be mutually beneficial—what is good for the follower is good for the organization.

Motivation theories may be used by leaders improve follower productivity throughout the organization. Three classic theories currently used by organization are:

- Vroom's Expectancy Theory presupposes that followers will evaluate outcomes associated with potential performance and then will work at the level that they perceive will create the greatest personal reward. It is important that the followers believe that they can achieve the desired outcome and that the reward matches the effort expended.
- Herzberg's Motivation-Hygiene Theory argues that follower job satisfaction and dissatisfaction are two independent factors. Certain motivation factors such as increased responsibility or enhanced opportunity for achievement status may result in job satisfaction while a different, independent set of factors may cause follower dissatisfaction (organization bureaucracy, inadequate salaries, or poor working conditions).
- McClelland's Need for Achievement (*n-Ach*) Theory claims that followers have a strong desire to succeed within an organization. However, followers may have different innate motivations,

i.e., achievement, affiliation, or power. For example, high achievers want challenging work with positive and constructive feedback, and high affiliation individuals require a cooperative environment, while power seekers have an innate desire to manage or control other people or resources

In the book, *Certain Trumpets: The Nature of Leadership,* the author writes,

Most literature on leadership is Unitarian. But life is Trinitarian . . . leaders, followers, and goals make up the three equally necessary supports for leadership." The goals must be shared, no matter how many other motives are present that are not shared.[7]

Motivation is essential for the long-term health of an organization. In the book, *Beyond Leadership: Balancing Economics, and Ecology,* Warren Bennis, Jagdish Parikh, and Ronnie Lessem argue that organizations should guard against a decrease in follower motivation and associated productivity. The authors state that when followers "feel that the work is devoid of intelligent content and therefore experience a kind of qualitative under-employment; they feel reduced to a number, a mere extension of the system."[8] Consequently, followers begin to lose their identity with the overall organizational vision and are likely to decrease production over time. To prevent this scenario, leaders must learn how to motivate their followers effectively.

Effective Organizations

Effective organizations achieve their vision, goals, and objectives efficiently while balancing relationships and tasks successfully. Pictured typically with organizational charts and wire diagrams that demonstrate the visible relationships between people and responsibilities, the performance of organizations actually hinges on these interactions. It is essential to understand the strengths of the interconnections in order to identify the organization's potential for success. It is an enormous challenge to recognize the traits that encourage success and separate them from those that contribute to failure. Like a healthy person, a healthy organization presents the image of a vibrant mind and body, where all of the parts are interdependent and contribute to the overall well-being of the whole. This same analogy applies to the organization that stumbles. An ineffective organization is exemplified by the lethargic and the weary. For the unhealthy body, just getting through the day is a challenge.

If an organization has a hidden culture that hinders forward progress, nothing gets done. While not readily apparent, the hidden culture demonstrates a failure to support the major body organs that productively sustain the health of an organization. It is this potentially negative element that must be unveiled before significant improvement can be achieved. The Organizations that display ineffective interdependence are best described as dysfunctional.

Dysfunctional Organizations

Dysfunctional organizations are described quite differently from successful organizations. They are ineffective, or at best, marginally effective while exhibiting multiple inefficiencies, rigidity, and disappointments highlighted by a lack of cooperation. It is not uncommon to find that many organizations are simply unable to provide positive outcomes, no matter how hard they try. Moreover, leaders of a dysfunctional organization persistently deny that internal problems exist and attempt to place blame on external forces. The dysfunctional organization usually ignores problems it refuses to identify or "fix." The conclusion that genuine change can only occur by inserting an external event or person into the organization to analyze the organizational patient and confer the diagnosis. In the end, training is scheduled, consultants are hired, and systematic diagnostic processes are implemented. To all appearances, it seems reasonably straightforward to expect an outside agent to analyze, review, and develop strategies to respond to the perceived visible barriers in a normally dysfunctional organization because these barriers are well—visible.

However sincere this "criticize, analyze, and revise" activity appears, frequently it is the symptoms that are obvious, not the cause. Neither does it always need to be an outsider who determines the source of the symptoms. It takes more than just identifying the underlying cause of the problem that is critical. Identifying and implementing the "fix" may not be so easy. It requires an absolute willingness to undergo a thorough self-examination and the courage to respond once the invisible barriers are recognized.

The Invisible Barriers to Organizational Effectiveness

Invisible barriers are those actions and processes going on behind the scenes and under the surface. They include the subversive tendency by some people to forestall any desired success, innovation, or change while feigning agreement (sometimes enthusiastically). While the visible barriers are usually evident, in order to spot those that are invisible, leaders will have to honestly be willing to look for them, and then be willing to question (and answer) what made it so. Here we identify and explain ten of the critical invisible barriers found in many organizations that serve to blockade organizational effectiveness.

- **Malicious Compliance** is specific behavior of a follower who appears to meticulously comply with a management decision while actually subverting the spirit of the order through inaction, minimal support, subversion, or overly strict adherence of rules, policies, or regulations; thus intentionally causing a decrease in productivity and damage to the organization's mission or reputation.
- **Mirroring** is subconscious behavior of a leader or manager to employ, mentor, and promote a follower with like characteristics, economic status, academic background, ethnicity, behaviors, and personality type. Mirroring may lead to a mediocre follower advancing faster than a more qualified follower, which may result in lack of equity issues.
- **Self-Interest** is the principle that a follower's output is directly proportional to the follower's perception of relative personal reward. Therefore, a follower may elect to place their self-interest first, even at the expense of the organization's goals.
- **Slap Down the Idea Generator (SDIG)** is a type of follower that attempts to circumvent constructive critical thinking or block potential changes that are inconsistent with the status quo or not within the follower's self-interest. The additional potential consequence of SDIG is to halt the freedom of expression accepted in progressive organizations.
- **Malicious Mischief** is a specific behavior of a follower who intentionally causes disruption within the workplace through misbehavior, indifference, gossip, agitation, nuisance, and/ or malicious compliance. Malicious mischief may foster an organizational culture of mistrust and insecurity.
- **Lack of Diversity of Thought** is the subconscious behavior of an entire organization to consistently promote homogeneous thought and discourage independent critical thinking or constructive change.

- **Ethnocentrism** is the propensity to feel that their ethnic group, culture, values, and beliefs are intrinsically superior to other cultures. An ethnocentric follower may discount valuable contributions from other followers within the organization simply based on a conviction of cultural superiority.
- **Intergenerational Conflict** is a basic divergence of cultural, social, or economic values and norms that can result in an unspoken intolerance between two separate generations. This conflict can result in a lack of workforce harmony within an organization. The perception is that once recognized, dysfunctional organizations are also thought to be easy to repair.
- **Organizational bureaucracy** that discourages personal responsibility and knowledge sharing is characterized by a lack of trust. The vacuum created in this situation impedes creativity and originality.
- **Alexithymic personality** is characterized by an inability to understand the impact of emotions on decision-making. This is due in large part to two functions of emotions. First, emotions are appetitive motivations connected to a strong wish or urge. Secondly, the affect system processes information differently from the more logical intellectual system and is therefore more likely to overlook important information. An organization with abundant "alexithymia" is likely to be overwhelmed accomplishing functional tasks.

While certainly de-motivating, all of these invisible barriers serve to subtly block organizational effectiveness, even when appearances may be to the contrary. If so, how does management begin to maximize the human assets in an organization when everyone's motivating factors are different? How does management deal with everyone as individuals and align their values with corporate objectives?

Literature suggests that diversity is not simply an issue of race, ethnicity, gender, and age. It is the multitude of unique personas found in every organization. It is the trigger for building cooperation or the grounds for dissention. Organizational effectiveness is found in the blend of the variety of people and ideas and is exhibited by honest respect, one for the other.

Conclusion

Motivational factors are dependent on the issues, values, motives, and goals of every follower, and just like the followers, they are very diverse. This means the workplace solutions one develops have to be even more creative. It is an enormous task to undertake when motivation is low or when the problem is persistent.

It is actually easier to recognize the invisible barriers than it is to repair them. Where the actions are well established, subtle, and pervasive, it requires diligence to counteract the long-term effects of the ineffective relationships. These measures need to be undertaken; not solely to maintain competitive advantage or to satisfy transforming organizations, but because it is the right thing to do.

Clearly, the foundation of the solution originates in ongoing, multi-directional communication that establishes the need for deep organizational and individual introspection. While the tendency to "do nothing" will be strong, that is exactly what the followers who created these invisible behaviors expect—avoidance. And they win again. Embrace change; model the desired behavior and attitude; be positive; finish what has been started; be trustworthy; be thorough; and no matter how painful, develop a long-term plan for transparent solutions to the invisible barriers.

Notes

1. George Goethals, Georgia Sorenson, and James Burns, *Encyclopedia of Leadership, Vol. 1.* (Thousand Oaks, CA: Sage Publications, Inc., 2004), 181.
2. Robert Kaplan, *Warrior Politics: Why Leadership Demands a Pathan Ethos* (New York: Vintage Books, 2002), 47.
3. Ulysses Pierce. *The Creed of Epictetus* (Boston: The Beacon Press, 1916), 58.
4. Robert Lussier, and Christopher Achua. *Leadership: Theory, Application, and Skill Development* (Mason, OH: Thomson Higher Education, 2007), 95-96.
5. Ibid., 383.
6. Bernard Bass, Bruce Avolio, Dong Jung, and Yair Berson, "Predicting Unit Performance by Assessing Transformational and Transactional Leadership," *Journal of Applied Psychology* (2003): 207–218.
7. Gary Wills, *Certain Trumpets: The Nature of Leadership* (New York: Touchtone,1994), 17.
8. Warren Bennis, Jagdish Parikh, and Ronnie Lessem, *Beyond Leadership: Balancing Economics, Ethics, and Ecology* (Cambridge, MA: Blackwell Publishers, Ltd.1994), 225-226.

John Plifka and Wayne Ditto

Leading Change Through Investment

Introduction

In February 2003, the Army Training and Leader Development Panel (ATDLP) Report Phase IV (Civilian Study)[1] revealed that "the Army has no well-developed and executed, integrated systemic approach for Civilian education and leader development." This prompted the leadership of the Army to commit and invest in the development of a centralized Army system integrating Civilian and Military individual training, education, and development.

Although Army Civilians have historically made significant contributions in the execution of the Army's mission, today the reliance on Civilians is more pronounced. As the transforming Army responds to new "operational" requirements, Army Civilians will assume a higher degree of increased leadership roles and responsibilities to support Army operations and the modular force. As the modular force increases the combat power of the Active force and the size of the Army's overall pool of available forces are reallocated, assignments of Civilians to non-fighting combat support/ combat service support leadership positions will become more pronounced. In addition, Military-to-Civilian conversions will release many Military leaders from current garrison and support type roles within the institutional

Army. As Army Civilian positions continue to increase in responsibility and authority, this will mandate a system to ensure professionally developed and highly productive Civilian leaders.[2] Navigating the strategic direction of any organization is a complex undertaking. This challenge is exacerbated when making future decisions for an institution like the United States Army.

The Army currently finds itself reexamining the decision it made to invest in and commit to the Civilian Education System (CES) by asking itself, "If the Army knew then what it knows now, would it again commit?" The method in which this is occurring is through the consideration of questions as well as a comparative analysis of other organizations that rival the size and operations of the Army.

During the initial decision to commit scarce resources to CES, the Army faced significant Civilian leadership and management training and education challenges as it still does today. To overcome these challenges, the Army mandated the much-needed transformation based on the results of a comprehensive study showing an incomplete education and development system, a limited reach to its population, and a necessity to replicate the successes of the established Professional Military Education Systems. This mandate led to the rationale for a significant initial fiscal investment. The resulting design and development of the Army's CES has put in place the fundamental elements and architectural framework necessary to provide leadership and management development across the Army Civilian Corps' to meet present and future developmental needs of its Civilian workforce.

In addition to the previous and current challenges faced, the Army also examined the planning requirement assumptions associated with committing to and investing in CES. Though most of the initial assumptions have occurred, the Army now faces a new set of planning requirement assumptions as it reconsiders its renewed commitment and investment. Evaluative data is still being collected for an accurate longitudinal assessment of return on investment. Similar to colleges and universities, the Army's return on investment cannot be successfully analyzed without making the connection to the results that its followers provide to the organization. Kirkpatrick's classic model[3] to evaluate training/education offerings is used to look at four specific levels of assessment—student reaction, learning, behavior, and business results. With the current operational tempo, the Army must constantly examine decisions to commit more scarce resources and funding toward CES. Kirkpatrick's model is one model that enables leaders to revisit planning requirement challenges. However, to understand the Army's decisions regarding its investment in CES and to underscore the importance of Civilian leader development investment, it is essential to address and understand its historical evolution.

Historical Perspective

Army Field Manual 6-22, *Army Leadership*, dated October 2006, "combines the lessons of the past with important insights for the future to help develop competent Army leaders."[4] During the last 20 years, the Army has been progressive in words and actions in the development of Army Civilian Corps Leader to sustain and meet future leadership requirements. Though leader development courses and programs have been in place long before the 1980s, it was during this time that the Army began making a concerted effort toward building a progressive and sequential system that was an investment for the future.

The 1980s

A 1986 Department of the Army Inspector General report on the Army Civilian Personnel Management System found that, "Army leaders are failing to provide effective leadership to the 484,000 Army Civilians (almost 40 percent of the total active Army) . . . Their concern is primarily for the Soldier, not the Civilian member of the Army Team."[5]

"Leadership by Army Civilians had been a special concern of HQDA since a 1985 study revealed deficiencies in this area. To address this and other personnel matters, the Civilian Personnel Modernization Project (CPMP) was created."[6] The CPMP was initiated with a draft concept dated December 2, 1986, titled "Modernizing the Army Civilian Personnel System–A Conceptual Design."[7] "Known as the Civilian Personnel Modernization Project, this initiative is aimed at strengthening Military and civilian leadership and management of the large complement of Civilian followers who play a vital role in housing, equipping, training and caring for soldiers throughout the world."[8] The investigation, findings, and recommendations (along with the initiation of the CPMP), and an emphasis by Military and Civilian senior leaders became the genesis for the first comprehensive development of a Civilian Leadership Training Core Curriculum (Figure 1 next page).

Civilian Leader Development Courses

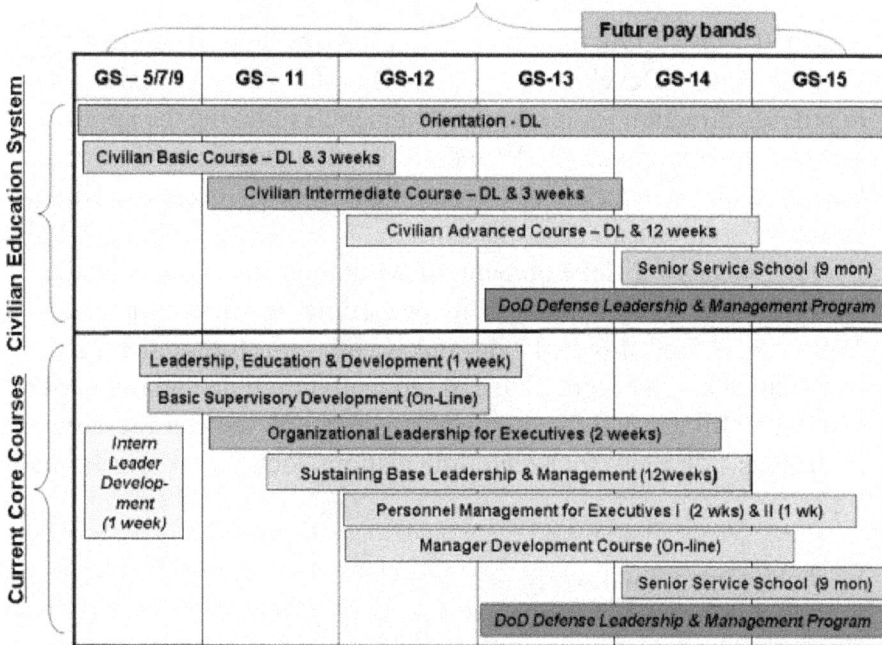

Future pay bands

	GS – 5/7/9	GS – 11	GS-12	GS-13	GS-14	GS-15
Civilian Education System	Orientation - DL					
	Civilian Basic Course – DL & 3 weeks					
		Civilian Intermediate Course – DL & 3 weeks				
			Civilian Advanced Course – DL & 12 weeks			
					Senior Service School (9 mon)	
				DoD Defense Leadership & Management Program		
Current Core Courses		Leadership, Education & Development (1 week)				
		Basic Supervisory Development (On-Line)				
	Intern Leader Develop-ment (1 week)		Organizational Leadership for Executives (2 weeks)			
			Sustaining Base Leadership & Management (12weeks)			
				Personnel Management for Executives I (2 wks) & II (1 wk)		
				Manager Development Course (On-line)		
					Senior Service School (9 mon)	
				DoD Defense Leadership & Management Program		

Figure 1

On November 14, 1987, General Carl E. Vuono, Army Chief of Staff, speaking to senior officers and Civilians stated,

> One of the things I think we have recognized too late–in my view, we should have done it several years ago– that the development of leaders is not restricted to Military. The criticality of ensuring that we've got the right competent Civilians in our force is equally as critical as having the right competent Colonel in our force. You do not develop the Civilian leader overnight. He, as well as the Military, has to be given the opportunity for training and education. We have just begun to see that come forward, and I'm delighted with it. I intend to continue to pursue the development of both Military and Civilian leaders in the Army.[9]

Even though the Civilian Corps training programs had been developed and integrated into the Army training programs during the 1980s with the importance of leader development being emphasized by senior leadership, the training programs were still not well-defined and fully-integrated into the workforce.

The 1990s

On 10 April 1990, the Chief of Staff, Army, approved the Army Civilian Leader Development Action Plan (CLDP), a cohesive plan to provide direction for leader development. Following the approval and implementation of CLDP, the officer, noncommissioned officer (NCO), and Civilian leader development systems became parallel systems for America's Army.[10]

The successful development of Military and Civilian leaders is key to the Army's success in peacetime and in combat. The Army recognized this early on and became the forerunner in the establishment of a progressive and sequential training common core to ensure Military and Civilian leaders are ready to meet these new challenges....Twenty four recommendations focused on four broad areas:

1. Achieving a Total Army Culture
2. Adopting a Civilian Leader Development System
3. Developing and Delivering Civilian Leadership Training
4. Resourcing the Program

One key recommendation of the CLDAP in 1990 was 'to provide essential leader training, (progressively and sequentially) to parallel leadership training afforded to Military officers.[11]

"In 1991, the Leader Development *Investment* Strategy study developed principles and imperatives to synchronize leader development initiatives as the Army downsized."[12] This study in the early 1990s recognized the Army's commitment to the development of leaders (Military and Civilian) at all levels. It began to shape the thinking about how Civilian counterparts fit into the Army's Leader Development Model, circa 1994 (Figure 2),[13] which comprises three distinct pillars—Institutional Training and Education; Operational Assignments; and Self-Development. The CLDAP focused on improving Civilian leadership and management development through formalizing an institutional training and education system.

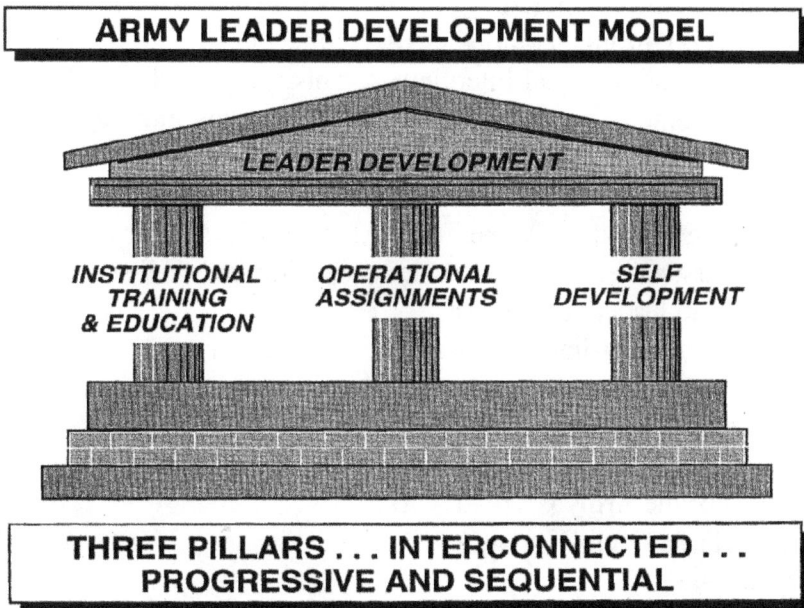

Figure 2: DA Pam 350-58, 13 October 1994

These recommendations reinforced and continued to emphasize the importance of providing a systematic, progressive, and sequential program to close the gap between concept and execution. "The Army commitment to develop competent, confident leaders will remain constant as we address future challenges. Our three-pillared leader development model will continue to serve as the foundation for the future leaders of the Army."[14] This statement further reinforces the words and actions of senior leadership addressing the importance of leader development for the Civilian component.

The 2000s

At the beginning of the new millennium, the Army began and completed a significant study in support of the Army's Vision of Transformation, examining its leader development and educational program for Officers, Warrant Officers, Noncommissioned Officers, and Army Civilians. On February 24, 2003, Lieutenant General James C. Riley, Commanding General, Combined Arms Center, sent a memorandum to the Army Chief of Staff in reference to the Army Training and Leader Development Panel (ATLDP) Report (Civilians). This report contained the results of the extensive Army study to identify training and leader development requirements for current and future Army Civilians. Data was collected from more than 40,000 Army

Civilians and Soldiers (including Senior Executive Service members and General Officers) through comprehensive written and online surveys, focus group sessions, and personal interviews.[15] This study produced four major imperatives that the Executive Panel believed the Army must address:

- Accountability—Make developing Army Civilians a high priority . . .
- Lifelong Learning—Make lifelong learning the standard . . .
- Interpersonal Skills—Acknowledge that interpersonal skills are pivotal to leader competence.
- Army Culture—Integrate Army Civilians fully into the Army culture.

As noted in previous reports and studies, the "repeat offender" is the requirement to achieve a total Army culture that fully invests in the development of the Army Civilian workforce.

Dr. Pamela Raymer, Dean of Academics at the Army Management Staff College, states,

> There has been a lack of sustained momentum in growing Army Civilian leaders. It is evident that the Army has been aware of its shortfalls in developing Army Civilian leaders, but for whatever reasons— resources, mission requirements, and operational pace, other priorities, internal/external resistance, etc.— the Army has not made the changes recommended in previous studies. This history of marginal action and the many conclusions from these studies indicate that the Army has not been effective in developing Army Civilian leaders and that the Army's current programs do not prepare Army Civilians to become leaders.". . . 'In June 2005, the Army Management Staff College (AMSC) received the mission to design, develop, and implement the new program.[16]

The leadership and faculty of AMSC formally began the development, design, and implementation of the new Civilian Education System (CES), which consists of four progressive and sequential levels of leadership and management training for the Civilian workforce—Foundation, Basic, Intermediate, and Advanced courses (Figure 3). Pilot programs were developed in 2006, with the implementation phase beginning in Fiscal Year 2007, in conjunction with the issuance of the Army Civilian Education System Policy, dated November 2006, by Headquarters, Department of the Army, Deputy Chief of Staff, G-3/5/7 Training Directorate.

Civilian Leader Development Overview

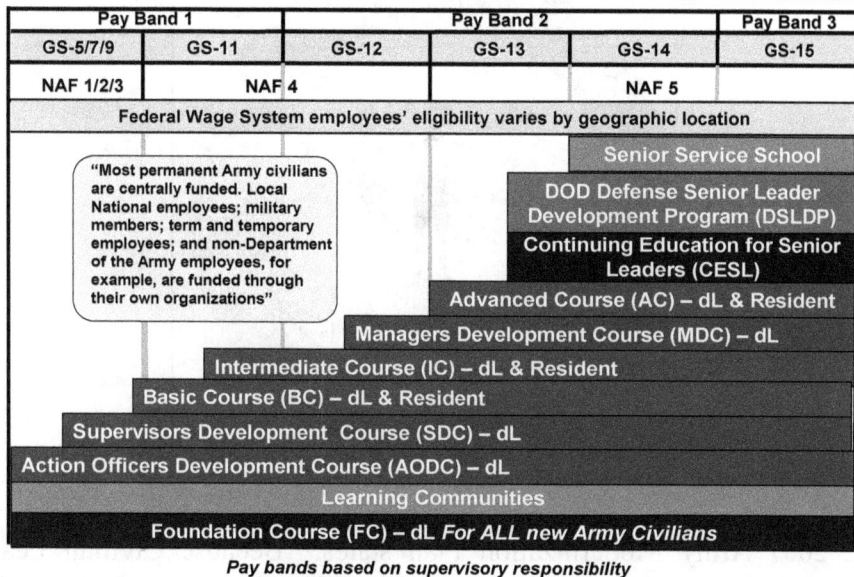

Pay Band 1		Pay Band 2			Pay Band 3
GS-5/7/9	GS-11	GS-12	GS-13	GS-14	GS-15
NAF 1/2/3	NAF 4			NAF 5	

Federal Wage System employees' eligibility varies by geographic location

Senior Service School

DOD Defense Senior Leader Development Program (DSLDP)

Continuing Education for Senior Leaders (CESL)

Advanced Course (AC) – dL & Resident

"Most permanent Army civilians are centrally funded. Local National employees; military members; term and temporary employees; and non-Department of the Army employees, for example, are funded through their own organizations"

Managers Development Course (MDC) – dL

Intermediate Course (IC) – dL & Resident

Basic Course (BC) – dL & Resident

Supervisors Development Course (SDC) – dL

Action Officers Development Course (AODC) – dL

Learning Communities

Foundation Course (FC) – dL *For ALL new Army Civilians*

Pay bands based on supervisory responsibility

Figure 3, Civilian Leader Development Overview (http://www.amsc.belvoir.army.mil/ces/)

In November 2006, the Army released a report titled "Army Leaders for the 21st Century," which represented the results of the Army's Review of Education, Training, and Assignments for Leaders (RETAL). This study confirmed that the current Army Training and Leader Development Model (Figure 2) is "effective and provides agile, innovative leaders successfully . . . however, it has not kept pace with change."[17] Recommendations for the Civilian workforce included, "Make the investment in Civilian Leader Development."[18] On March 8, 2007, the Army issued the revised Army Regulation 600-100, *Army Leadership*, identifying the new leader development model that shows the important interactions for training Soldiers and developing leaders,[19] which has been adapted to reflect the civilian component (Figure 4).

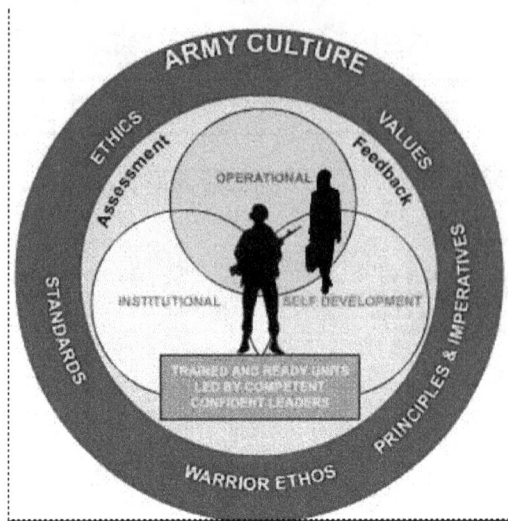

Figure 4. Army Training and Leader Development Model (http://www.amsc.belvoir.army.mil/ces/)

The 2007 Army Modernization Plan states, "Because Civilian Leader development is significantly less established than the Military's, it requires new initiatives to give the Civilian Corps a unique identity."[20] This emphasis was reinforced through the Army's Strategic Communications referencing Army Leaders for the 21st Century (AL21); "Leader development is an investment not a cost in the Army and our Nation's future."[21]

More than 20 years ago, the Army recognized the need to develop and manage the Civilian workforce effectively, but it will take time as indicated by the words from Vuono in 1987, "You do not develop the Civilian leader overnight."[22] These words, along with a variety of studies, concepts, initiatives, and actions over the years, have moved the Army closer to a "cradle to grave" approach that incorporates an effective, progressive, and sequential civilian leadership and management development program. The idea of random, periodic, or non-sequential training development opportunities of the past is changing in both words and actions. The emphasis by the Army to develop a training and education system that integrates a culture of institutional training, operational assignments, and self-development from the day a Civilian follower is administered the Oath of Office to the day that follower retires is moving forward.

Change Through Investment Takes Time

The Civilian Education System now provides a culmination of the best practices identified and used by other comparable organizations such as General Electric, Motorola, Pepsi, Federal Express, Johnson and Johnson, Sony, etc.[23] The IBM Global Human Capital Study[24] reported that companies such as these (with 80 percent or more of managers in management development programs) had approximately three times the profitability of companies with 0 to 60 percent. A 2005 survey conducted by Bersin & Associates[25] found that successful organizations such as these spend as much as 30 percent of their corporate training dollars on leadership development. Although the Army is not a profit-oriented organization, it is still challenged with conducting complex, intense, and global operations with an appropriated budget to provide the best return on investment with America's tax dollars.

As long as the Army continues to recognize and stay clear of what Ready and Conger[26] calls the three pathologies of why leadership development efforts fail...

- The "Ownership is Power" Mind-Set
- The Productization of Leadership Development
- Make-Believe Metrics

...as well as not falling into the six major pitfalls that Parker[27] addresses,

- Urgency overrides preparation
- Participants fail to engage emotionally
- The CEO cannot contain himself
- Awkward issues are not confronted
- Trendy triumphs over consequence
- Culture is not receptive to change

recommitting scarce money is a solid investment that promises beneficial returns. Most leadership development programs focus on developing a great program. Another point to remember is that the program is a small part of the overall likelihood of successful returns on investment. A course or program is an event, but learning that includes leader development is a process.[28] So if we know that leader development is a worthy investment for any organization, what is the resistance?

Measuring Return on Investment

Similar to the U.S. Army, colleges and universities are aggressively scrutinizing costs and tightening budgets. To fully appreciate how return on investment pertains to the Army, it is important to discuss and present the research that has already been conducted by colleges and universities. In order for colleges or universities to further invest in their programs and degrees, it is prudent to prove that their educational offerings are worth a student's investment.

Administrators within colleges and universities continually analyze their investment in programs, personnel, technology, and infrastructure versus the impact on not investing for these things as well as for the cost of the individual student education. Administrators are continually challenged with the resources they invest in their programs. This process becomes easier if administrators know that the outcome their institution provides is positive and that more students will want to enroll to achieve that same positive outcome. The positive outcome the scholastic institution provides is then used for individual benefit as well as adding to the benefit to society. When statistics and data show that there is an individual return on education, there should be less risk for more educational institutions to invest more money in their programs, especially in the programs that are proven to provide an individual return on investment. However, this does not seem to be the case for many colleges and universities due to a weak evaluative process, the lack of data, or sometimes a changing institutional standard.

Successful planning becomes tremendously difficult if the institution cannot accurately measure how effective its programs are. The delicate balance between investment and cost is further complicated when performance-based funding is used, which leads to the process of improving the institutional standard.[29] Improving educational standards requires greater investment and more resources. The decision to improve educational standards is normally based on the rationale of measurable success that individuals have upon their return to society and the labor market.[30]

The Army does this through the use of cyclic survey instruments and periodic studies. The Army's measurement philosophy is analogous to that of colleges and universities. College and university systems typically agree that return on investment cannot be successfully analyzed without making the connection to the results that individuals provide to the labor market and society. Within CES, these are the results that individuals provide to their organizations and the Army on a whole.

As mentioned earlier, the classic model to evaluate training/education offerings developed by Kirkpatrick,[31] looks at four levels of assessment—student reaction, learning, behavior, and business results. There are several methods to evaluate education offerings based on financial return, and these methods include both quantitative and qualitative assessments.[32] According to Roth,[33] the quantitative assessments used to determine financial returns on education are benefit-cost ratio, return on investment, and forecasting. These provide a measure of the value of the offering utilizing a cost/benefit approach. There are both quantitative and qualitative ways to determine a return on investment, however, not all colleges and universities use this, and there is a certain amount of disagreement regarding the accuracy of what these assessments measure. One of the most significant issues pertains to the questionable market value of education, especially when considering the type of degree obtained and the institution from which it is obtained. There seems to be little known about overall labor market returns due to the associated individual variables and motivations.[34] The knowledge that education benefits the individual student in terms of increased earnings is widespread, but information is incomplete about the benefits that increased education has on society.[35] However, in the same report, *Investment in Education: Private and Public Returns*,[36] to the Joint Economics Committee, U.S. Congress found that increasing the years of schooling, training, and experience of a follower has a significant effect on the earnings of the individual and society at large. In the context of training the Army Civilian workforce, one could postulate that increased schooling, training, and experience would further advance the Army as a whole.

In a different vein, there does seem to be commonality regarding the concerns of student quality at different colleges and universities. Private colleges and universities typically have higher admission standards on college admission exams such as the SAT and ACT than public colleges and universities. This may influence studies, which will determine the results between private and public individual return on education.[37] Though this seems to be a common concern when attempting to accurately measure individual return on investment, Monks[38] points out that there is weak evidence that private colleges are any better than public. This directly rebuts the common concern of student quality. In the same report previously cited, it seems that the individual benefit that education provides is linked to its impact on society as quoted:

> Investment in education contributes to enhanced labor force productivity and enables individuals to become better citizens and parents in addition to being better followers. The effectiveness of American education will have an important impact on U.S. economic performance for the foreseeable future.[39]

Another argument surrounding the balancing act between the investment and cost issue relates to the significant returns to college quality. Graduating from a graduate degree granting or research institution as compared to a liberal arts college denoted a significant return difference.[40] This disparity highlights the investment strategy differences because liberal arts colleges understand that their commitment to the various core values they abide by all have a cost, usually with a person attached to it.[41] To deliver and operate by the values and commitments liberal arts colleges convey, significant effort is used to attract and retain the faculty required. This process demands greater focus of the budget because the faculty salary and benefits cost more. This is where Palmer[42] discusses the risk and leadership style associated with investment.

The balance between conservative risks versus aggressive investment can positively or negatively impact the sustained success of an institution. In the example of liberal arts colleges, aggressive investment seems to be required to recruit and retain the best faculty so that they may continue to thrive and offer an education that does provide a return on investment. Collectively it seems that studies indicate that investing in a scholastic institution is worthwhile because college dropouts earn higher wages than high school graduates who accumulate no college credits.[43] It is the nature of these very studies that federal, state, and local governments all recognize the importance of education and share a common goal to ensure that all citizens have access to quality education.[44] When data supports that education provides a return on investment and the Army recognizes the importance of leader development from the 1980s to present, what factors are not being addressed when assessing the return on investment of previous educational systems?

Politics, Ego, Emotions, and Money (PEEM)

There seem to be four enduring principles that impact all systemic decision making and developmental efforts. Politics, Ego, Emotions, and Money (PEEM–Figure 5) are four axioms that are intertwined and influence organizational decision making. There are literally thousands of books on the shelf regarding leadership and management, and the common thread found in almost every one of these works is the ability to make effective decisions. When studying leadership and management, an area that is normally not identified as part of the decision making process is a leader's ability to look beyond the theoretical steps or process and identify the qualitative issues of Politics (at all levels), Egos, (theirs and others around them), Emotions, (theirs and others around them), combined with Money, (a limiting quantitative concern and usually viewed as the cost of any actions resulting in a decision made).

Whether sustaining system operations or creating new ones, leaders must make decisions for improved continual growth and effectiveness. It seems that systems typically fail because leadership fails to address the PEEM involved with their system development decisions. We typically spend a great amount of energy analyzing the fiscal quantitative aspects versus the implicit qualitative ones to make decisions.

Politics: According to Wikipedia, politics is the process by which groups make decisions. It is the authoritative allocation of values. Although the term is generally applied to behavior within governments, politics is observed in all human group interactions, including corporate, academic, and religious institutions.[45] Politics are associated with every system, across the spectrum from the local to international level. Politics can be described as a bargaining process or a formal process of checks and balances. Specifically, politics may bind an issue or alternative that we generate either individually or are directed to explore. We may select a particular alternative based solely on its political implications, and sometimes the unpopular choice is selected for the right reason. Though they may be closely related, politics and ego can compound the challenge of making effective decisions.

Ego: Popularly defined as an over-inflated sense of self-importance, egos can present major leadership challenges.[46] When faced with systemic decision making, egos can wreak personal and organizational havoc. Instead of placing organizational interests first, an unchecked and unbalanced ego may steer an organization in the wrong direction—especially in the case of taking greater risks for more investment. Vital for organizational growth, egos have drive and energy, and if used appropriately can be highly productive. Balancing our egos may be extremely difficult since self-confidence and a strong ego are often factors in executive success. If we release the need to be in control, to be right, or to have all the answers, we will foster better decisions and build organizational capacity.[47] This is easier said than done, especially considering cultures such as the U.S. Army.

Emotions: Our emotional involvement can have a tremendous impact on decisions we make. Interrelated with politics and ego, emotions are very powerful and can easily interfere with our ability to be objective. Consider for a moment the leaders who have been in an organization for a long period of time, and imagine how that investment alone links directly to their emotions. Throughout history, nations, families, and individuals have fought because of their unwillingness to get beyond the emotional aspects of the event that may have occurred and affected them. Emotions are a contributing factor to any paradigm shift in thinking and actions. If leaders are unaware of the emotional aspects of systemic decision making, subjectivity may cloud their ability to make the most effective decision.

Money: It must be considered in almost every systemic decision a leader or organization makes. Monetary resources will always be limited; there will be competing interests, and maximizing a focus to be more effective and do more with less. As cited earlier, Kirkpatrick's model addresses the importance of money and is a quantitative aspect of PEEM. Unlike politics, egos or emotions, determining a true return on investment must not be limited to analyzing dollars and cents. This gets to the heart of why considering all aspects of PEEM are critical. If we make decisions going forward on the Civilian Education System on numbers alone, we are missing the recurring error of full integration of the Civilian workforce into the organizational culture of the Army.

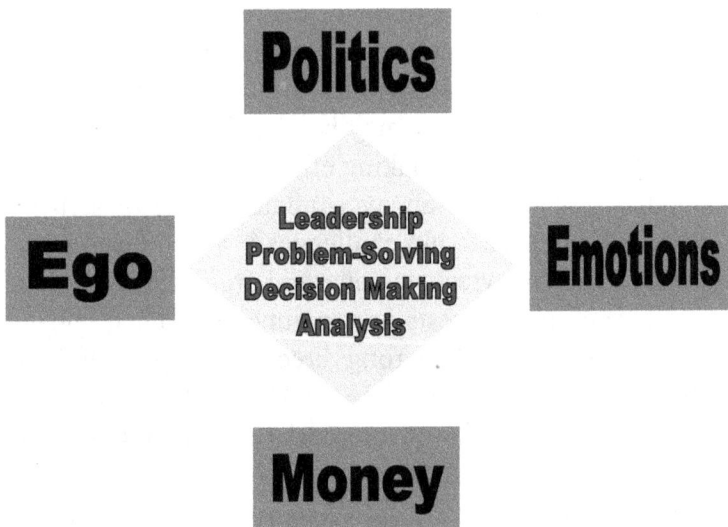

Politics

Ego

Leadership
Problem-Solving
Decision Making
Analysis

Emotions

Money

Figure 5. PEEM Model

Politics—Is the issue limited within internal or external
       organizational paradigms?

Ego—Is the issue self-serving or for the organization?

Emotions—Are personal emotions set aside for the organization?

Money—What is the cost of not investing?

Conclusion

Readdressing the initial questions that posed a reconsideration for continued investment, confirms that the Army's CES is congruent with industry best practices, while at the same time having the awareness to avoid the common pitfalls associated with failing programs in other institutions. The information presented leads to a recommendation that the Army (through its continued investment) leverages the best practices and avoids the pitfalls to continue meeting the intent of educating Department of the Army Civilian leaders and, more importantly, achieve the Army's goals. The investment versus cost for education from the individual and the organizational perspective is important. Knowing a true return on investment helps leaders plan effectively and invest in their programs and futures. However (before doing so) it is prudent to prove that educational and developmental offerings are worth the individual and organizational investment. Even though there are different views on what are educational returns, investing effectively requires organizations to focus on those programs and degrees that yield the greatest individual return on investment for continual growth. Based on all the issues and accompanying arguments presented, it seems that educational investment from the organizational or individual perspective is money well-spent because it will yield results.

At the same time the Army must address the elements of politics, ego, and emotions appropriately in its strategic planning initiatives and decision making. The Army's 300,000 Civilian Corps members directly contribute to the Army's readiness and its ability to accomplish the mission at every level. Avoiding the failures of not fully integrating the Army Civilian Corps into the culture and leveraging the best practices will continue a successful return on investment for meeting the Nation's business. We, as leaders, have a responsibility to exercise our judgment to make the most effective decision for our continual investment efforts for the success of the Army. If we fail to recognize the importance of investment and its associated challenges, we will fail as leaders of today and hinder our leaders of tomorrow.

Notes

1. *The Army Training and Leader Development Panel Report Phase IV (Civilian Study),* (Fort Leavenworth, KS: U.S. Army Combined Arms Center, 2003), 2.
2. *Civilian Education System (CES) Concept* (Fort Monroe, VA: U.S. Army Training and Doctrine Command, 2004).
3. Donald L. Kirkpatrick, *Evaluating Training Programs: The Four Levels,* 2nd ed. (San Francisco: Berett-Koehler Publishers, Inc.,1998), 19-25.
4. *Army Leadership: Competent, Confident, and Agile* [Field Manual 6-22], (Washington, DC: Department of the Army, 12 October 2006), viii.

5. Dallas Van Hoose, "Developing Civilian Leaders for Force XXI," *Military Review* (January-February 1996): 56.
6. William Joe Webb, Charles Anderson, Dale Andrade, Mary Gillett, Glen Hawkins, Dave Hogan, Thomas Popa, Rebecca Raines, and James Yarrison, W. Scott Janes (Eds.), *Department of the Army Historical Summary, Fiscal Years 1990 and 1991*, (Washington, DC: U.S. Army Center for Military History, 1997), 39.
7. Headquarters, Department of the Army, Deputy Chief of Staff, G1, memorandum dated 2 December 1986, subject: "Modernizing the Army Civilian Personnel System: A Conceptual Design, Civilian Personnel Modernization Project."
8. *Army Personnel Bulletin* (Washington, DC: Department of the Army, Deputy Chief of Staff, G1, September 1987), 3.
9. "Vuono Sets Sights on Maintaining Army with Momentum, Impact," *Army Times,* 14 December 1987, 18.
10. Webb et al., *Department of the Army Historical Summary, Fiscal Years 1990 and 1991*, 39.
11. *Army Civilian Leadership Training,* Civilian Human Resource Agency (CHRA), Europe; available on the Internet at http://cpolrhp.belvoir.army.mil/eur/training/aclt.htm (accessed 4 April 2008).
12. *The Enduring Legacy –Leader Development for America's Army* [DA Pam 350-58], (Washington, DC: Department of the Army, 13 October 1994), 1.
13. Ibid., 2.
14. Ibid., 32.
15. *The Army Training and Leader Development Panel Report Phase IV*, 3-4.
16. Pamela Raymer, "The New Army Civilian Education System," *U.S. Army Journal of Installation Management* 3 (Winter 2008), 84.
17. *Army Leaders for the 21st Century Final Report* (Washington, DC: Department of the Army, Deputy Chief of Staff, G-3/5/7, November 2006), 5.
18. Ibid., 7.
19. *Army Leadership* [AR 600-100], (Washington, DC: Department of the Army, 8 March 2007), 5.
20. *2007 Army Modernization Plan*, (Washington, DC: Department of the Army, Deputy Chief of Staff, G8, March 2007), 38; available on the Internet at http://www.army.mil/institution/leaders/modplan (accessed 19 February 2008).
21. "StratComm: Areas of Interest," 18 April 2007, available on the internet at https://www.us.army.mil/ suite/doc/8342378 (accessed 19 February 2008).
22. "Vuono Sets Sights," *Army Times.*
23. David V. Day and Stanley M. Halpin, "Leadership Development: A Review of Industry Best Practices," U.S. Army Research Institute Technical Report 1111, (Alexandria, VA, February 2001), 31-56.
24. Mari Sako, "Global Human Capital Study 2005: The Capability Within," IBM Global Business Services; available on the Internet at http://www.ibm.com/services/us/gbs/bus/html/2005_human_cap_mgt_gen.html (accessed 14 April 2008).
25. Josh Bersin, "Leadership Development: Moving from Priority to Action," *Chief Learning Officer,* December 2006; available on the Internet at http://www.clomedia.com/content/templates/ clo_article.asp?articleid=1596&zoneid=187 (accessed 14 April 2008).
26. Douglas A. Ready and Jay A. Conger, "Why Leadership Development Efforts Fail," *MIT Sloan Management Review* 44, no. 3 (2003), 83-88.
27. Stephen Parker, "Effective Leadership Development: Avoid Six Common Pitfalls,"

Leadership Excellence (November 2007): 18.
28. Kevin Eikenberry, "Why Most Leadership Development Efforts Fail," *EzineArticles*, May 25, 2006; available on the Internet at http://ezinearticles.com/?Why-Most-Leadership-Development-Efforts-Fail&id=205917, (accessed 5 March 2008).
29. Daniel T. Layzell, "Linking Performance to Funding Outcomes for Public Institutions of Higher Education; The U.S. Experience," *European Journal of Education*, 33, No.1 (1998): 103-111
30. United States Congress Joint Economic Committee, *Investment in Education: Private and Public Returns* (Washington, D.C.: January 2000), 1-13.
31. Kirkpatrick, 19-25.
32. L. Roth, "Determining Return on Investment in Training/Education," electronic article from Johnson Center at Grand Valley State University, Non-Profit Leadership Institute, 2008; available on the Internet at http://www.careertools.org/pdf/AdvancedROI.pdf (accessed 5 March 2008).
33. Ibid.
34. James Monks, "The Returns to Individual and College Characteristics: Evidence from the National Longitudinal Survey of Youth," *Economics of Education Review* 19, Issue 3 (June 2000): 279-289.
35. Ibid.
36. United States Congress Joint Economic Committee, 1-13.
37. Monks, 279-289.
38. Ibid.
39. United States Congress Joint Economic Committee, 1-13.
40. Monks, 279-289.
41. "Mission, Market, Value, and Excellence: The New Economics of the Liberal Art," electronic article from Center of Inquiry in the Liberal Arts, Wabash College (Crawfordsville, Indiana), 2007; available on the Internet at http://liberalarts.wabash.edu/cila/home.cfm?news_id=5190 (accessed 5 March 2008).
42. James C. Palmer, "Funding the Multi Purpose Community College in an Era of Consolidation," in Glenn M. Nelson, Eugenie A. Potter, John C. Weidman, John L. Yeager and Thomas G. Zullo (Eds.), *ASHE Reader on Finance in Higher Education* (Pearson Custom Publishing, 2001), 207-218.
43. Thomas J. Kane, and Cecilia Elena Rouse, "Labor Market Returns to Two-Year and Four-Year College," *American Economic Review* 85, no. 3 (1995): 600-614.
44. Ibid.
45. *Politics*, Wikipedia, available on the Internet at http://en.wikipedia.org/wiki/Politics (accessed March 2008).
46. Susan Debnam, "Office Egos Uncovered," *Management-Issues.com*, 2006; available on the internet at http://www.management-issues.com/2006/10/19/opinion/office-egos-uncovered.asp (accessed March 2008).
47. Ibid.

AUTHOR

BIOGRAPHIES

David S. Burdick is a Professor of Installation Management at the Army Management Staff College, Fort Belvoir, Virginia, with expertise in antiterrorism, force protection, and homeland security. His leadership experience includes service as a director or deputy director within various operations, security, and law enforcement directorates on Army installations, and active Military service as an Army field artillery officer. Mr. Burdick is completing his MA degree program in homeland security with the Naval Postgraduate School and holds a BA in political science from Brigham Young University, where he was recognized as a Distinguished Military Graduate.

Fiona J. Burdick, Ph.D., is a Professor of Civilian Leader Development at the Army Management Staff College, Fort Belvoir, Virginia, with expertise in Army family programs. Her leadership experience includes serving as Director of Army Child Care, Army Drug and Alcohol Counseling, and Army Community Service organizations. Dr. Burdick received a Ph.D. in organizational leadership from the University of Oklahoma, a MEd in human resource education from Boston University, and a BS in psychology and sociology from Cameron University.

Wayne Ditto is a Professor of Civilian Leader Development at the Army Management Staff College, Fort Leavenworth, Kansas. He is currently assigned to the Basic Course with expertise in curriculum, presentation, development, design, and research. He retired from the U.S. Army in 1992 and has conducted leadership training and workshops for over 20 years. He received extensive training in leadership and management development from Blanchard Training & Development, Inc., Personal Strengths Publishing, Inc., and BCon WSA International. He is a certified instructor of the Phase I Human Element Program. Mr. Ditto holds a MS in human resource development from Pittsburg State University and a BS in management from Park College.

Alton Dunham is a Professor of Civilian Leader Development at the Army Management Staff College, Fort Belvoir, Virginia. Prior to joining the College, he served in the Air Force as a missile officer, command & control officer, and support officer. His research interests include organizational development and motivation. Mr. Dunham is a Ph.D. candidate in education studies at the University of Nebraska-Lincoln and holds a MHR. in human relations from the University of Oklahoma, an MSSI. in strategic intelligence from the Joint Military Intelligence College, a MBA in business management from Golden Gate University, and a BBA in business management from Texas Christian University.

Roy Eichhorn is the Director of Research and Development at the Army Management Staff College. He has been actively involved in Army Civilian Leader Development since 1983 and has previously written and presented on critical thinking, civilian development, systems thinking, and Army deception operations in World War II. He is a graduate of the Army Management Staff College and the Army Command and General Staff College. Mr. Eichhorn holds an MA in anthropology from Northern Illinois University and a BA in anthropology from Beloit College.

Jim Geter is a Technology and Operations Specialist at the Army Management Staff College, Fort Belvoir, Virginia. He is an Air Force retiree with a specialty in information management. Mr. Geter holds a BS in management from the University of Maryland, University College.

Darrin P. Graham, Ed.D., is a Professor of Civilian Leader Development at the Army Management Staff College, Fort Belvoir, Virginia. He is currently an adjunct faculty member with six Universities and Colleges. His professional career reflects over 22 years of education, training, leadership, program planning, and assessment. His teaching experience includes 5 years of university teaching, both face-to-face and online, in the areas of curriculum and instruction, education administration, educational leadership, educational technology, teacher education at all graduate levels and 3 years of teaching in public school special education. Dr. Graham holds a BS in psychology, a MA in adult education, an EdS in curriculum and instruction, and an EdD in curriculum and instruction.

James Jarrett is a Professor of Civilian Leader Development at the Army Management Staff College, Fort Belvoir, Virginia. As a retired Army officer, he served in a variety of command and staff positions throughout the United States, Europe, and Asia. He is currently enrolled with Central Michigan University, with a focused area in organizational leadership. Mr. Jarrett holds a BA in business administration from North Carolina A&T State University and a MS from the University of Central Texas in business management.

Arthur McMahan, Ph.D., is Director of Education Services and Strategic Planning at the Army Management Staff College, Fort Belvoir, Virginia. His responsibilities include strategic planning, institutional research, quality assurance, performance management, and the balanced scorecard. He is a Malcolm Baldrige National Quality Award Examiner (2007), has served on the U.S. Amy Training and Doctrine Command Accreditation team, and is a past member on the Board of Directors Washington Area Corporate University Consortium. He has written and presented on strategic planning, the balanced scorecard, change management, and diversity. Dr. McMahan has a Ph.D. in adult education and training from Virginia Commonwealth University, a MS in urban education from the University of Nebraska-Omaha, and a BA in humanities and social sciences from the University of South Carolina.

Judy Thompson-Moore is a Professor of Civilian Leader Development at the Army Management Staff College, Fort Belvoir, Virginia. She previously worked with Vice President Gore's National Performance Review Team as a doctoral research analyst. Judy is a graduate of the Sustaining Base Leadership and Management Program from the Army Management Staff College and a current Ph.D. candidate in adult learning and human resource management at Virginia Polytechnic & State University. Ms. Thompson-Moore has a MS in adult learning and human resource development from Virginia Tech, a MS in business administration from Strayer College, and a BS in business administration from Strayer College.

Angela R. Parham, Ph.D., is a Professor of Civilian Leader Development at the Army Management Staff College, Fort Belvoir, Virginia. She has over 15 years of Government service in finance, research, program development, and teaching. Dr. Parham has a Ph.D. in political science from Howard University, an MPA from Troy State University, and an AB in political science from University of Georgia.

John Plifka is the Director of the Basic Course at the Army Management Staff College, Fort Leavenworth, Kansas. He joined the college in January 2003 and taught the Sustaining Base Leadership Management program. He played an integral part in the development of the Army's Civilian Education System. He is currently pursuing his Ph.D. in adult education leadership at North Central University. Mr. Plifka holds a MS in public administration from Troy State University and a BS in management from National-Louis University.

Pamela L. Raymer, Ed.D., has served as the Dean of Academics at Army Management Staff College since January 2007. Previous assignments include the Quality Assurance and Staff and Faculty Director at both the Fires Center at Fort Sill, OK and the Armor Center at Fort Knox, KY. She has over 15 years of university teaching experience. Dr. Raymer holds a EdD in supervision, with a subspecialty in training and development from the University of Louisville, an MS in instructional systems technology from Indiana University, an MA in counseling from Baylor University, and a BA in history and political science from the University of Kentucky.

Sidney Ricks, Jr. is a Professor of Civilian Leader Development at the Army Management Staff College, Fort Belvoir, Virginia. He is a member of the Advance Course and the Distance Learning Program. As a retired Army Reserve officer, he served in a variety of command and staff positions throughout the United States and Korea. Mr. Ricks holds a BA in mass communications/journalism from Hampton University and a MS in human resource management from Pepperdine University.

Karen Spurgeon, Ed.D., is a Professor of Civilian Leader Development at the Army Management Staff College, Fort Belvoir, Virginia. Her research interests include learning organizations and entrepreneurship. Dr. Spurgeon has an EdD in educational leadership from Vanderbilt University, a MEd from Trevecca College, and a BEd from University of Georgia-Columbus.

Kathy Strand is a Professor of Civilian Leader Development at the Army Management Staff College, Fort Belvoir, Virginia. Kathy has been designing leadership curricula since 1998 and has worked with a variety of Military Academies, colleges, and institutions on officer, NCO, and civilian leadership curricula. She recently joined the Intermediate Course team and has worked with AMSC Faculty Development and Curriculum Development since July 2007. Ms. Strand is pursing a Leadership Certificate with Cornell University and holds a MS in education from the University of Oklahoma.

Charles Stokes is a Professor of Civilian Leader Development at the Army Management Staff College. Fort Belvoir, Virginia. During his Military career, he served primarily as a Special Forces Operations and Intelligence Specialist in South East Asia. Mr. Stokes holds a MEd in education from Virginia Tech and a BS in education from Seton Hall University.

Colonel Garland H. Williams, Ph.D., is the Commandant of the Army Management Staff College, Fort Belvoir, Virginia. As a combat engineer, he has served in a variety of command and staff assignments throughout the United States, Europe, and Asia and has commanded at all levels through brigade. He holds a BA in journalism from Auburn University and a MA and Ph.D. from Duke University in political science. Colonel Williams has published numerous articles and written one book titled *Engineering Peace.*

Deloris Willis is a Professor of Civilian Leader Development and Team Leader at the Army Management Staff College, Fort Belvoir, Virginia. She is experienced in Human Resource and Personnel Management Programs and is a Certified Facilitator for Franklin Covey-Seven Habits of Highly Effective People and Principle Centered Leadership. Deloris has over 24 years of Government service in academic and organizational leadership. Prior to joining the College, she worked as a Quality Advisor for the 15th Civil Engineer Squadron, Hickam Air Force Base-Hawaii as a facilitator and consultant to the Base Deputy for education and training program development. She began her career as a Supervisor in the Civil Aircraft Registration Branch of the Department of Transportation, Federal Aviation Administration. Ms Willis holds an MS in management from the University of Maryland University College and a BS in business management from Excelsior University.

Constance Yelverton is a Professor of Civilian Leader Development at the Army Management Staff College, Fort Belvoir, Virginia. She specializes in training, strategies, and distance learning, with over 25 years of experience in education as a teacher, instructor, and developer. Ms. Yelverton holds a MEd in curriculum and instruction from National Louis University and a BA in early childhood education from Fayetteville State University.

AMSC
HISTORY

AMSC has been in the forefront of Army Civilian Leader Development for over 20 years. Our history began in 1985 after the Army concluded that Civilians in or entering into leadership positions were ill-prepared for the challenges they faced, while their Military counterparts received leadership training in Military staff and senior service colleges. The Army needed a comprehensive program to educate Military and civilian leaders in Army-specific subjects geared to the sustaining base. These factors led to the creation of two related efforts—AMSC at Fort Belvoir, Virginia, and the Civilian Leader Development Division (CLDD) in the Center for Army Leadership at Fort Leavenworth, Kansas.

AMSC offered an integrated resident program to civilians called AMSC. CLDD offered the Organizational Leadership for Executives course and then the Intern Leader Development Course and Leadership Education and Development. Names and missions changed over the years. In 1989, CLDD was changed to Civilian Leadership Training Division (CLTD) to accurately reflect its mission. AMSC as a course was changed to Sustaining Base Leadership and Management when the Garrison Precommand and General Officer Installation Command courses were added in 1994 and 1995. In

1997, our Command Programs office piloted the Garrison Command Sergeants Major Course. After the September 11, 2001, terrorist attacks, the Army required a number of changes for antiterrorism and force protection measures worldwide. As a result, the Installation Force Protection Exercise Program was launched in October 2006.

In 2005, CLTD merged with AMSC to develop the Civilian Education System (CES) Leader Development Program for the Army Civilian Corps. AMSC and CLTD both brought together extensive experience from teaching thousands of Army leaders. The merger has resulted in a wealth of expertise that will only serve to intensify the educational experience for the Army Civilian Corps and magnify the success of CES for the Army. CES was launched in January 2007 and provides enhanced leader development and educational opportunities for Army Civilians throughout their careers.

By the fall of 2007, AMSC piloted the first Continuing Education for Senior Leaders. Command Programs kicked off 2008 by launching two new courses—the Directorate for Plans, Training, and Mobilization Course and the Army Installation Antiterrorism Executive Seminar. AMSC faculty and staff are excited to be part of developing leaders for the Army, DoD, and other Federal Government agencies. Through CES, Command Programs, and our Research and Development program, AMSC is consistently Transforming Leaders through Education.

United States Army
Army Management Staff College
Fort Belvoir, Virginia
Fort Leavenworth, Kansas

ISBN 978-0-9820387-0-3

www.ingramcontent.com/pod-product-compliance
Lightning Source LLC
Chambersburg PA
CBHW081149270326
41930CB00014B/3089